Saint Germain des Prés

Library and Archives Canada Cataloguing in Publication

Bonal, Gérard, 1941-
[Saint-Germain-des-Prés. English]

    Saint Germain des Pres : the heart of Paris 1945-1955 / Gerard Bonal; translated by Leonard Rosmarin.

Translation of: Saint-Germain-des-Prés.
Issued in print and electronic formats.
ISBN 978-1-77161-168-8 (paperback).--ISBN 978-1-77161-169-5 (html).--ISBN 978-1-77161-170-1 (pdf)

    1. Saint-Germain-des-Prés (Paris, France : Quarter)--History--20th century. 2. Saint-Germain-des-Prés (Paris, France : Quarter)--Intellectual life--20th century. 3. Saint-Germain-des-Prés (Paris, France : Quarter)-- Biography. 4. Arts--France--Paris--History--20th century. 5. Paris (France)--Intellectual life--20th century. I. Rosmarin, Léonard, translator II. Title. III. Title: Saint-Germain-des-Prés. English.

DC752.S25B6513 2016   944'.361   C2016-901127-5
                                                                                   C2016-901128-3

No part of this book may be reproduced or transmitted in any form, by any means, electronic or mechanical, including photocopying and recording, information storage and retrieval systems, without permission in writing from the publisher, except by a reviewer who may quote a brief passage in a review.

Pubished by Mosaic Press, Oakville, Ontario, Canada, 2016.
MOSAIC PRESS, Publishers
Copyright © 2008 Gerard Bonal, Editions du Seuil.
Translation copyright © 2016, Mosaic Press & Leonard Rosmarin.

Interior design and layout by Eric Normann

Cover Image: "Young women at the terrace of the Café de Flore. Paris (VIth arrondissement), boulevard Saint Germain, June 1959" by Bernard Lipnitzki / © Bernard Lipnitzki / Roger-Viollet

ONTARIO ARTS COUNCIL
CONSEIL DES ARTS DE L'ONTARIO
an Ontario government agency
un organisme du gouvernement de l'Ontario

We acknowledge the Ontario Arts Council
for their support of our publishing program

We acknowledge the Ontario Media Development Corporation
for their support of our publishing program

Funded by the   Financé par le
Government   gouvernement
of Canada   du Canada

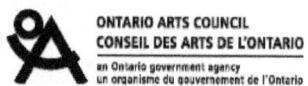

MOSAIC PRESS
1252 Speers Road, Units 1 & 2
Oakville, Ontario L6L 5N9
phone: (905) 825-2130

info@mosaic-press.com

Saint Germain *des* Prés

The Heart of Paris
1945-1955

Gérard Bonal
translated by Leonard Rosmarin

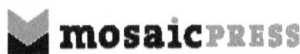

One of the beautiful things about Paris is that one neighbourhood among many becomes a focal point. It used to be Montmartre and Montparnasse. Today it is Saint-Germain-des-Prés.

Jean Cocteau

Preface

" Jean-Paul Sartre lives at the Hôtel La Louisiane, on the rue de Seine. M. Sartre gets up early in room no. 17, on the first floor. The interior, made up of a somewhat faded big red couch and several scattered pieces of furniture, recalls the décor of his play *Huis-clos* (*No Exit*) representing, as everyone knows, the very image of hell. In the early morning the philosopher is pleased to find his clothes scattered about, some ash-filled saucers that happen to be overturned, and scribbled pages that are sometimes uncovered deep inside his bed. Indeed, M. Sartre never stops writing, he writes anywhere and anytime, whether he is standing up or lying down, dressed or in pyjamas. M. Sartre is unfortunately afflicted with a divergent squint and his heavy eyeglasses cannot correct the vagueness of his gaze. He constantly smokes a pipe. Under his pillow one often comes upon a cup of tea or a fork against which he has fallen asleep. He prefers canned goods to fruits ripened by the sun and cold cuts to rare meat ..."[1]

Immediately after the war newspapers overflowed with grotesque, even malicious and, in the final analysis, profoundly imbecilic stories like these. Just like this anecdote, obviously a complete fabrication, and related with smug self-satisfaction by *Samedi-Soir*: "To an American journalist who asked him the question:—What is Existentialism, M. Sartre?—He replied, it's what keeps me alive." And this other, that happens to be true: Jean-Paul Sartre was in Stockholm, a journalist rushed towards him: "Monsieur Sartre, le Tabou has just been closed, what do you think?" The philosopher's disillusioned comment: "I am one of the Tabou's persecuted

---

[1] *Samedi-Soir*, November 17 1945. Is it necessary to emphasize that the editor of *Samedi-Soir* has obviously never set foot in Jean-Paul Sartre's room?

people."² Even the venerable critic Émile Henriot couldn't refrain from making an indignant comment in *Le Monde*: "Beasts driven by their instincts, enveloped in deceitful words, this is what we are, according to M. Jean-Paul Sartre, professor of Existentialism and, as such, admired master of part of the young generation today..."

As for the titles of articles that were splashed across newspapers and the way they used the word "Existentialist," they afford us insights into the minds of the editors: "The scandalous Chronicle of Saint-Germain-des-Prés," "First Existentialist Crime," "Existentialists are Jealous, Dirty and Vulgar"... Moreover the phenomenon was not limited to the Parisian press; an Algiers newspaper, Dernière Heure, that could only give evidence by hearsay, asserted: "This neighbourhood, once strict and quiet, has become the meeting place of snobs intent on enjoying the decadent pleasures sponsored, God only knows why, by Jean-Paul Sartre and the Existentialist movement." It is obvious: from *Le Monde* to *Samedi-Soir*, from middle-class newspapers to populist press, Jean-Paul Sartre was the target of every criticism.

This animosity, this nastiness that turned the philosopher into some kind of public enemy no. 1, was undoubtedly the price to be paid for the notoriety that suddenly swooped down on him as well as the Existentialist movement just after the war. Until then, neither the creation of *Les Mouches* (*The Flies*) at the Sarah Bernhardt Theatre in 1943, nor the publication, that same year, of *L'Être et le Néant* (*Being and Nothingness*)—a veritable Existentialist manifesto, even though the abhorred word was never utilized in it—unleashed such a tidal wave, even if some people could sense right away the importance of this book: "The work was massive, unorthodox, overflowing with an irresistible force, full of exquisite subtleties, encyclopaedic, superbly technical, with an intuition of diamond-like simplicity running through it from one end to the other. There was no doubt possible: we had been given a system."³

But, in the autumn of 1945, the situation had changed. Having rid itself of all forms of censure since the month of June, the press was henceforth able to deal without reprisals with subjects that were "lighter" than beforehand. Above all, it was able to become the echo chamber of a literature that was coming back to life as best it could. The sounds this echo

---

² Le Tabou was a famous cellar nightclub on rue Dauphine. It opened in 1947; see infra, more specifically chapter 10.

³ Michel Tournier, *Le Vent Paraclet*, Gallimard, 1977.

chamber emitted were all the louder because France, reduced to the status of a second-rank power after its defeat and four years of occupation, had scarcely any other riches except its culture to offer to the admiration of the multitudes. "The most modest text aroused cheering, a big fuss was made over its author: being kindly disposed, foreign countries were moved by this tumult and amplified it."[4] Thus, without anything else to lay its hands on, newspapers got hold of the Existentialist phenomenon and blew it up way out of proportion. In their defence, perhaps the newspapers vaguely guessed the importance that the works of Jean-Paul Sartre were going to acquire, even though they could not yet fathom their impact.

The fame that overwhelmed Sartre and the little group of friends and disciples surrounding him would have a bitter taste. It was the kind of ambiguous glory that he had not sought out, that he was not hoping for, that he would end up deploring: "Famous and scandalous at the very same instant, Sartre felt uneasy about accepting a renown which, while going way beyond his original ambitions, contradicted them."[5] In short, there was a misunderstanding.

In truth, within a few weeks Paris witnessed a kind of Existentialist offensive. Right from the month of September, Simone de Beauvoir opened fire with her second novel, *Le Sang des autres* (*The Blood of Others*), which drew the critics' attention; Jean-Paul Sartre followed suit and published one after the other the first two volumes of his large-scale novel, *Les Chemins de la liberté*[6] (*The Roads to Freedom*). On October 15 appeared the first issue of the review *Les Temps Modernes*, accompanied by an editorial signed by Jean-Paul Sartre. It made a big stir in the world of letters and in it appeared, already, in implicit terms, the notion, dear to the heart of the philosopher, of the engaged writer: "The writer is in a real-life situation in his time: every word has its repercussions. Every silence as well ... The writer is involved in his age, whatever he does, he is marked, compromised, even in the remotest of his retreats." This issue is also, in its way, an authentic Existentialist manifesto: "Man is first and foremost, and only afterwards is he this or that; man must create for himself his own essence." On October 29, Sartre gave a lecture at the Club Maintenant in front of a highly excited gathering, in a hall too small to accommodate the crowd pushing to get in: "Existentialism is a

---

[4] Simone de Beauvoir, *La Force des choses*, Gallimard, 1963.
[5] *Ibid.*
[6] *L'Âge de raison* and *Le Sursis*, Gallimard, 1945.

humanism."⁷ The next day, *Les Bouches inutiles* (*Who Shall Die?*), Simone de Beauvoir's first play, began its career at the Théâtre des Carrefours.

"Not a week went by without the newspapers talking about us. *Combat* commented favourably on everything that came out of our pens and our mouths. Everywhere were echoes that we and our books had touched off. On the streets, photographers would click away madly at us, people would approach us. At the Café Flore they would look at us, they would whisper."⁸ Which made a journalist of the magazine *Arts*, annoyed by this Existentialist omnipresence, say: "In the same week, we have heard Sartre's lecture, attended the dress rehearsal of *Les Bouches inutiles* and read the first issue of *Les Temps Modernes*." For its part, *Samedi-Soir*, commenting on the same events, is more direct if not more brutal: "Since Barnum, we had never witnessed such a triumph of publicity. Existentialism is a philosophy. It is also excellent business. Today, Existentialists dominate the Puritan stronghold of the *Nouvelle Revue Française*. They invade the theatres, secure faithful followers in the press, enslave publishing houses, and publish a review: *Les Temps Modernes* (*Modern Times*), whose title is borrowed from Charlie Chaplin, and they convince American capitalists that they hold the monopoly on French thought."⁹

Samedi-Soir was right: Existentialists were everywhere. *Samedi-Soir* was all the more right because the newspaper itself, without any scruples, had been an important factor in making Existentialism fashionable. Create a scandal, invent one if necessary, you will reap its consequences in the form of newspapers sold... For example, the success of cellar nightclubs, especially the Tabou, was assured in large part by the articles the magazine had devoted to them. But those Existentialists were not necessarily the ones who read Sartre...

With the end of the war, a new generation of writers who had been forced into silence during the Occupation, came to the foreground—Sartre's generation to be exact. The pre-1939 old celebrities had had their day: out of sight now! Or send them to the museum. Readers wanted to feed on new names, faces, ideas. Especially ideas. Now they demanded that these newcomers explain the world to them: this new, incomprehensible world that was born out of the rubble of the old one, pulverized by the extermination camps, the bombing of Hiroshima, the

---

⁷ This lecture is given a caricatured treatment by Boris Vian in *L'Écume des jours*.

⁸ Simone de Beauvoir, *La Force des choses, op. cit.*

⁹ *Samedi-Soir*, November 17, 1945.

Cold War... Sartre, Camus found themselves in the position of arbiters. Or, to put it more prosaically, they suddenly became personalities in the public eye consulted on everything and anything. The popular press was quick to scent a good deal: Existentialism could bring in lots of cash. Provided that it was stripped of its philosophical content and was left with only a few clichés—and was viewed as a fashion rather than a set of moral values.

Existentialism? That's no doubt using the word too quickly. Because in the first place Sartre refuted it: "My philosophy is a philosophy of existence; Existentialism? I don't know what it means," he insisted during the course of a public meeting organized by the philosopher Gabriel Marcel. But it was useless: the press, the public wanted only to hear about Existentialism; the word became fashionable, it was now launched and on everybody's lips.

The misunderstanding had just begun. "They hoist a writer up on a pedestal only to examine him better and conclude that they were wrong to perch him there," thought Simone de Beauvoir, on recalling that period in *La Force des choses* (*Force of circumstances*). In fact, Sartre and Existentialism were now attacked from all sides, most often by people—ordinary or journalists—who had never read a single line of *L'Être et le Néant*... Philosopher of despair, of emptiness, of mud, of filth as much on the physical as on the moral level, etc, were expressions that emanated from the writings or the mouths of commentators. "At that time Existentialism was called a nihilistic, miserabilist, frivolous, licentious, despairing, ignoble philosophy," went on Simone de Beauvoir.

Next the Communists got involved, no doubt fearing that the public might see in Existentialism a substitute ideology. On December 28, 1945, the newspaper *Les Lettres françaises* published a violent attack against the philosopher—there would be others just as virulent—under the title *A False Prophet: Jean-Paul Sartre*," while afterwards other titles, Marxist or not, continued this job of denigration. Here is an example: "This morning in *Cavalcade*, an idiotic and venomous article on Sartre by Monnerot. Reactions to Mounin's article implying that he delivered a knockout blow to Sartre..."[10] As for the foreign press, particularly the Soviet one, it also had a field day.[11] Witness these words that *Samedi-Soir*

---

[10] Simone de Beauvoir, *La Force des choses*, op. cit. Jules Monnerot, 1909-1995, essay writer and sociologist; Georges Mounin, 1910-1993, linguist.

[11] In this connection we should remember that Pravda will merely announce in three lines the death of Sartre in its issue of April 16 1980. A very tenacious grudge.

published delightedly in January 1949: "Two Soviet journalists have just published in the *Literatournaïa Gazeta* the impressions they garnered during their sojourn in Paris. The Tabou scandalized them. 'You can see here,' they say, 'girls in pants and tramps in shirts but without pants. This is the poverty-stricken youth. They live in filth. Here are the dregs of Paris: a strange kind of mould made up of hatred, jealousy, stupidity and the most vulgar sexuality. Such is the face of the Existentialists. The literary creations and the style of the Existentialists are reflected in a slanderous play by Sartre, *Les Mains sales* (*Dirty Hands*), and the book by Boris Vian, *J'irai cracher sur vos tombes* (*I will Spit on Your Graves*), examples of the most abject and perverse pornography.'" The relationship between Existentialists and Communists—be they Stalinist or post-Stalinist—would be, during the next thirty years, nothing but a long succession of violent and heated exchanges.

It was obvious, then, that from the literary or political standpoint everyone was out for blood. Jean-Paul Sartre would say, "Fame, for me, was hatred."

As we have seen, one of the first, the weekly tabloid *Samedi-Soir*—"Big Weekly of World News," as its publicity stated, founded in June 1945 and boasting in its editorial staff young writers like Marcel Haedrich or Kléber Haedens—*Samedi-Soir*, then, was one of the first to rush into the breech; henceforth, hardly a week would go by without it slamming in its pages, most often in the coarsest of terms, Existentialism and the man who had already been designated as that movement's "pope": Jean-Paul Sartre.

As an example we can refer to an article entitled "This Is How the Cave Dwellers of Saint-Germain-des-Prés Live," published in May 1947 and launching, so to speak, in the public consciousness the scandalous legend of Existentialism in Saint-Germain-des-Prés. The article associated definitively in the minds of its readers Jean-Paul Sartre and Saint-Germain-des-Prés, Jean-Paul Sartre and the young frequenters of the cellar night clubs...Here are some choice excerpts: "From ten p.m. till midnight the Existentialists get together at the Bar Vert, on rue Jacob, where they engrave Existentialist graffiti in the bathrooms and the phone booth. Neither obscenities nor arrow-pierced hearts. But solemn thoughts that all deal with the void, the grave, suicide and Bikini.[12] Here are,

---

[12] It was on the Bikini Atoll, northwest of the Marshall Archipelago, that the first underwater atomic explosion took place on June 30, 1946.

chosen at random, some of these sombre aphorisms: 'I dream, day and night, about the animals on Bikini'—'When you hear hello, hello! don't you think of the Seine river?'—'Ask for a mint cocktail with arsenic to slake your thirst for eternity'—'An Existentialist is a man who has Sartre between his teeth'... The cellar nightclub, 'Le Tabou,' at around two a.m. is an entrance to hell. The tavern is so smoke-filled that one would think a locomotive has just crossed through and left its vapour there. On some nights the Existentialists, whom one can only glimpse through a fog, throw themselves, howling, into frenzied jitterbugs and boogie-woogies. But most often, completely prostrate, they remain seated and stare into their glasses of lukewarm water. At that moment one is struck by their young faces that are so pale, by their wilted gazes, by the discouragement one sees in all of their gestures... What financial resources do the Existentialists have? No one knows anything about it. They sell some books, contract some debts, play some manservant in a play by Sartre... Maybe, basically, it suffices to be an Existentialist in order to exist..."

"The Existentialists get together," "the Existentialists throw themselves, howling," "the Existentialists are prostrate": it's as though we were reading the observations of a naturalist evoking the behaviour of a group of unknown anthropoids. As a supplement in the same issue, *Samedi-Soir* proposed a "Description of the Existentialist," a caricature of the Saint-Germain fauna, as it was already called: "Masculine sex: tousled hair, falling in locks over the forehead; shirt open down to the navel, in winter as in summer; bright coloured socks with multicoloured horizontal stripes. Female sex: hair falling straight down till the chest; a few tamed white mice in her pants pockets; the use of makeup is strictly forbidden."

Boris Vian protested against such methods all the more because, all things considered, they drew a plausible portrait of these young people; he assailed, not without humour but not without vehemence, those whom he called "rubbish churners," that is to say the journalistic clique of *Samedi-Soir* as well as other "Françamedimanchesoir"(France-Saturday-Sunday-Evening newspapers), as he said amusingly. "In short, all this propaganda pursued one goal and one only: to spread a false conception of Existentialism in the world and place the victims of the propagators' slogans at the mercy of the latter."[13] According to Vian, these slogans

---

[13] *Manuel de Saint-Germain-des-Prés*, Pauvert, 1997. (Société Nouvelle des Éditions Jean-Jacques Pauvert, 1997; Librairie Arthème Fayard, 2002, for the edition of the complete works.)

became established little by little in the public's mind and ruined the reputation of the true residents of Saint-Germain-des-Prés.

Thus, taking advantage of the misunderstanding, underscoring it when necessary, the press—at least that part of the press similar in every respect to the one we call today *people* tabloids—went to great lengths to confuse, in the same jeering reprobation fuelled by salacious allusions and ribald innuendos, the Existentialist philosophy and the behaviour and clothes of a certain post-war class of young people. "Obviously, those who wanted to attack modern youth as well as those who wanted to attack me have made use of the same error. Those who wanted to attack young people have said: 'They are dirty, cynical, desperate because they are Existentialists.' Those who wanted to attack me have said: 'Look at what Sartre has done, he is responsible for the cynicism, the behaviour and the dirtiness of the youth of today.'"[14]

This "youth of today," which, let us not forget, suffered for four years under the yoke of the Nazi occupier, was the one "letting off steam" at present, in the cellars of Saint-Germain-des-Prés where they rediscovered and even reinvented having a good time. Yes, really, they reinvented having a good time: because, between the jazz in the cellars in 1947 and the fox-trot that people still danced at popular balls in 1939, more than a decade had elapsed. It was more like a century...

So the word "Existentialism" would become synonymous with smoke-filled, dark basements, wild jitterbugs and be-bops, night club addicts, checked shirts, filthy, uncombed and overly long hair, jazz and alcohol, easy sleeping around and sinful practices, sloppiness, lazy lounging about at sidewalk cafés...Synonymous with debauchery. The "Existentialist's Schedule," published by *Samedi-Soir* in its issue of May 3 1947 bears this out. Here it unsubtly caricatures the so-called laziness of the "Existentialists": "In the spring and summer, from 11 a.m. till 1 p.m. the Existentialist takes a sunbath at the Café Flore; at 1 p.m., lunch most often on credit, in one of the neighbourhood bistros. One of these bistros on the rue Jacob, is jokingly called The Assassins; from 3 p.m. to 6 p.m., coffee at the Flore; from 6 p.m. till 6:30 p.m., work; from 6:30 p.m. till 8 p.m., Flore; from 8 p.m. till midnight: Bar Vert; from midnight till 10 in the morning, Tabou."

Such a reputation, blared out from all the rooftops, did not fail to attract very rapidly tourists and voyeurs who came, as one would say, to get an

---

[14] Jean-Paul Sartre, words noted by Othilie Bailly in Marcelle Routier, *Saint-Germain-des-Prés*, Éditions RPM, 1950.

eyeful in Saint-Germain-des-Prés; Boris Vian for one dated the arrival of these not always well intentioned invaders to the year 1946: "Many young girls, many young boys would lend themselves to the lewd games of the flash-photographers, always eager to place them in compromising positions and profit from these to imprint on bromide paper various poses the involuntary immodesty of which resulted entirely from the biased choice of an unusual shooting angle capable of shedding light on spots that, according to the strict morality that still reigned among the cave dwellers, should have remained concealed and hidden from the gaze of participants who were rather blasé towards this kind of spectacle and more concerned with the cerebral than the erotic. All this, reinforcing the impression of lust engendered by the trash of hack reporters, helped draw foreigners..."[15]

Although it was expressed in Vian's inimitable style, all this stressed the unwholesome curiosity to which Saint-Germain-des-Prés was subjected from the very beginning, a phenomenon that the press exploited unscrupulously. Seeing the profit that could be made from the situation, certain people quickly devised a "marketing strategy" that would rapidly transform the neighbourhood into an Existentialist reserve where tourists would come to observe at leisure—whereas the original Saint-Germain natives would, on the contrary, flee towards more tranquil places... The strangest thing about this affair is that some of the long-time residents were not afraid to participate in these public relations operations—for what purpose? We know for example that Anne-Marie Cazalis, who, as one would say today, was more or less in charge of "publicity" for the Tabou, took advantage of her connections within the editorial board of *Samedi-Soir* to fully inform, in an underhand way, the editor selected to draw up the famous article we have quoted that appeared on May 3 1947.[16] Later, when she grew older, she said her *mea culpa* in her own way, but not without a certain virtuous hypocrisy: "Saint-Germain-des-Prés was a commercial invention, the brainwave of several big capitalists and two or three newspaper directors."[17] This is what one would call having a short memory!

---

[15] Boris Vian, *Manuel de Saint-Germain-des-Prés, op. cit.*

[16] The editor in question was none other than the novelist Jacques Robert (the author of *Marie-Octobre* among others), who would moreover win the prize of the Tabou shortly afterwards. Anne-Marie Cazalis, besides, is the source of an unkind article published in France-Dimanche during the same period and titled "Le scandale Sartre"...

[17] Anne-Marie Cazalis, *Les Mémoires d'une Anne*, Stock, 1976.

Simone de Beauvoir got it right: "Certain masculine gazes wounded me; they offered the Existentialist woman, hence the fallen one that I was, a villainous complicity."[18] Because here indeed lay the source of the misunderstanding—but did those who kept it going do so out of pure malevolence or only out of incomprehension of Sartre's theories? When the latter wrote: "The profound choice that determines our everyday decisions is at one with our self-awareness,"[19] he seemed to justify those who labelled rightly or wrongly as Existentialists young people who lived according to rules they had chosen and rejected bourgeois morality. This fails to follow Sartre's lesson to the very end and ignores—or, rather, pretends to ignore—that the liberty he accords man is quite relative, and that he brings immediately into his reasoning what he calls "responsibility."

Sartre, however, endeavoured to explain himself: "I believe that the word 'Existentialism' has given rise to an error that comes from the simplistic interpretation attributed to it: people have believed that Existentialism signifies creating one's existence, that is to say, living one's life; people 'in the know' have, in turn, become 'Existentialists.'"[20] And he cited the example of a boy declaring to the girl he is courting: "I'm a bon vivant, a girl-chaser. I'm an Existentialist." He also related that one of his lady friends who pinched her finger in a door, let out a resounding cry of "Shit!" before simpering: "My God, here I am becoming an Existentialist!..."

Very soon, conscious of the danger that lay in wait for him, the writer would strive to escape from this sinister amalgamation—"The idiotic glory that had swooped down on Sartre had something vexatious about it," noted Simone de Beauvoir in *La Force des choses*. But, whatever he said or did, it was already too late, above all, no one wanted to listen to his reasons; everybody, beginning with the press, was blocking his ears: "It is quite obvious that Existentialism—as a philosophy—has absolutely nothing to do with the Existentialism of Saint-Germain-des-Prés. It would be interesting to know, however, if those whom one calls 'Existentialists' call themselves, in turn, Existentialists...I don't think so, and those whom I have questioned about it deny it. Very few among them had heard about *L'Être et le Néant*, and most of them knew absolutely nothing

---

[18] *La Force des choses, op. cit.*

[19] Jean-Paul Sartre, *L'Être et le Néant*, Gallimard, 1943.

[20] Jean-Paul Sartre, conversation, in Marcelle Routier, *Saint-Germain-des-Prés, op. cit.*

about the philosophy called 'Existentialism.' So I think other people have labelled as Existentialists young people in checked shirts for whom life means having fun. By 'other people' I mean above all journalists."[21]

Certainly. Except that the journalists' zeal did not stop at "young people in checked shirts." Everything and everyone was henceforth Existentialist in Saint-Germain-des-Prés: the Tabou was an Existentialist cellar night club and its hostess, Anne-Marie Cazalis, was an Existentialist hostess; the Flore, an Existentialist café as were les Deux Magots or le Bar Vert; Juliette Gréco would soon be an Existentialist singer, Annabel, an Existentialist model, Michel de Ré, an Existentialist actor, and the Rose Rouge, an Existentialist cabaret... Even starlets would become Existentialists under the pen of unscrupulous journalists: "Mesmerized by Jean-Paul Sartre, Miss Latium wants to become an Existentialist," related *Samedi-Soir*, in its issue of December 18, 1948, under the photo of a still unknown Italian actress, but who would not take long to get people talking about her. "Jean-Paul Sartre is all the rage in Italy. This young beauty is his latest victim. Her name is Gina Lollobrigida. She's a starlet. All she dreams about, apparently, is to visit Paris, frequent the Existentialist cellar night clubs of Saint-Germain-des-Prés. Gina claims that her passion for Existentialism is sincere. 'The proof of it,' she says, 'is that I drink nothing but fruit juices whereas before being an Existentialist I adored liquors.'" In short, people said "Existentialist" the way they used to say "Zazou" in 1940 or "Incredible" and "Marvellous" at the time of the Directoire...

Jean-Paul Sartre was not taken in by a renown that had been created at his expense. And which, in a certain way, minimized his work—when it did not try to ridicule it. Nevertheless, he tried once more to make things clear: "My books and the Existentialist philosophy were fashionable among snobs. *Samedi-Soir* got hold of the word, it soon caused a furor and people described as Existentialist the whole crowd of youngsters that frequents Saint-Germain-des-Prés. They have nothing to do with me, I have nothing to do with them. Here you have a quite extraordinary adventure that has happened to a philosophy."[22]

An extraordinary adventure, indeed. It happened not only to a philosophy but to a whole neighbourhood. Saint-Germain-des-Prés, henceforth,

---

[21] *Ibid.*

[22] *Ibid.*

would become, in the eyes of everyone, for better or for worse, the headquarters of Existentialism. The golden age of Saint-Germain-des-Prés—a term used readily to characterize this period, that is to say, the decade running from 1945 to 1955, that saw the burgeoning and the full flowering of most of the talents and ideas which would mark the thirty years to come—the golden age of Saint-Germain-des-Prés, then, began in incomprehension, even in shame and general disapproval. Saint-Germain-des-Prés is a misunderstanding.

1

"The young will carry off with them Saint-Germain-des-Prés and their fathers will embody Montparnass, their grandfathers Montmartre…"

"Two blocks of houses, that is all of Saint-Germain-des-Prés."[1] It's true, barely a big village huddled around its old church tower and its main street—Boulevard Saint-Germain. The writer Léo Larguier, the loving chronicler of a neighbourhood the provincial aspect of which he took pleasure in emphasizing, was already saying "Saint-Germain-des-Prés, my village," long before the Second World War: "The Café de Flore at the time was frequented only be a few old regular customers. An ancient waiter would bring them *Le Journal des débats*, *La Revue des deux-mondes* or *La Revue bleue*, and they would sometimes indulge in a game of dominos."[2] Léo Larguier lived at 5 rue Saint-Benoît, that is to say, in the very heart of a village of which he proclaimed himself the "honorary country policeman." A little later, it is at this very address that we will find Marguerite Duras.

Several blocks of houses, then, that the Seine, to the north, enclosed as though behind a moat: quai Voltaire, quai Malaquais, quai de Conti… To the south, the rue du Vieux-Colombier and the rue Saint-Sulpice; to the west, the rue des Saints-Pères… But the frontiers remained fluctuating, even emotional if not sentimental, no geography ever fixed them and

---

[1] Simone de Beauvoir, *Lettres à Nelson Algren. Un amour transatlantique (1947-1964)*, text established, translated from the English and annotated by Sylvie Le Bon de Beauvoir, Gallimard, 1997 (letter of July 26 1948).

[2] *Saint-Germain-des-Prés, mon village*, Plon, 1938.

each person redrew them according to his liking—indeed, according to his mood; more than one street in the Seventh or Fifth districts called itself part of Saint-Germain-des-Prés—kinds of enclaves, colonial trading posts spread out in foreign territory... The rue du Bac, for example, and its famous Bar Bac, where Jacques Laurent, Antoine Blondin and even Léo Ferré quenched their thirst; the far-off rue des Carmes, on the slope of Mount Sainte-Geneviève, where the very first cellar night club, animated by Claude Luter and his orchestra, opened as early as June 1946, one year before the famous Tabou, in the basement of the Hôtel des Carmes: the hotel's owners were Bretons from Lorient. For this reason it became the Club des Lorientais; half of the profits were directed to the disaster victims of the Lorient region. The orchestra as well as the musicians all became Lorientais.[3] Or even smack in the Latin Quarter, the rue Champollion, with the Théâtre des Noctambules, which witnessed the débuts of Arthur Adamov, Jacques Audiberti, Henri Pichette, Eugène Ionesco...

Does every war give birth, then, to a new spot? Let's say, rather, every post-war period. The one in 1870 made Montmartre fashionable—for a long time. The Montmartre of painters and cabaret singers: Bruant, Rodolphe Salis and Toulouse-Lautrec, the French cancan and the Moulin Rouge; the Montmartre of the Lapin Agile, that little cabaret located half way up the slope of la Butte, at the corner of the rue Saint-Vincent and the rue des Saules. It was a former inn for cart drivers where every night, shoulder to shoulder till dawn, would meet up writers, actors, poets, painter and models, many of whose names have gone down in history: Roland Dorgelès, Pierre Mac Orlan, André Warnod, Max Jacob, Pablo Picasso, Francisque Poulbot, Charles Dullin... At the Lapin Agile, they drank, recited verses, sang, and got into fights, too... Under the low ceiling, they were sheltered by inside shutters that closed off windows with small glass panes. Smoke piled up here, but so did human warmth and friendship. This did not prevent some terrible brawls from taking place. One morning, while sweeping, the cleaning lady found a human eye on the floor among the debris of bottles and glasses... Simone de Beauvoir got the anecdote from Dullin himself and related it in *La Force de l'âge* (*The Prime of Life*).

---

[3] Conversation with Claude Luter published in *Saint-Germain-des-Prés, 1945-1950*, Pavillon des Arts, 1989. It is the Club des Lorientais, entirely rebuilt in the movie studio that served as the décor for Jacques Becker's film *Rendez-vous de juillet* (1949).

After World War I Montparnasse became the fashionable neighbourhood. The famous Montparnasse of the Roaring Twenties—Modigliani, Van Dongen, Foujita, Kiki de Montparnasse...Artist studios hidden under the trees, in the backyards of the rue Campagne-première or the rue Notre-Dame-des-Champs, the Closerie des lilas, the big, noisy cafés of the Vavin crossroad: the Dôme, the Coupole, the Rotonde...

In 1945, during the euphoria following the Liberation, Saint-Germain-des-Prés resumed its role as witness. As the poet Maurice Fombeure—he resided on the rue du Vieux-Colombier—reported on the spot: "From these last years the young will carry off with them Saint-Germain-des-Prés, and their fathers will remember Montparnasse, their grandfathers Montmartre. They will stop there, not having enough ancestors to establish a link with Maupassant's boaters." Or Jean Cocteau: "One of the beauties of Paris is that one neighbourhood always takes the lead. In the past it was Montmartre and Montparnasse. Now it is Saint-Germain-des-Prés. Viewed from the outside, it is a neighbourhood that lazes around. That is not true. Youth does its best work when it lazes about, dreams, discusses, gorges itself on extremes and injustices."[4] As proof, Cocteau recreated on the movie set a kind of replica of the Café de Flore that he called simply the Café des Poètes, the rendezvous of young people in his film *Orphée* (*Orpheus*)—casting was entirely filled by the denizens of Saint-Germain-des-Prés.

Why Saint-Germain-des-Prés? Why this infatuation with "two blocks of houses," as Simone de Beauvoir emphasized? Who hastens nevertheless to add, to conjure up the feverish atmosphere of the neighbourhood following the Liberation: "But within this perimeter, finding a place to sit in the bars, cafés, or even on the sidewalk is problematic."[5]

Yes, why? Because here, between the tutelary church tower, "a storm-coloured, old piece of furniture, a piece of Romanesque armour,"[6] and the cafés with their spacious sun-filled terraces, opening up like fans onto the boulevard Saint-Germain, the spirit of the place, as one would say, had been circulating for a long time. "Saint-Germain-des-Prés Square is one of the spots in the capital where one feels most in the know, closest to the real events, to the men who know the inside

---

[4] Quoted in Marcelle Routier, *Saint-Germain-des-Prés, op. cit.*

[5] Simone de Beauvoir, *Lettres à Nelson Algren, op. cit.*.(letter of July 26 1948).

[6] Léon-Paul Fargue, "Saint-Germain-des-Prés", in *Le Piéton de Paris* (1939), Gallimard, "L'Imaginaire .»

workings of the country, to the world and to art. Indeed the square lives, breathes, vibrates and sleeps thanks to three cafés as famous today as state institutions: les Deux Magots, le Café de Flore and the Brasserie Lipp. Art and politics hold hands there."[7] Léon-Paul Fargue wrote this during the thirties. Already. And he even stressed: "Whether there has been a cabinet meeting during the day, a boxing match in the state of New Jersey or some dispute, the regular customers at the cafés on Saint-Germain-des-Prés Square are the first ones to be informed of these meetings or these competitions, either by a courier or through a mysterious telegraphic system."

Saint-Germain-des-Prés was waiting its turn, patiently; time was working in its favour. The spirit of the times. And when this turn came—at the end of the Second World War—it was thanks to one detail: the opening and closing times of a modest bar on the rue Dauphine. The Tabou, just like its Montmartre ancestor, the Lapin Agile, was a bistro for night shift workers: people in the press distribution service would congregate at the counter until the wee hours of the morning. It was the only establishment in the neighbourhood that didn't close down at midnight. Soon the blue collar workers were joined by the nocturnal revellers, the night pirates –the thirsty and talkative ones of all categories, thrown out unceremoniously at the stroke of midnight from all of the bars in a hurry to close the lights, pile up the chairs and pedestal tables: "Once they left Flore and the Bar Vert, the night people would go to the rue Dauphine where they were sure of finding something to drink."[8] The poets, painters, actors followed and all the others after them, just as they had done in Montmartre not long ago. The Tabou, open until dawn, thus went down in legend. And the whole neighbourhood with it. There was no spontaneous generation in Saint-Germain-des-Prés.

The line can be traced back very far. From Spain, where Childebert I, son of Clovis, laid siege to Saragossa in 542. He wanted to dislodge the Visigoths who had barricaded themselves there. Their supplies exhausted, the besieged townspeople gathered on the ramparts and hit upon the idea of brandishing at arms length the tunic of Saint Vincent, the deacon of the city, who had been martyred two centuries earlier under the

---

[7] *Ibid.*

[8] Bernard Lucas, quoted in Boris Vian, *Manuel de Saint-Germain-des-Prés, op. cit.*

reign of Diocletian. And the stratagem worked. On seeing the precious garment, the King of the Francs was overcome by a saintly and virtuous fright. Without delay he negotiated the lifting of the siege in exchange for the relic that he carried off in his baggage. He had to appear victorious, however: So Childeric added a large massive gold cross laden with precious stones, thirty or so gold chalices, as many patens and richly decorated boxes for carrying the Gospels... So ended the Spanish episode.

The second act took place in Paris. On the advice of the Bishop Germain—the future Saint Germain—Childebert ordered the building of a basilica destined to receive the sacred trust. Grégoire de Tours told the story in great detail in his monumental *Historia francorum*—more than forty volumes...

The building was consecrated on December 23, 558. Strange coincidence: Childebert I died on the same day. He would be buried in his church. As Léon-Paul Fargue reminds us, four centuries later: "It is on the terrace of the Café Les Deux Magots that one can ponder over the ashes of Childebert and Descartes."[9] Indeed, other remains, just as famous, would soon join the Franc King's under the flagstones: Descartes, of course, but also Boileau, and long before them these scholars who ensured the renown of the abbey, and whose memory is recalled by the neighbourhood streets: Mabillon, Montfaucon... Last but not least Saint-Germain himself who would give his name to the building.

Monks established themselves there. Their community prospered: following the left bank of the river, their possessions extended till the Petit-Pont. Gardens, cultivated fields, vast meadows where one could see flocks grazing—this would give the abbey its definitive name of Saint-Germain-des-Prés. As the years went by, a veritable village—the town of Saint-Germain, where lived the numerous people working for the clergy—developed around the monastery that had become one of the richest in France. The memory of this population has not yet been lost, at least not in the maps of Paris today. "Street names remind us of the kingly rights that the Abbey exercised over its citizens: the rue du Vieux-Colombier, where the rulers' pigeon houses had been set up, the rue du Four, opening onto the place where an ordinary bake oven stood..."[10]

---

[9] "Saint-Germain-des-Prés", in *Le Piéton de Paris, op. cit.*

[10] André Miramas, in *L'Almanach de Saint-Germain-des-Prés*, set up under the direction of Henri Philippon, Éditions de l'Ermite, 1950.

At the time of the former Saint-Germain Fair—it is said that Henri IV spent many gold coins there, to his minister Sully's great displeasure—here is where the city of Paris came to have fun, near the present Saint-Sulpice Square, from the beginning of February till the end of Lent. Jugglers, bear trainers, tumblers, outdoor stages...For at least two centuries. The ancestors of the Opéra-Comique and of the Comédie-Française were born in these narrow streets. So was the Café Procope, the first literary café—well before the Deux Magots or the Café de Flore—founded in 1686 by Francesco Procopio, who chose to Frenchify his name in order to give it to the establishment he had just opened. The philosophers of the Age of Enlightenment congregated there: Voltaire, Rousseau, Diderot; and, after them, the philosophers of the Shadows: Marat, Robespierre...Just as, two centuries later, the philosophers of Existentialism would meet at the Café de Flore.

During the darkest hours of the Revolution, the monks were driven out and the Abbey, closed down, became a prison. A memoir, preserved in the National Archives, handwritten by the caretaker-clerk, François Delavaquerie, itemized the cost of work done on the framework "to set up a prison in the former refectory of the monks";[11] another document scrupulously summarized the operations for counting the prisoners. The official accounts, the circulars and certificates relate, from day to day, the horror of the "September massacres" that unfolded in the prison of the Abbey in 1792.[12] On the evening of September 2, the commissioners sent to the place told the Assembly that they were unable to calm the rioters who had forced the doors. The next day, the Committee of Public Safety in turn informed the departments that a number "of the conspirators were put to death by the people in the prison." Three hundred and eighteen individuals. Two commissioners were again sent to the Abbey, on September 4, to try "to stop the avenging arm that was striking down the criminals." In vain: "M. Wittgenstein, Lieutenant General, imprisoned in the Abbey on August 11, was judged by the people on September 4 and executed immediately," related a certificate signed by François Delavaquerie. Savage violence had spread across the capital. Six other commissioners, sent to the de la Force prison, were not any luckier than their colleagues: the Princesse de Lamballe, dragged out of her cell, was massacred right on the spot. The account of the event given by the municipal guard Daujon showed the full

---

[11] This refectory occupied the place of the present rue de l'Abbaye.

[12] These documents are preserved for the most part in the National Archives.

extent, or rather the excesses, of the scenes of carnage that were covering Paris in blood: "Two individuals were dragging by its legs, with its back over the ground and its stomach opened up till its chest, a naked, headless corpse. At the end of a pike was a head that often touched my face as a result of the movements the bearer made when gesticulating. To my left a more horrible person held, in one hand, the entrails of the victim and in the other a large knife. Behind them a large coalman held, hanging from a pike over my head, a strip of a shirt soaked in blood and mud."[13]

Soon, the Reign of Terror reached its peak in the Abbey prison and elsewhere. It mattered little that Madame Rolland, imprisoned in the month of June 1793, denounced with all her might in a loud, clear voice the illegality of her arrest, the blade of the guillotine would silence her. Canon powder was stored under the vaults of the church. It became a saltpetre factory and an armament workshop; the forges were fed by the reserves of coal deposited in the Abbey palace...A fire ensued that ravaged the former refectory of the monks in the month of August 1794.

The Benedictines would never return to their dishonoured abbey, of which remained only the palace, the church and the old Romanesque steeple that guards Saint-Germain-des-Prés like a watchtower.

Yes, everything changes...Who would have suspected that the famous sign Les Deux Magots, at the corner of the square and the boulevard Saint-Germain, once housed a hosiery and fabric shop? Chinese silks, muslin, batiste, percale—rolls of brand new fabric unfolded with a sharp move of the hand, under the greedy eyes of the customers, in an acid odour that makes one's mouth water...Jean-Paul Caracalla, in his *Saint-Germain-des-Prés*,[14] tells the story of this shop presenting new models, set up first on the rue de Buci, then transferred to the square in 1873, undoubtedly to stimulate a business weakened by the success of the department stores. In vain. The venture collapsed. The management of Printemps transferred its shipping services there after the fire that ravaged the building on the boulevard Haussman in 1881. Then handed over the place definitively, in 1885, to a café selling syrupy wine that would keep the same store sign. Soon Oscar Wilde, Léon Daudet, Alfred Jarry would be seen there...

---

[13] "Daujon's Account", in G. Lenôtre, *La Captivité et la Mort de Marie-Antoinette*, Librairie académique Perrin, 1914.

[14] Flammarion, 1993.

In June 1893, the very year of her first marriage, Colette, who was still just Colette Willy, moved unenthusiastically into the building at 28 rue Jacob. A grey street with monotonous facades, a third floor without sunlight, between two courtyards... "Most of the houses that line the rue Jacob, between the rue Bonaparte and the rue de Seine, date from the 18th century. I was much too young, at the time of my first move, to find any virtue in them. I saw them as sad."[15] In actual fact, it is a garden that drew all of her attention: "Of this garden I could only glimpse the tip of a tree, by leaning hard over the windowsill. I didn't know that this boundary of agitated leaves marked the dwelling of Remy de Gourmont and the garden of his 'Amazon.'"[16]

Ten years later, Remy de Gourmont, one of the founders of the review, *Mercure de France*—the strange Gourmont, ugly, stuttering, afflicted with tubercular lupus and an impossible love for his "Amazon," solicited by other passions—was still there. Léo Larguier remembered having enjoyed an aperitif with him, around 1903, at the Café de Flore... Another era! Because the 20th century had begun, and Saint-Germain-des-Prés could shake off the dust of the years.

Balzac had invested in a printing house on rue Visconti only to ruin himself financially. A literary review is what André Gide, Jean Schlumberger, Jacques Copeau and several others would found. Even though the adventure began elsewhere, near the Madeleine, on the rue de Sèze to be precise, before emigrating briefly to the rue Henri-Monnier, at the bottom of the slope of Montmartre, *La Nouvelle Revue Française* belonged, with all its being, to Saint-Germain-des-Prés. Besides, it would seek right away to draw closer to that neighbourhood, as though following a natural inclination. After a failed attempt, the first issue was put together at the home of Jean Schlumberger, at 73 rue d'Assas. Twenty years later, it took up residence definitively on rue Sébastien-Bottin, after a short stay on rue Madame, and another on rue de Grenelle.

"The profound imprint Copeau left on the theatre overshadows somewhat the role he played in the revue,"[17] Jean Schlumberger rightly reckoned

---

[15] Colette, *Trois...six...neuf...*, Corrêa, 1946.

[16] *Ibid*. The "Amazon" was, of course, Natalie Clifford Barney. Colette is mistaken: this "boundary of agitated leaves" did not mark the dwelling of Remy de Gourmont (he lived at 71 rue des Saint-Pères), but that of Natalie Clifford Barney, who would move in there in 1910. By that time, Colette would have left the rue Jacob long before.

[17] "Cinquantenaire", *Nouvelle Revue Française*, February 1959.

when he evoked, in 1959, on the occasion of its fiftieth anniversary, the birth of the famous *Nouvelle Revue Française*—the NRF—of which he himself was the godfather, in February 1909, in the company of his comrades. Jacque Copeau was barely thirty years old when he embarked on this great editorial adventure. "At the time I was a salesman at the Georges Petit gallery, on rue de Sèze," he relates in his *Souvenirs*.[18]

"The little square gallery soon became a kind of literary centre. I received people there. One was sure of finding me. 'It was very convenient,' said Gide, 'to have a friend so centrally located.' It was there that were held the first meetings of the *Nouvelle Revue Française*, in which Andre Gide, Jean Schlumberger, Michel Arnault, Henri Ghéon, André Ruyters and Eugène Montfort participated."[19] One could indeed find these names in the table of contents of the first issue, in the month of February 1909, all fugitives from various other literary reviews of the moment: *L'Ermitage, Antée, La Phalange, La Revue blanche* ...

"*La Nouvelle Revue Française* appeared on a small number of pages, with few collaborators but the way we wanted it, pure, firm, a bit rigid in its rigorous uniform..."[20] What did they want, these austere young men, hooked on rigor and rigidity? To change literature radically? To dispose of the old-fashioned writers, principally Anatole France or Paul Bourget? No doubt. But also to forge links between writers, to create a kind of writer's guild: "What brought together, around 1907, the original group of the *Nouvelle Revue Française*, was perhaps less a clearly defined intellectual aspiration than a sentiment of common professional esteem. We wanted to do good work together, to engage freely in work both decent and entirely disinterested."[21] The founders would then feature, logically, in the table of contents of the revue, from the very first issues, the names of authors as yet little known to the general public: Romain Rolland, André Suarès, Paul Claudel, Valery Larbaud, Jacques Rivière... In actual fact, a kind of club—very closed—was in the process of being constituted. This prompted Roger Martin du Gard to say, as early as 1913: "Strong impression of a coterie. You have to belong to it. Once you do, the slightest bit of crap is a marvel." And, later on, he

---

[18] In *Revue hebdomadaire*, November 23 1929. The gallery belonged to the Belgian painter-sculptor Georges Petit.

[19] Jacques Copeau, *Les Registres du Vieux-Colombier*, "Registre I", Gallimard, 1979.

[20] *Ibid.*

[21] *Ibid.*

said to Emmanuel Berl: "There has always been this biased notion at the *NRF* according to which when one did not inhabit the left bank near the rue Vaneau, that is to say in an austere and somewhat provincial neighbourhood, one was a rather dubious individual... And not a genuine writer."[22]

"Good work," "decent work," certainly, but risky work: "The *NRF* had perhaps a hundred readers at that time. Our ongoing situation was tight and very difficult," reckoned André Gide. All the more because Copeau, its director, was farsighted, without however making the slightest concession. Wild about the theatre, he did not play the card of facility, but rather of strictness—an inflexible strictness that could even be easily mistaken for a kind of provocation. As early as the fourth issue, in the month of May, he did indeed produce a darkly humorous chronicle that he titled "Le métier de theatre" ("The Theatre Trade") where he stigmatized the vulgarity, pretences and mercantilism of the Paris stage. This chronicle came after a series of articles that appeared in a variety of publications, where already was very clearly affirmed the strictness of the man whose "Jansenism" his detractors would emphasize—to the point of nicknaming the Théâtre du Vieux-Colombier, where Copeau would pitch his tent several years later, "The Calvin Follies"... More than strictness: a veritable code of ethics. In fact, with Copeau began one of the great French theatrical adventures of the 20th century, undoubtedly one of the most beautiful, along with those of the Compagnie Renaud-Barrault and the TNP (Théâtre National Populaire) directed by Jean Vilar—Vilar who, by virtue of his emphasis on the great classical repertoire, his rejection of décors and stage machinery, would be in a way Jacques Copeau's direct heir.

Because that man preached the return to simplicity, naturalness and objected to intrusive stage machinery, heavy décors—"Let the other glamorous illusions vanish and, for the new concept, let them leave us with bare boards."[23] On writing these lines, Jacques Copeau, of course, was thinking of André Antoine, another pioneer of the theatre who, in 1906, became the director of the Théâtre de l'Odéon where he imposed his naturalist theories at great expense: 125 supernumeraries, 60 musicians, 70 stagehands—no less—in order to ensure the performances of Shakespeare's *Julius Caesar*. Of Antoine but also of Meyerhold and Reinhardt, European theoreticians of the theatre from whom Copeau had distanced himself:

---

[22] *Interrogatoire par Patrick Modiano,* Gallimard, 1976.

[23] "Manifeste du Vieux-Colombier", in *Nouvelle Revue Française*, September 1913.

"The more the theatre appeared degraded to me, the more strongly did I feel the need to devote myself to it. I believed that only someone foreign to the stage could save it."[24] During the course of a lecture he gave in Geneva in March 1918, Jacques Rivière, another major figure in the *NRF*, attempted to define Jacques Copeau as accurately as possible: "In his own eyes he appeared not as a stage director, not as an actor, but as an organizer of dramas. He felt something emerging from his person, a flame that he kindled in the minds of his actors, that transformed everyone from the star to the most humble stagehand, that penetrated even the play he had them study." Would Rivière have spoken any differently about a great mystic? Probably not. And Copeau seemed to bear him out: "My theatrical vocation has never been anything else except the imperious need to commit myself to a cult." In this domain he would even go much further, since he would convert to Catholicism in 1924.

In short, the director of the *NRF* had only one idea in mind: to possess, to make a theatre come alive. But a theatre his heart and mind craved, that is to say, pure theatre: "We must produce something sound, uplifting and heartfelt, rather than something original. We will strive to draw attention to ourselves only through fundamental and durable qualities. Our first concern will therefore be to break with the theatrical behaviour of our time, to protect ourselves from all forms of theatricality."[25]

Little by little, the project evolved and assumed its definitive form in the mind of Jacques Copeau, who laid out his ideas in writing: "A small enterprise. Low costs. Few sets. Repertoire. Plays in alternation. Tradition and renewal. Above all, a clean stage, de-industrialized, shorn of its over-acting. A theatre stripped bare. The development of a little family of artists."[26] Such a program, that implicitly extolled bareness, found favour immediately with Charles Dullin, a die hard anarchist, opposed to the forces of money, to "the powerful commanding tribe," as he called it. The two men hit it off at once, as though they had been waiting for one another. "A monk enclosed in his cell, an organizer, and a street preacher, the one complemented the other," commented Caryathis the dancer—the future Élise Jouhandeau,—who was for a time Charles Dullin's companion. A lively friendship drew them close at once: "We would walk back and forth, for hours, at night, on the asphalt

---

[24] Excerpt from a lecture presented in New York, March 1917.

[25] Jacques Copeau, *Les Registres du Vieux-Colombier*, "Register I", *op. cit.*

[26] Notes for a Lecture, Geneva, April 1916.

of the boulevard, exchanging thoughts in which were concentrated all the unselfish energies of our youth, all the hopes of our pure spirits, all the confidence of our hearts that were still intact. And from these conversations would emerge, some time later, the first projects for the Vieux-Colombier."[27]

Because Dullin, impassioned, fired up by his impatience, urged Copeau to take action. Letter of June 1912: "It can't go on like this, if we don't attempt something…" January 1913: "You must undertake something. You are the only one in Paris able to do it. In your own interest you must." And without waiting any longer, as though he wanted to force Copeau's hand, he started looking for a theatre, supported by the *NRF* team, Jean Schlumberger and Gaston Gallimard—the latter having taken over the management of the publishing house of the *Nouvelle Revue Française*, founded in 1911 as an extension of the review: "Gaston Gallimard amassed funds and negotiated, and was in charge of the first books edited under the aegis of the *NRF*."[28]

The search was directed towards Saint-Germain-des-Prés: "We were attached to the left bank," Jean Schlumberger would say later on. First it was Salle Récamier, located in a blind alley opening onto the rue de Sèvres and sublet to a movie house, seven hundred and fifty seats. "Not bad, but too high a rent," judged Schlumberger. Just then Dullin discovered, on the rue du Vieux-Colombier, at number 21, another place, a large hall that its owner rented by the day to middlebrow and amateur troupes. Because of its proximity to Saint-Germain-des-Prés, it was called l'Athénée-Saint-Germain. "Do you remember l'Athénée-Saint-Germain? A hideous hall, rented out to companies putting on melodramas or shabby musical hall shows. With its overblown Louis XV style, it looked like the drawing room of a small-town bordello."[29] Charles Dullin got carried away, however: "I have just visited l'Athénée-Saint-Germain and seen one of the administrators," he wrote to Copeau right away, "it's just right." Jean Schlumberger, for his part, insisted: "I visited l'Athénée-Saint-Germain, it's much better."

The months of May and June were entirely devoted to finding the funds necessary to open the theatre. To endeavour to find them, at least,

---

[27] Jacques Copeau, *Les Registres du Vieux-Colombier*, "Register I", *op. cit.*

[28] José Cabanis, *Dieu et la NRF*, Gallimard, 1994.

[29] Guillaume Hanoteau, *Ces nuits qui ont fait Paris*, Fayard, 1971. (Librairie Arthème Fayard, 1971.)

because potential patrons needed to be coaxed: Anna de Noailles, the poet and Countess, Princess Bibesco, the actress Simone, some high society women... This triggered the following unkind thought by Copeau: "The snobbism of these light theatre people consists precisely in wanting to appear as intellectuals."[30] Here he was mistaken, inasmuch as the light theatre people in question would end up by letting themselves be convinced and investing in the enterprise to the tune of 200,000 francs, distributed over two hundred shares, each one costing 1000 francs.

And while the little group worked itself into the ground, some to bring together a solid troupe of actors—Suzanne Bing, Valentine Tessier, Romain Bouquet, Lucien Nat, Julien Carette...—the others to gather up the necessary money, Jacques Copeau, in seclusion at his home in Limon, a village near La Ferté-sous-Jouarre, planned the repertoire of the future theatre. The classics, "a constant example and the antidote to bad taste:" Molière, Racine, Musset, Aeschylus, Mérimée. The modern ones: Becque, Renard, Courteline, Claudel, Ghéon. Though not to the exclusion of some foreign playwrights: Heywood, Shakespeare, Ibsen, Shaw...

Gil Blas was the first among the newspapers to give coverage to these preparations, and the following comment was attributed to the philosopher Alain: "The theatre?... I don't go there anymore, I'm waiting for the opening of Copeau's Vieux-Colombier." Because it was finally under that name, borrowed from the street, that the ex- Athénée-Saint-Germain was baptized. With, as a sign, two doves facing one another, discovered by Maria van Rysselberghe, Gide's friend, "the Little Lady," on the cobblestone of the church of San Miniato, in Florence. The hall was renovated, and a proscenium, added to the stage, brought actors and audience closer. Francis Jourdain, son of the architect who had conceived la Samaritaine, took charge of the renovations. This did not prevent the gossips from asserting that the Vieux-Colombier—with its walls covered by a kind of beige batik adorned with a black border, its parsimonious lighting, its green rep curtain ("it's not a curtain, it's a billiard!" exclaimed the most venomous among them)—was as warm as a sacristy: "Imagine a narrow passageway, at the end of this passageway are four boxes from which one must see nothing. On the ceiling there is no chandelier, but some kinds of lanterns shedding light that is sadder than an old macramé. Reading a newspaper is impossible in this equinoctial lighting. As a result, the spoken words themselves are deadened.

---

[30] *Les Registres du Vieux-Colombier*, "Register I", *op. cit.*

This is done on purpose. Jacques Copeau demands that his audience collect its thoughts before the curtain rises."[31]

July 1 1913: the actors were summoned at 9h30 to the home of Jacques Copeau, in Limon, where they would spend a studious summer—physical exercises, rehearsals, readings... As of June 30, they were all present. In the lead was Charles Dullin, of course, accompanied by a newcomer with odd diction, who called himself Louis Jouvet.[32] This was the first time that actors were getting ready to live in this way, as a quasi-community, cutting off all links with their usual lives, working, improvising, rehearsing, reading, collating texts, taking their meals together... "To change the actor's surroundings. To indoctrinate the actor. To subject him to an influence superior to that of mere professional teaching. To awaken within him questions unrelated to the daily grind. It is the actor we must strive to render worthy of the text," Copeau remarked in his notebooks. He would be heeded: "First and foremost, Jacques Copeau taught those who followed him the eminent dignity of his art."[33]

During July, were studied, among other works: *Britannicus, La Nuit des rois* (*Twelfth Night*), *L'Avare* (*The Miser*), *L'Amour médecin* (*Love the Doctor*), *Barberine*... and *Femme tuée par la douceur* (*A Woman Killed with Kindness*) by the Elizabethan author Thomas Heywood, that would constitute the opening performance of the Vieux-Colombier, on the following October 22. The roles were exchanged, went from one performer to another; the same actor tried out several roles in the same play. Everyone tested his resources, explored the breadth of his sensibility, discovered the field of unsuspected expressive potentialities that was his own body.

What was elaborated there, in that Seine-et-Marne hamlet, were the very foundations of a dramatic art, of a radically new conception of the stage; a revolutionary doctrine regarding the actor and the troupe, from which would emerge the whole French theatre of the 20th century. From Dullin to Barrault, from Copeau to Vilar, all the while passing through Jouvet—and leading to Ariane Mnouchkine's Théâtre du Soleil.

All the actors were able to find lodgings in the village. Blanche Albane, for example, and her husband, the writer Georges Duhamel, found refuge at the home of a carpenter: "Our room overlooked a small rustic courtyard that in turn opened up onto the gardens. We would leave the

---

[31] Guillaume Hanoteau, *Ces nuits qui ont fait Paris, op. cit.*
[32] Louis Jouvet would keep this written form of his name till 1918.
[33] Robert Brasillach, *Animateurs de théâtre*, Corrêa, 1936.

window wide open at night. The characters of Shakespeare, Claudel, Molière or Musset would lament, laugh or fight during our dreams. With their cries mingled the sighs of animals, the calls of nocturnal birds, the fragrant breath of this happy hill."[34]

Every morning, the actors gathered in the former mill that Copeau, his wife and their three children inhabited. At the end of a large garden planted with boxwood trees and enclosed by walls clad with espaliers, it was an old edifice from which one's gaze could take flight freely over the valley of the Marne. To the side was a little building where Copeau had installed his office. The schedule was strict. On August 21, for example, the day's program was set up in this way: 9:30 a.m., *Une femme tuée par la douceur*; 12:30 p.m., photographs; 15 hours, work; 16 hours, physical exercises. Indeed, as of July 26, a memo informed the artists that they would henceforth have to do a half-hour of physical exercises every day under the direction of their comrade Roger Karl, named professor of gymnastics for the occasion. "We are going to try to give our pupils the knowledge and experience of the human body. It is necessary to get normally developed bodies to acquire suppleness, to lend themselves to any action they perform. It is necessary that the pupils' every movement be accompanied by an intimate state of consciousness linked to the movement that has been executed."[35]

One is struck today by the modernity of Copeau's views, this "despot" with the profile of Dante, as certain not always well-intentioned contemporaries used to call him. Body language, in the years 1910-15, was still a rarely explored—even non-existent—aspect of the actor's art. Performers were much more interested in the voice, in declamation, in noble attitudes, in gestures... The body, the body's language, were the mime's specialty. The Conservatory of Dramatic Art itself was at the time no more than a mere department of the National High Conservatory of Music and Declamation.

Nevertheless, all of Copeau's lessons would be heard, taken up, developed: "Ever since that evening of October 1913, in a former middle-brow hall, where a forgotten English playwright, Thomas Heywood, was revealed, with *Une femme tuée par la douceur*, his name has not ceased to appear as the supreme recourse of genuine theatre against the simony of shopkeepers."[36] But the beginnings were difficult, since, aside from

---

[34] Georges Duhamel, *Le Temps de la recherché*, Paul Hartmann, 1947.

[35] Jacques Copeau, *Les Registres du Vieux-Colombier*, " Register I", *op. cit.*

[36] Robert Brasillach, *Animateurs de théâtre, op. cit.*

the enthusiasm of a few people, the experience of the Vieux-Colombier was at first met only by indifference. Until the triumph of *La Nuit des rois* (*Twelfth Night*), in May 1914, which marked a major date, in France, in the history of the staging of Shakespeare's plays: "One remembers the emotion that was generated, on the eve of the war, by the famous presentation of *La Nuit des rois*, by Shakespeare, that seemed to bring forth a world in itself. After the war, during which Copeau performed in America for French propaganda, the Vieux-Colombier was resurrected. For only a few years, since it closed its doors at the end of the 1924 season."[37]

Others would celebrate this cult that Copeau claimed to serve through his theatrical vocation—Dullin, Jouvet... People did not fail to wonder why Copeau left: "Being a born legislator, a theoretician of the theatre, perhaps this extraordinary man preferred, for an instant, school and experience to the harsh constraints of reality. I personally fear that there exists in him a certain taste for danger, perhaps mixed with a taste for misfortune, a certain penchant of his mind that leads him to failure, to the exquisite delight of failure, and also to bravado, a certain asceticism consisting in the pleasure of not succeeding. Whatever attempts he made to explain himself, this remains his secret."[38]

The Vieux-Colombier had not yet lowered its modest rep green curtain when a new theatre was already opening its doors, at 143 boulevard Saint-Germain. An odd theatre, that looked in part like a shed and in part like a fairground stall, hastily constructed in a kind of recess on the boulevard, that little square where a statue of Diderot stands today. Here is where Gaston Baty set up his troupe, les Compagnons de la Chimère (The Chimaera's Companions), after having wandered from shelter to shelter—Comédie des Champs-Élysées, Théâtre des Maturins... The "Baraque de la Chimère" (The Chimaera's Stall), as it would be called, deserved its name. It would appear quickly for what it was: a chimaera; better still, a veritable utopia. And would disappear just as quickly.

Three hundred and forty seats, most of them uncomfortable, a façade painted by Boris Metchersky in the naïf style. The real originality of the theatre lay rather in its artistic functioning, with a reading committee

---

[37] *Ibid.*

[38] *Ibid.* What followed in Jacques Copeau's career, notably the short time he held the position of Administrator in Chief of the Comédie-Française, in 1940, seems to bear out Robert Brasillach's judgment.

composed of thirteen members, almost all of whom belonged to the new generation of dramatic writers, the post-war one: Saint-Georges de Bouhélier, Denys Amiel, Jean-Jacques Bernard, Gabriel Marcel, Jean Sarment, Henri-René Lenormand... But there was the rub, because the committee didn't have any real power, it was a kind of recording chamber; Baty made all the decisions, and above all he chose the plays! "Either out of admiration for Baty or out of weakness stemming from fellowship, we ended up agreeing to things that should have revolted us, such as that *Sainte Geneviève* penned by a sanctimonious provincial lady," Henri-René Lenormand recalled in his Memoirs.[39] The committee's tastes, as one could imagine, favoured rather plays like *Chacun sa vérité* by Pirandello or *Empereur Jones* (*Emperor Jones*) by Eugene O'Neill... that Baty ruthlessly rejected. What he wanted were texts that illustrated the theory he developed elsewhere, in his writings or lectures—what he called the "integral drama"—in order to subject them, on stage, to the test of reality.

In short, not one of the works selected by the reading committee would see the light at the Baraque. Discouragement? Lack of perseverance or stubbornness? Bad artistic choices? Grave financial problems?... After having mounted rather unsuccessfully *Je veux revoir ma Normandie* (*I want to see my Normandy again*) by Lucien Besnard, *Cyclone* (*Cyclone*) by Simon Gantillon, *Le Voyageur* (*The Traveler*) by Denys Amiel, Gaston Baty threw in the towel suddenly and closed the Baraque de la Chimère: "That spelled the end of his uncomfortable stalls, his décors, his luminous orchestra pit, his projectors, and all his little marvels of lighting and machinery."[40] Opened on May 2 1923, the theatre was put up for auction less than a year later, February 19 1924. It was sold for 60,800 francs—"The modest and perfect tool had cost triple the amount," Lenormand concluded—and was right away earmarked for the wreckers' pick axes. The adventure lasted only nine months. And the Chimère, deprived of a shelter, resumed its wandering: the Théâtre de l'Odéon, the Studio des Champs-Élysées... The audiences at the Baraque nevertheless had the opportunity to discover a rare actress, whose destiny would, for a long time, be inseparably linked to Baty's: Marguerite Jamois.

But already Adrienne Monnier had opened her bookstore, la Maison des Amis des Livres (The House for Friends of Books), 7 rue de l'Odéon. This House was almost a convent, in any case a kind of workroom in a con-

---

[39] *Les Confessions d'un auteur dramatique*, Albin Michel, 1950.
[40] *Les Confessions d'un auteur dramatique*, Albin Michel, 1950.

vent, behind the austere grey store window, and Mlle Monnier—she was just 23 years old when she set up her business—was its lay nun, devoted to the cause of books, with her round face devoid of makeup, disdainful of all coquettishness, in which two clear eyes were shinning, with her soft voice, her long dress of grey cloth...Besides, this is how certain people called her: "The Servant of books." Beforehand, she had spent three years with Yvonne Sarcey, the founder of the Université des Annales (the University of Annals), as her secretary—long enough for her to discover that she was dreaming of a literature completely different from the kind that was being created at the Annals. At the Maison des Amis des Livres, she would not only find it but even bring it to life. One of the first to push open the door of her bookstore was Guillaume Apollinaire, behind whom rushed in Jules Romains, André Gide, Blaises Cendrars...It was with them that she did her probationary period. Henceforth, her poor were the known as well as unknown writers she gathered around her: André Breton, Louis Aragon, Philippe Soupault, Léon-Paul Fargue, François Mauriac, Valéry Larbaud (he called the Maison des Amis des Livres "the divine shop"), Paul Éluard, Claude Roy...; her good works were the help, the support she gave them. She brought together, in the spring of 1939, André Gide and Jean-Paul Sartre; the two men would talk about American literature. Paul Valéry probably owed her a good portion of his glory;[41] it is at her place that, in 1941, he read *Mon Faust* (*My Faust*) for an audience of initiates. And the final scene of *Tête d'or* (*Golden Head*) (the dialogue between Simon Agnel and the Princesse), by Paul Claudel, was given there for the first time, in 1919. Hers was a life entirely devoted to letters, to discoveries: "It was the bookstore for literature's young sap, new wine, fresh salt."[42] Musicians were also welcomed at Adrienne Monnier's place, Erik Satie, Darius Milhaud often previewed their works there.

In *L'Almanach de Saint-Germain-des-Prés* (*The Almanac of Saint-Germain-des-Prés*), a collective work published in 1950, where are notably evoked the great figures, past and present, of the neighbourhood, the writer and journalist Marius Richard draws a gripping portrait of her: "I can see her, in her grey cape, as a kind of Mother Superior of the Book, painted by Philippe de Champaigne. I have always found in her traits that bear a resemblance to Marguerite Audoux's portraits. They are women with the same sensibility. What respect and tenderness

---

[41] Paul Léautaud affirms this in his *Journal littéraire*.
[42] Marius Richard, "Les Librairies", in *L'Almanach de Saint-Germain-des-Prés, op. cit.*

in the transparent paper with which she covered the books she would lend us![43] Since 1915, she has been there, faithful to her love, and, it seems, without having made a fortune, unlike some of the authors to whose fame she contributed."[44]

Four years after Adrienne Monnier, Miss Sylvia Beach, an American, the daughter of a Presbyterian minister, born in Princeton in 1887, set herself up in turn on the rue de l'Odéon. Henceforth, at number 12, the sign "Shakespeare and Company" would face the Maison des Amis des Livres.[45] For at least thirty years, Shakespeare and Company became the preferred rendezvous of Anglo-Saxon writers passing through Paris and made them known to French readers. One would see Ernest Hemingway, James Joyce (Sylvia Beach would be the first to publish *Ulysses* in French), F. Scott Fitzgerald, Ezra Pound, Thornton Wilder...

Sylvia Beach belonged to that generation of American lesbians at the beginning of the 20th century in Paris, where their singularity seemed better accepted than in the puritanical society of the United States. Saint-Germain des-Prés would be their asylum. Rich heiresses for the most part, they had a common penchant for literature and the arts and, quite often, a genuine literary talent. For example, Gertrude Stein, with her hair close-cropped, and the face and build of a Roman tribune. A woman of letters—she influenced the Lost Generation—as well as a shrewd art collector (Picasso, Juan Gris, Matisse, Braque), she was born in 1874 in Allegheny, in Pennsylvania, into a family of wealthy industrialists. At first she lived at 27 rue de Fleurus, where she received the Paris smart set of writers and painters, before setting up residence on the rue Christine. There was also Natalie Clifford Barney, the "Amazon," two years younger than her, the daughter of a railway magnate, who moved into rue Jacob, around 1910, in the house that the Maréchal de Saxe had built formerly for Adrienne Lecouvreur, the illustrious tragedian, and whose garden hid, under its foliage, the fragile "temple of friendship." In addition, one could find the poet Renée Vivien, born Pauline Tarn, of an American mother; Alice B. Toklas, who landed in Paris from San Francisco in 1907; the painter Romaine Brooks. Finally, there was Winaretta Singer, born in

---

[43] The Maison des Amis des Livres included a lending library. In his work *Saint-Germain-des-Prés* (*op. cit.*), Jean-Paul Caracalla tells us that, on February 12 1916, Aragon borrowed *L'Annonce faite à Marie*, by Paul Claudel, and Jacques Lacan, on January 16 1919, *Le Neveu de Rameau*, by Diderot.

[44] "Les Librairies", in *L'Almanach de Saint-Germain-des-Prés, op. cit.*

[45] The two women would form a partnership.

1865, the daughter of the manufacturer of the Singer sewing machine, the future Princesse Edmond de Polignac and a music patron, whose "definitive blue gaze and conquering chin" Colette evoked kindly in her memoirs.[46]

Between the two of them, Sylvia Beach and Adrienne Monnier, dissimilar but complementary—"One had white hair. A bluish outfit with a masculine cut and a short skirt[...]. The other woman with her quiet demeanour, in grey, with her skirt sweeping the ground"[47]—would encourage writers to find their way to Saint-Germain-des-Prés; they would never forget it.

On leaving the Maison des Amis des Livres, turn to the left—to the right if you come out of Shakespeare and Company; go down the rue de l'Odéon. Right away, you come upon the crossroad. Then the boulevard and Danton's monument. Turn to the left again. Follow the boulevard Saint-Germain. On the other sidewalk, the church stands out behind the metal gate of a dusty little square. Here is the spot, here are the sidewalk cafés "that gurgle like a French fries oven,"[48] over which, when it is hot, the large cloth awnings are lowered... It was there, on the caned chairs, that Surrealists and dissident Surrealists, estranged from Montparnasse, set up their headquarters. Michel Leiris, Georges Bataille, Jacques Baron, Robert Desnos, Jacques Prévert, Georges Ribemont-Dessaignes, Roger Vitrac... All of these, unable to endure any longer André Breton's fits of tyranny, would soon slam the door. Not before drawing up, on the pedestal tables of the Deux Magots, in 1930, the anti-Breton satirical tract, *Un cadavre* (*A Corpse*). Each one put in his two cents with a provocative dart: Ribemont-Dessaignes called him a "tadpole in a baptismal font," Prévert conferred upon him the title of "illustrious kisser of the western world"...

Vain disputes, little authors' quarrels, jealousies, feelings of bitterness, acts of pettiness, that did not in the least trouble the daily tranquillity of the Saint-Germain residents. Nor their nights, for that matter: "If, in 1938, on a given night, after the Brasserie Lipp closed, a night reveller had been blackballed in the neighbourhood of Saint-Germain-des-Prés

---

[46] Colette, "Un salon 1900" in *Journal à rebours*, Fayard, 1941.
[47] Remark made by the cinema director Sergei Eisenstein related by Adrienne Monnier herself in her book *Rue de l'Odéon*, Albin Michel, 1960.
[48] Léon-Paul Fargue, "Saint-Germain-des-Prés", in *Le Piéton de Paris, op. cit.*

and forbidden to leave, he would not have found even one place to slake his distressed thirstiness."[49]

Tranquillity? Yes and no. In his *Manuel de Saint-Germain-des-Prés*, Boris Vian conjures up the evenings at Lipp, during the '20s, as they were related to him: "On the ground floor the Lipp had only one hall, the first. The one at the back did not exist. There were already earthenware decorations,[50] but the ambiance was more intimate. The clientele: Jouvet (every evening), Valentine Tessier, Gaston Gallimard. In a corner, André Gide, huddled up in his wraps, would be reading in a corner, and Léon-Paul Fargue who despite his legend as a drinker would invariably take—get this—a quarter bottle of Vichy warmed up in a double boiler! Much later on, historical scenes unfolded at the Lipp."

Because the peaceful, almost provincial atmosphere of the place would be replaced by a more lively, if not more violent climate, fuelled by the events of the day: the Stavisky Affair, the riots of February 6 1934... And soon the Front Populaire.

At the turn of the century, the Café de Flore had been one of the birthplaces of Action Française: "The AF met there at the time of the Dreyfus Affair. Maurras used to present his doctrine there."[51] Thirty years later, the Brasserie Lipp became the rendezvous of politicians of all shades: "left wing cells, right wing compartments, various Freemasons, young people going from the most narrow-minded patriotism to the most generous internationalism, and vice-versa. A kind of interior sea where mingled all the streams, all the political rivers of this singular 20th century. Thus one should not be astonished that storms broke out sometimes and darkened the sixth district of Paris."[52] Like the one that Charles Maurras' fanatical henchmen unleashed, one evening in 1935, when they booed Léon Blum who was dining in the back hall: "Cries rose up: 'Death to Blum, Blum to the gallows!' Perched on a table, Robert Desnos protested against this incitation to murder, and Picabia copiously chewed out the troublemakers. Blocking their path in front of his cash

---

[49] Guillaume Hanoteau, *L'Âge d'or de Saint-Germain-des-Prés*, Denoël, 1965.

[50] These ceramic and mosaic decorations, executed at the beginning of the 20th century, are the work of Léon-Paul Fargue's father and uncle, both specialized engineers. See Léon-Paul Fargue, *Le Piéton de Paris, op. cit.*

[51] Léon-Paul Fargue, *Le Piéton de Paris, op. cit.*

[52] *Ibid.*

desk, Cazes (he was a strapping man), prevented the ten or twelve aspiring assassins from getting close to Léon."[53]

Léon-Paul Fargue, who was watching the fight from his table, concluded: "Within a few minutes, the brawl became generalized and I myself received, I, a spectator who hadn't left his place, a reactionary pitcher thrown at full force, at an acute angle, like a tennis service that was a bit stiff, and that literally opened a gash in my leg."[54]

---

[53] Boris Vian, *Manuel de Saint-Germain-des-Prés, op. cit.* Marcellin Cazes was the owner of the Brasserie Lipp.

[54] *Le Piéton de Paris, op. cit.*

2

"Painting, affirmed Picasso while he was finishing Guernica, is not meant to decorate apartments, it is an instrument of war"

Really, Saint-Germain-des-Prés was changing. 1933, 1934, 1935... "Saint-Germain has begun imperceptibly to replace Montparnasse as the literary and artistic place to be, just as Montparnasse had taken over from Montmartre. People would meet at the Flore, and les Deux Magots supplanted la Rotonde and le Dôme as the painters' hangout."[1] Now, at the neighbourhood sidewalk cafés, "American women show their beautiful muscular legs and smoke cigarettes while drinking café crèmes or elixirs that are unknown back home, vermouth-cassis or Pernod."[2]

This was the time Jean-Louis Barrault chose to "cut the umbilical cord," as he said. Breaking, so to speak, with Charles Dullin, his master, he left Montmartre and the Théâtre de l'Atelier, where he had just enjoyed his first success.[3] He joined up with his new friends, including Robert Desnos, on the left bank.

In the heart of Saint-Germain-des-Prés, he unearthed—he is the one who asserts this—"a magnificent place." An attic, located on the last floor of a 16th century building, part of the ground floor of which was occupied by the Union of Bailiffs. 7 rue des Grands-Augustins: a car-

---

[1] Marcel Duhamel, *Raconte pas ta vie*, Mercure de France, 1972
[2] Léo Larguier, *Saint-Germain-des-Prés, mon village*, op. cit.
[3] June 4 1935, at the Théâtre de l'Atelier, Jean-Louis Barrault mounted *Autour d'une mère*, a dramatic adaptation of William Faulkner's *Tandis que j'agonise* (As I lay dying).

riage entrance leading to the street, a cobblestone courtyard, at the back a few steps leading to a weaver's workshop with its old looms. And, above, at the top of an old stone staircase, on the second and last floor, three vast rooms with sloping ceilings, crowned by a magnificent oak framework, paved with chipped red hexagonal tiles. These premises, "the Attic of the Augustins," as it would be called, would occupy a place of utmost importance first in the history of the theatre, then in painting. Here is where Jean-Louis Barrault would henceforth work and live. Amidst an incredible cohort of friends and collaborators. And spongers. A kind of community.

Marcel Duhamel, the future creator of the "Série Noire," has left us an on-the-spot sketch, done in broad strokes, of the Attic of the Augustins and its fauna: "It is freezing cold there, despite a stove that snorts only intermittently in the middle of the room, because the tenant doesn't earn much at Dullin's. As for furniture, there is a large table with benches, a portable stove in a corner and a few mattresses in certain areas, under the roof timbers, that serve as bedrooms. In addition to Jacques, Lou and Jean-Louis, those present include Maurice Baquet, Roger Blin, Gazelle, Raymond Bussières..."[4] There followed a long list of names, where one remarked those of many actors, labourers, barmen... "They have dinner. Everyone brings what he can. Bad red wine in abundance."[5] And those who did not have anywhere to sleep set up camp under the roof.

Margot Capelier would still recall these dinners, or rather picnics, sixty years later: "I would give a lot to go back to that place. Big dinners would unfold every week, everyone brought something, according to his means. The table was covered with victuals. The hall was lit by candles..."[6] Just like Maurice Baquet, another guest: "Fifty, sixty people would gather there on some Wednesday nights... There were non-stop comings and goings. Many just passed by. One got the impression of a big mess. For example, those opened trunks filled with clothing scattered about. There were also costumed evenings..."[7]

---

[4] *Raconte pas ta vie, op. cit.* "Jacques" is Jacques Prévert, "Lou", is Lou Tchimoukow, "Gazelle", Duhamel's wife.

[5] *Ibid.*

[6] Conversation with the author, 1998. Margot Capelier (1911-2007), after a career as a cinema script girl, then as an assistant director of production, became a casting director.

[7] Conversation with the author, 1998. Cellist and actor, Maurice Baquet (1911-2005) appeared in a hundred films.

This mess shocked Madeleine Renaud, a brilliant member of the Comédie-Française, very popular at the time, whom Jean-Louis Barrault had just met during the shooting of a film and whom he would marry in 1940: "He camped out in an apartment on the rue des Grands-Augustins. The Bohemian life seemed pale and quaint compared to this original and avant-gardist phalanstery. A kind of prefiguration of hippie communities. An extraordinary place. Matresses were spread out everywhere, because all those who did not have a room, or a home, came to sleep at Barrault's place. The jumble made me suffocate. I never slept there. My place was not there."[8]

One of the many frequenters of the Attic of the Augustins was none other than Jacques Prévert, who never went anywhere without his friends, "Prévert's Gang," as it was called at the Café de Flore, or else "The Préverts." Not that he was well known. In 1935, Prévert had as yet written practically nothing—his first collection of poems, *Paroles* (Words), would not be published before 1946. To his credit, he had just one of those film scripts that would make him famous: *L'Affaire est dans le sac* (*It's in the Bag*), directed by his brother Pierre in 1932. It was only with *Le Crime de M. Lange* (*The Crime of M. Lange*), by Jean Renoir, and *Jenny* by Marcel Carné, that his name would appear on the credits of important films.

"Prévert's Gang," otherwise known as the Groupe Octobre (The October Group), was a working class theatrical troupe, openly Marxist. These were numerous during that period, and brought together under the aegis of the FTOF (Fédération du théâtre ouvrier français/Federation of French Working Class Theatres): Masses (Masses), a company directed by Roger Legris; Douze (Twelve), led by Jacques Chabannes; Mars, run by Sylvain Itkine; and also Combats, Regards (Glances)...To which one must add the district troupes and groups from the suburbs. Most of them did not carry out excessive research, and so conceived their shows in the form of spoken choruses, where the social or political demands of the moment were commented on in an obviously schematic fashion. A kind of rap well before its time.

When mounting short plays, the Groupe Octobre quickly distanced itself from this simplifying tendency. They presented sketches where the audience could find, in addition to a ferocious denunciation of capitalism—the Front populaire (Popular Front) was emerging—the pleasure

---

[8] Madeleine Renaud, *La Déclaration d'amour*, Éditions du Rocher, 2000.

of an authentic show for which contemporary events would provide a daily supply of varied misfortunes and disappointments.

The 1930s saw the questioning, followed by the death of the old economic order inherited from the 19th century, in the convulsions of a crisis that preceded the painful establishment of new rules of productivity. And the theatre, a sensitive barometer of all of society's transformations, could not steer clear of such changes for long. Whereas an organizer like Erwin Piscator, who directed the Voksbühne (The People's Stage) in Berlin, had already understood this evolution—"Pure art has begun to demand of the theatre a response to the political and social issues of its time"[9]—in France the Groupe Octobre would meet the challenge. First under another name, since in 1927, during the period when the first nucleus of the group was constituted, it was called Prémices (Beginnings): about thirty members, all amateurs—young people, workers and employees for the most part—who, weary of exclusively aesthetic forms of research, wished to commit themselves to social struggle. In truth, rather than getting involved in the theatre, what interested them was starting a revolution. They could do so by participating in labour unrest, in popular meetings, in short, in political action. The approaching legislative elections of May 1932 would incite ten or so among them to leave Prémices in order to move towards a more radically proletarian kind of theatre. Thus was born the "Groupe de choc Prémices" (The Beginnings Shock Group). Among its founding members: Raymond Bussières, at the time a draftsman at City Hall, who would later on have a brilliant career in supporting roles in the cinema and on stage, Arlette Besset, a law student, Lazare Fuchmann, an accountant's assistant... Workers from all walks of life.

So the question of repertoire came up. Arlette Besset and Bussières informed Paul Vaillant-Couturier about this problem and asked him to write texts for them. The chief editor of *L'Humanité*, a writer himself, barely had the time to react to the young people's request. He directed them to a cinema critic who was then an authority and who, besides, was a specialist in the history of the theatre: Léon Moussinac. The latter referred them in turn to Jacques Prévert. Why Prévert? Indeed, during that period, his brilliant career as a poet and scriptwriter had not yet materialized. Because Prévert could talk! And even talk non-stop! "His true works had never been committed to writing, he had 'spoken' them. No one had ever seen Jacques awake and silent. With him, the spoken

---

[9] Erwin Piscator, *Le Théâtre politique*, L'Arche, 1972.

word was an attribute of his physique, just like his ears or his nose."[10] Not that he was a brilliant talker, far from it, but his words exuded a kind of magic: "He stammered. He even babbled. The charm of his conversation lay elsewhere, in its inner movement. A word barely pronounced gave rise to another word, another image, another idea. By expatiating, Prévert would reveal what would normally remain hidden in the deepest recesses of poets, the very mechanisms of creation."[11]

Consequently Bussières and Arlette Besset turned up at Prévert's place. He inhabited at the time a cheap residential hotel at 39 rue Dauphine: "In this seven story building transformed into a refuge for penniless artists, Jacques Prévert led a Bohemian existence. He willingly shared with his friends an omelette or spaghetti with tomato sauce."[12] They were equipped with little more than their total enthusiasm as activists—"We knew what we wanted: a sketch about the press, made up of clippings from the newspapers of the period and illustrating the themes of our propaganda: capitalism brings on war and poverty; social democracy has two faces, one demagogical, the other in the service of money."[13] Agreement was immediate between the future poet and his visitors, even though Prévert's ambition to reform society—assuming that he entertained this ambition—seemed closer, as his biographer Jean-Claude Lamy pointed out humorously, to the vague desires of anarchy and revolt of a Groucho Marx than to the pure and hard Marxist line applied by the French Communist Party.[14] He read them nonetheless the beginning of a play he was in the process of writing, in order to ascertain that they appreciated his manner and style.

Several days later, that is to say, towards the end of the month of April 1932, the Beginnings Shock Group was holding a meeting on the avenue Mathurin-Moreau, in the offices of the CGTU, la Confédération générale des travailleurs unitaires (The Principal Confederation of Unitarian Workers), a union close to the Communists, when Jacques Prévert arrived, bringing his work with him so to speak. It was a text he had baptized *Vive la Presse!* (Long Live the Press!) and it unleashed at once the enthusiasm of the troupe.

Very quickly Prévert would make his young comrades aware of the strengths—and weaknesses—of proletarian theatre. On the occasion

---

[10] Guillaume Hanoteau, *L'Âge d'or de Saint-Germain–des-Prés, op. cit.*

[11] *Ibid.*

[12] Jean-Claude Lamy, *Prévert, les frères amis*, Robert Laffont, 1997.

[13] Arlette Besset, quoted by Michel Fauré, *Le Groupe Octobre*, Christian Bourgois, 1977.

[14] See *Prévert, les frères amis, op. cit.*

of meetings organized in the former dancehall, Bal Bullier[15], where the cohorts of the FTOF, in overalls, were content to shout out dreary revolutionary slogans, they became, on the contrary, aware of the necessity of reinforcing the effectiveness of their message with the help of dramatic art's resources. And to appoint a genuine stage director as a collaborator. This was how Lou Thimoukow, who had scarcely anything Slavic about him except his pseudonym, joined the group. He was chosen as a token of their admiration for the Bolsheviks...

Lou Thimoukow, whose real name was Louis Bonin, had a passion for the theatre. He had contracted its virus as a child, had spent his childhood in the wings of the Théâtre de la Porte-Saint-Martin where his father was the stage manager. He was the one who hit upon the definitive name for the group: Octobre. It was one more way of paying homage to the Russian revolution of 1917. In any event, it was a name proclaiming loud and clear the political identity of a troupe that seemed thus, in advance, to adopt Roger Vitrac's declaration: "At a time when the world functions as it can, the theatre must function as it must. It is in the vanguard of human preoccupations, it underscores profound changes. In France, we are at last preparing the revolution in the theatre. And here is a formula that can reverse itself just like an hourglass."[16]

The Groupe Octobre went straight to work, making appearances at "goguettes,"[17] in the backrooms of bistros in working-class neighbourhoods like Belleville, at the cité Popincourt, where a few tables drawn together made a stage, as well as during popular celebrations... *Vive la Presse!* was given for the first time at the Fête de l'Humanité (the celebration organized by the newspaper *L'Humanité*), in May 1932. This was the first of Prévert's works to be performed on stage. A crowd-pleaser, sustained by contemporary themes, more substantial than a simple collage of slogans, the show won a huge popular success:

> *To die for one's country is to die for Renault,*
> *For Renault, for the Pope, for Chiappe,*

---

[15] The Bal Bullier, at the corner of the boulevard Montparnasse and the avenue Denfert-Rochereau, was situated opposite the Closerie des Lilas.

[16] *La Flèche*, July 11 1936.

[17] The name referred to recreational evenings organized in the hope of drawing sympathizers.

For the meat dealers,
For the arms dealers...
[...]
The work is hard, underpaid, very hard, very underpaid,
And when you go out into the street, the street doesn't belong
to you,
The street belongs to the cops,
The street belongs to the clerics...

In the cast were Jean-Paul Dreyfus, who would later direct films under the name of Jean-Paul Le Chanois, Raymond Bussières, of course, Paul Grimault, Jacques-Bernard Brunius, Guy Decomble... "Début greeted with applause. *Vive la Presse!* would be performed many times in halls and outdoors before popular audiences and sometimes before very young children who enjoyed themselves as much as at a puppet show."[18]

Hatred of cops, hatred of the clergy, hatred of arms dealers... At the very outset, Jacques Prévert hit upon the tone that would henceforth constitute his moneymaker. And Saint-Germain-des-Prés discovered a style that would be around for a long time. The shows presented at Agnès Capri's cabaret, at the end of the 1930s, or on the little stage of the Rose Rouge, ten years later, would come straight from those put on by the Groupe Octobre. Because after *Vive la Presse!* there would be *La Bataille de Fontenoy* (*The Battle of Fontenoy*), *La Famille Tuyau de Poêle* (*The Stove Pipe Family*), *Le Palais des Mirages* (*The Palace of Mirages*), *Suivez le druide* (*Follow the Druid*)...

The scriptwriter Jean Aurenche remembers these manifestations vividly: "I would attend performances of the Groupe Octobre. *La Bataille de Fontenoy* was deeply moving, it was like nothing we knew. When Jacques Prévert wrote for the cinema, I recognized his poetry, but in a form less forceful, less free perhaps than at the Groupe Octobre."[19]

Would Jacques Prévert and Jean-Louis Barrault be henceforth inseparable? One might have believed this on reading the article that *L'Humanité* published on December 1 1935, an interview with Jean-Louis Barrault where he stated: "I am going to mount two interludes by Cervantès that Jacques

---

[18] Guillaume Hanoteau, *L'Âge d'or de Saint-Germain-des-Prés*, op. cit.
[19] *La Suite à l'écran. Entretiens*, Institut Lumière/Actes Sud, 1993.

Prévert will adapt."[20] And it was at the actor's place, a month later, under the handsome framework of the Grenier (Attic), that Jacques Prévert—with his friends, of course—spent New Years Eve. One member of "Prévert's Gang," Jean Rougeul, captured the scene: "It must have been three or four o'clock in the morning, and we remained until daybreak. These few hours left me with a strange impression. Prévert was talking. The night's face was receding, going away, beyond the faded walls, far from this magnificently miserable place, immense and almost empty, where we sat astride shaky chairs, and listened. Some boards placed on trestles made up a long table lost in the midst of this bare space. It was very simple, it was only a conversation. A conversation with Prévert, during which he gave no one the opportunity to answer him, but we didn't feel the need to answer. I scarcely remember what he said. I have simply kept the image of a night where the familiar forms of daily life became illuminated as though they were secrets we had discovered. We understood everything. We were in agreement. This old world in which we were living became so affectionate that even in the depths of our poverty we really loved it."[21]

In truth, a real dramatic team was created at the Grenier des Augustins, where Barrault, for that matter, had set up a stage as best he could. Improvisations, readings of plays, physical exercises, courses in mime: "At the Grenier, I took courses in improvisation given by Jean Dasté."[22]

After announcing their collaboration in the press, Prévert and Barrault got to work. *Le Tableau des merveilles* (*The Tableau of Marvels*), based on Cervantès, relates the story of wandering actors who arrive in a city. When received by the Prefect, the Assistant Prefect and the Captain, the thespians inform them that only those citizens whose conscience is clear will be able to see the performance. It will remain invisible for all the others. Obviously, there is no performance. Standing before the empty stage, Chanfalla, the puppeteer, simply describes imaginary scenes: Samson shaking the columns of the Temple, a furious bull, a horde of escaping rats... Scenes that all the inhabitants, nevertheless, will claim to have seen! In the role of Chanfalla was Barrault himself, surrounded by unknowns who, for the most part, would become famous: Marcel Mouloudji, fourteen years old at the time—and who thus staked out his territory in Saint-Germain-des-Prés, where he would be one of the

---

[20] In reality, he will only mount one, *Le Tableau des Merveilles* (The Tableau of Marvels).

[21] *L'Écran français,* September 25 1946.

[22] Margot Capelier, interview with the author, 1998.

important figures after the war—Roger Blin, the future stage director for Samuel Beckett and Jean Genet, Fabien Loris, the Avril in Marcel Carné's *Les Enfants du paradis* (*The Children of Paradise*)...

Presented first on the Grenier's little stage, before an audience of buddies—"This is the play I saw, among some close friends, under the maritime forest of tangled beams"[23]—*Le Tableau des Merveilles* was then performed before a real audience, in the salle Adyar, 4 square Rapp, in February 1936, under the patronage of the AEAR (Association des écrivains et artistes révolutionnaires/The Association of Revolutionary Writers and Artists) of which Louis Aragon was the godfather. In its issue of March 1, the review *Esprit* devoted an article to the evening: "Jean-Louis Barrault's Grenier des Augustins presented a play whose adapter, Prévert could have turned into a masterpiece. The staging by Jean-Louis Barrault, very jerky, rich in strokes of inspiration, but sometimes a bit muddled, was considerably hampered by the narrowness of the performing space. One would like to see it again under better conditions." Pierre-Aimé Touchard, who wrote these lines, would be heard. Indeed, the big strikes of May-June 1936, that accompanied the installation of the Front Populaire government, would favour numerous repeat performances of the show. Most of the time these were given in support of the strikers, at the very workplaces the latter had occupied. *Le Tableau des Merveilles* was thus performed on June 13 at Montreuil's City Hall, then, a few days later, in the "First Communion" department of the Grands Magasins du Louvre, before being presented in front of the four hundred delivery and shipping employees of the Samaritaine depot, on boulevard Saint-Jacques, that had been occupied for twelve days...

But an era was ending. The group would fall apart under the pressure of political events, the issue of the Spanish Civil War would poison relationships between the various members. In fact, since the Laval-Stalin pact, in May 1935, by virtue of which the USSR approved the French national defence policy, the worm was in the fruit. Because the French Communist Party, submissive, as usual, to the diktats of Moscow, aligned itself with docility. And began if not to adore, at least to consider without unnecessary hostility what it had burned yesterday. Namely, the French army. From then on, Jacques Prévert distanced himself. And there were many who questioned the appropriateness of pursuing their activity. As Roger Blin explained: "For people like us,

---

[23] Guillaume Hanoteau, *Ces nuits qui ont fait Paris, op. cit.*

who were in the vanguard of the struggle against capitalist structures, no re-conversion was possible."[24]

And the Groupe Octobre broke apart.

As for himself, Jean-Louis Barrault, really enamoured of Madeleine Renaud, jumped with both feet over the Seine and went off to join his beloved on the right bank, near Auteuil, abandoning Saint-Germain-des-Prés and the attic on the rue des Grands-Augustins. The latter would not remain unoccupied for long. Dora Maar, a photographer, and Picasso's companion, was in fact looking for a studio for the painter.

It was at the Café des Deux Magots that Picasso and Dora Maar first met, introduced by Robert Desnos. A couple? No, if one is to believe Jean Cocteau. Rather a kind of improbable trio. Should one believe this? No doubt. Because Cocteau knew Picasso inside out: "Picasso is a profoundly entangled man and woman (just like in his paintings). It is a household. The Picasso household. Dora is a concubine with whom he betrays himself. From this household are born some marvellous monsters[25]." *Guernica* was one of those sublime and monstrous offspring.

The former Grenier des Augustins was where the artist, from the month of May 1937, undertook the composition of the tableau that is no doubt the most celebrated political painting of the 20th century. Several days earlier, on April 26, the airplanes of the Luftwaffe attacked the little town of Guernica, in the province of Biscay, in Spain.[26] For three hours, the Junker-52 of the German legion Condor, commanded by General Sperrle, dropped fifty tons of bombs on Guernica. The result: 1,654 victims. So Dora Maar, profoundly committed to the anti-Fascist cause, convinced Picasso to take a position publicly. She didn't have to work hard to persuade him. Because as soon as the pro-Franco declaration was issued, the painter chose his camp, shouting out his horror of the "military caste that has plunged Spain in an ocean of suffering and death," and thereby becoming, in a way, abroad, the symbol of Republican resistance.[27] The Republicans had asked him, in January 1937, to conceive

---

[24] Quoted in Michel Fauré, *Le Groupe Octobre, op. cit.*

[25] *Journal 1942-1945*, Gallimard, 1989.

[26] During the Spanish Civil War, the Nazi regime, in power in Berlin, in fact supported the Franquists.

[27] In July 1936, already, the Republican government named Picasso director of the Prado Museum. A strange museum, with empty halls. Because the paintings had been hidden in the storerooms and basements for fear of bombardments by the Nationalists.

a work meant to decorate the Spanish pavilion at the World Fair that would be held in Paris, during the course of the summer. That work—and masterpiece—for which recent tragic events would provide the subject—would be *Guernica* ...

But, without waiting for the summer, Picasso seized the opportunity offered by an exhibit of Spanish Republican painters in New York to publish a forthright declaration: "All my life as an artist has been nothing but a continuous struggle against repression and the death of art. How could one think, even for an instant, that I would be in agreement with repression and evil?"[28] Then he concluded: "I have always believed, and I still believe that artists who live and work with spiritual values can not, and must not remain indifferent in the face of a conflict where the stakes are the highest values of humanity and civilization."

And so, without further delay, at the beginning of the month of May, in the austere, almost empty studio of the rue des Grands-Augustins, under the boughs of the several centuries old framework, he went to work. There were neither pieces of furniture nor curtains on the windows that overlooked the rooftops, only the indispensable: the painter's tools—brushes, colours, canvasses, easels. Tens of canvasses, some facing the wall, the others visible. And the pipes of the old stove—the one used by Jean-Louis Barrault—running along the inside surface. Within a few weeks, he executed a hundred or so preparatory sketches. Before tackling the work itself. Monumental in size, it occupied a whole side of the studio, from the ground to the ceiling: white, grey and black. The colours of mourning. Perched on a large ladder, his palette in his hand, Picasso worked, with hatred in his heart: "Paintings are not meant to decorate apartments," he told Gertrude Stein, "they are instruments of an offensive and defensive war against the enemy."

In the meantime, Dora Maar, standing by him, captured, in her photos, the progress and above all the evolution of the work. "In modern painting," said Pablo Picasso, "every stroke has become a precise operation, is part of a clock-making procedure. You paint a personage's beard, it is auburn, and this auburn colour leads you to rework everything in the ensemble, to repaint, as though this were a chain reaction, everything that surrounds it."[29]

---

[28] The rumour had circulated for a short time that Picasso had gone over to the pro-Franco party. A rumour spread, of course, by that very party.

[29] *La Guerre et la Paix,* text by Claude Roy, Éditions Cercle d'art, 1954.

As was expected, *Guernica* would be presented in Paris, during the summer of 1937, on the occasion of the World Fair, in the pavilion of the Spanish Republic:[30] "Picasso doesn't relate facts. He even eliminated all anecdotes from his tableau. He conjures up, in a way, in this 3m 50 x 7m 80 panel, a mythical portrait of our era. Meaning is not outside the painting; it cannot be summarized in a narrative. Meaning and form are inseparable. Colour had to be sorrow there, line had to be terror or anger, and the composition had to be so strongly mastered that the work would be indivisibly a verdict and man's cry."[31]

Was it in this period—1937? 1938?—that Simone de Beauvoir, abandoning Montparnasse, pushed open for the first time the door of the Café de Flore? No doubt...The place had become the rendezvous of cinema people. One could see the Prévert brothers and their friends from the former Groupe Octobre, the director Jean Grémillon, the scriptwriter Jean Aurenche..."The Flore had its way of life, its ideology; the little band of faithful that met there daily did not belong entirely either to the bohemian or the bourgeois world[32]." And the little band in question only had eyes for Jacques Prévert: its god, it oracle...Certainly, Simone de Beauvoir and Jean-Paul Sartre had appreciated *L'affaire est dans le sac* shortly before and, more recently, *Drôle de drame* (*Funny Drama*). No matter, the couple felt only a very relative affinity towards the "Prévert Gang": "Their anti-conformism served above all to justify their inertia; they were very bored. They spent their day giving vent to their disgust in blasé little sentences interspersed with yawns. They never stopped deploring the bloody human stupidity!"[33] Just like this bit of dialogue, caught on the spot at Café de Flore's terrace: "Even when I get an erection I say to myself: What's the point?" or this young man's reflection in the presence of a beautiful girl: "Perishable!..."[34]

---

[30] After Paris, *Guernica* was presented in Scandinavia, in London, in the United States (where the picture would remain more than forty years, exhibited at the Museum of Modern Art, according to the wish of Picasso who hoped that it would return to Spain only when public freedoms were restored). Installed in 1981 in the Prado Museum, the canvass is now exhibited at the Reina Sofia Art Centre in Madrid.

[31] Roger Garaudy, *D'un réalisme sans ravages*, Plon, 1963.

[32] Simone de Beauvoir, *La Force de l'âge*, Gallimard, 1960.

[33] *Ibid.*

[34] Marcel Duhamel, *Raconte pas ta vie, op. cit.*

Simone de Beauvoir was hard on the survivors from the Groupe Octobre when she evoked, from a distance of more than twenty years, the atmosphere at the Café de Flore before the war: "One could also see very pretty girls there. The most striking one was Sonia Mossé whose face and superb body had inspired sculptors and painters. ... But the most prevalent feminine type was what we used to call 'the distressing ones': creatures with pallid hair, more or less ravaged by drugs, or alcohol, or by life, with sad mouths and eyes that never seemed to end."[35] And these "distressing ones," precisely, constituted the main preoccupation of the "idle youths at the Flore": "Every young man had, with every girl, in succession, a relationship of variable duration, but generally brief; once the circuit was completed, they would start all over again, which would be rather monotonous."[36] And, in fact, some very curious games of musical chairs were played out between Jacques, Janine, Fabien, Gazelle, Marcel, Germaine, Robert and the others...

Each group—each clan?—conscious of the stakes involved, seemed to distance itself from the other. One belonged to "Sartre's Gang" or to "Prévert's Gang," rarely to both. And this is how it would be for the whole duration of the Occupation. "At the outset, Saint-Germain-des-Prés is 'Prévert's Gang' and 'the Sartre Family.' But all the people mingled. I saw several times, but in truth not very often, Sartre and Prévert together. Having said this the notion of 'family' was very strong, especially for these two essential poles; 'the Prévert Gang,' with the Groupe Octobre as its base, and 'the Sartre Family,' that is to say Sartre, Simone de Beauvoir, Bost, Olga and Wanda Kosakiewicz, Mouloudji... But everything got complicated, because he, Mouloudji, was between the two: he was a former member of 'Prévert's Gang,' of the Groupe Octobre, and at the same time he was a protégé of Sartre."[37] Conscious of his position, Mouloudji would endeavour to bring about a meeting between the two clans: "My initiative remained vain, because as much as the Sartre people were open under closed appearances, as much Prévert under his open exterior..."[38]

Everything was in place, then, to make Saint-Germain-des-Prés the fashionable neighbourhood—if not the trendy one. The places, the décor,

---

[35] Simone de Beauvoir, *La Force de l'âge, op. cit.*

[36] *Ibid.*

[37] Robert Scipion, conversation, in *Saint-Germain-des-Prés, 1945-1950, op. cit.* Scipion himself belonged to the "Sartre Family."

[38] *La Fleur de l'âge*, Grasset, 1991.

the actors and supernumeraries, the ideas, the politics, the friendships and enmities, the intrigues... All of it was ready.

The spring of 1939, the last close-up on the faces at the Café de Flore: behind the lens, the focus, this time, is on "Prévert's Gang," and is provided by Marcel Duhamel: "Our table, preferably on the terrace, with Jacques, Pierrot, Gazelle, Loris, pals from the Groupe or ex-Groupe Octobre. Roger Blin, too. The ultra blond Sonia Mossé, beautiful and pale, in her eternal black dress. Who will disappear at the beginning of the war, taken away by the Gestapo. Nearby, Henri Filipacchi, with Ripault, both spurred on by the same caustic, sarcastic mind, with a sense of humour that, by dint of cruelty, became sometimes excessively funny. With them were the Bouthoul and Léaud, a film-maker. Pardo as well, an antique dealer, with Gégé, his wife, Robert Pontabry and Germaine, Pierre Boucher, Nicole Védrès, Marcel Cravenne, the future television director... And also Renaud de Jouvenel, Roland and Claude Malraux, Jean Aurenche, the scriptwriter, Louis Chavance, idem, Stéphane Aboulker, the film-maker, etc. And André Malraux who, one day, consulted us, Jacques and myself, on the validity of a panoramic shot in his film *L'Espoir*..."[39] One could hear them laughing, talking, getting up and calling to one another from one table to another, sit down again, carried away, in the heat of their discussions, by the steeple-chase of love and politics—in the shade of the large white awnings unfurled over the terrace.

The camera travels one last time over the buildings of the boulevard Saint-Germain, on the opposite side. One last glance before the approach-

---

[39] *Raconte pas ta vie, op. cit.* Jacques and Pierrot are, of course, the Prévert brothers; a painter, an actress, a model for the surrealists, the beautiful Sonia Mossé was a regular customer at the Café de Flore (on her tragic end, see chapter 6); Henri Filipacchi, the father of Daniel Filipacchi, would be, among others, the creator in 1953 of the Livre de Poche; Gaston Bouthoul, sociologist, journalist, published notably in *Les Lettres Nouvelles*, in 1958, an article titled "Jacques Prévert et un siècle de poésie martiale"; Pierre Léaud, film-maker, married to the actress Jacqueline Pierreux, was the father of the actor Jean-Pierre Léaud; Pardo and Gégé, friends of Simone de Beauvoir, are two names familiar to readers of *Mémoires d'une jeune fille rangée, La Force de l'âge* and *La Force des choses;* Robert Pontabry, close to the Groupe Octobre, was an architect; his wife, Germaine, would become the second wife of Marcel Duhamel; Pierre Boucher was one of the pioneers of modern photography, the Museum Nicéphore-Nièpce in Chalon-sur-Saône paid homage to him in 2004; Nicole Védrès is a film director, notably *Paris 1900;* Renaud de Jouvenel, the son of Henry de Jouvenel, was thus Colette's son-in-law—Guillaume Hanoteau, in *L'Âge d'or de Saint-Germain-des-Prés (op. cit),* described him as a patron of the Groupe Octobre.

ing horrors... The Hôtel Taranne, at number 153. On the last floor, under the rooftops, a very young man, barely arrived from his Languedoc province, was leaning on his elbows at the window. Nineteen years old, close in spirit to the Action française, he contemplated this square he had dreamed so much about from afar. It was a beautiful summer evening, on July 15 1939: "Like in October 37. From my window on the last floor I could see this surprising village church tower, which enchanted me. Below, another surprise, Stendhal's and Toulet's Le Divan.[40] On the other side I had the Flore of Maurras and Bourget. The Deux Magots didn't mean much to me yet, but the Paris I had dreamed about from far was beginning to reveal itself with every step I took through one of the innumerable names on its identity card. On leaving the hotel I had on my left the Café Biard in the middle of which stood an elongated U-shaped counter. In the basement I called to Thierry Maulnier at *L'Insurgé*.[41] 'You've arrived on time for the funeral,' he told me. 'We are putting the last issue to bed.' He informed me that on Tuesday from 6 a.m. the collaborators of *Combat*,[42] which was continuing, would meet at the Brasserie Lipp."[43]

Yes, everything was in place. Life continued. Except that Adolf Hitler, in Berlin, had decided otherwise. The curtain fell on Saint-Germain-des-Prés. An intermission that would last five years. Even though in the wings the resumption was being prepared.

---

[40] This is the bookstore Le Divan, which stood at the corner of the rue Bonaparte and the rue de l'Abbaye. The book dealer, Henri Martineau, was a great specialist of Stendahl.

[41] *L'Insurgé*, weekly founded in 1936 by Thierry Maulnier and Jean-Pierre Maxence, defended ideas favoured by the Action française.

[42] *Combat*, a monthly review founded by Thierry Maulnier and Jean de Fabrègues, would stop appearing on September 1939. It is not to be confused with Albert Camus' *Combat*, a daily stemming from the Résistance.

[43] François Sentein, *Minutes d'un libertin (1938-1941)*, Le Promeneur, 2000.

3

"It was warm at the Flore and one could spend hours over an ersatz coffee or a Viandox"

It was during the course of the winter of 1941-42 that Simone de Beauvoir and Jean-Paul Sartre would get used to frequenting regularly, and almost exclusively, the Café de Flore—or rather, should one say, would get used to taking refuge in the Café de Flore: "We always had a pleasurable shock, in the evening, when we would emerge from the cold shadows and enter this warm and illuminated hideout, bedecked with beautiful red and blue colours."[1]

They left Montparnasse without much regret. Too many greyish-green uniforms at the Dôme. And above all: "while I was swallowing an ersatz coffee, 'grey mice' had at their disposal at their table butter, jam, they entrusted real tea bags to the waiter."[2] Without any shame, any respect or compassion for the starving people who were watching them. Besides, the metro station Vavin was closed, which made necessary long treks on foot to reach the crossroad. The two writers would not lose on the deal. Neither would the Café de Flore and Saint-Germain-des-Prés: "I remember that the recent launching of Saint-Germain-des-Prés is to a large extent due to their literary renown, and that if the local hotel bosses had even the slightest amount of honesty, Simone de Beauvoir and Sartre would eat free of charge in all the bistros they launched."[3]

---

[1] Simone de Beauvoir, *La Force de l'âge*. Op. cit.

[2] *Ibid*.

[3] Boris Vian, *Manuel de Saint-Germain-des-Prés*, op. cit.

In 1941, they were not yet there. Sartre? There he was, at Gallimard's, sitting in Jean Paulhan's office: "Paulhan asks him what he is working on.—Finishing a philosophical work that he brought back from captivity.—The subject?—'Being and Nothingness.' He articulates his words dryly, but the gutturals make his throat tremble like a light goitre. I had heard about his ugliness, and I didn't find him disagreeable."[4]

In the "cold shadows" of Paris during the Occupation, deprived of heat, deprived of food, deprived of freedom, the Café de Flore would be for the two of them, like for many others, a veritable haven: "We not only found there a relative comfort: it was our *querencia* (dwelling); we felt at home, sheltered."[5] In 1950, in an interview, Jean-Paul Sartre, too, talked at length about this period, and not without a kind of nostalgia: "Soon, Simone de Beauvoir and I made ourselves at home there completely: from 9 o'clock in the morning till noon, we used to work there, we would have lunch, at 2 o'clock we would come back and would then chat with friends whom we would meet till four o'clock. Then we would work again until 8 o'clock. After dinner, we would receive the people to whom we had given a rendezvous. That may seem bizarre, but the Flore was our home."[6]

"We felt at home there...we were at our home." It is not a coincidence that the same words keep coming back, under the pens of Beauvoir and Sartre, to evoke the long hours spent at the Café de Flore. For years, and to be exact ever since they were appointed to Paris, after having taught philosophy for a long time in provincial secondary schools, they adopted a style of life that they would keep until fame would oblige them to give it up: the café life, the uncomfortable hotels, the random flats[7]...As Jean-Paul Sartre would explain in an interview he would grant, in 1972, to John Gerassi: "Up till then, I had always lived in hotels, worked in cafés, ate at restaurants, and not having any possessions was very important for me. It was a form of personal salvation; I would have felt lost—as is Mathieu—if I had owned an apartment all to myself, with furniture and objects belonging to me."[8]

---

[4] François Sentein, *Minutes d'un libertin (1938-1941), op. cit.* (dated October 23 1941).

[5] Simone de Beauvoir, *La Force de l'âge, op. cit.*

[6] Quoted in Marcelle Routier, *Saint-Germain-des-Prés, op. cit.*

[7] In October 1936 Simone de Beauvoir was appointed in Paris to the lycée Molière. Sartre joined the lycée Pasteur in Neuilly, when the school year began in 1937.

[8] Interview published in Jean-Paul Sartre, *Oeuvres romanesques*, "Bibliothèque de la Pléiade", 1981. (Mathieu is the hero of *L'Âge de raison*). It was only in 1946, in fact, that Sartre moved into an apartment on the rue Bonaparte that he shared with his mother.

Moreover he was not the only one. "Practically everybody used to live in a hotel. First of all because people didn't have enough money to own an apartment and also because they did not want to stay put. Also, having an apartment ran counter to their style of living. It was almost a 'must,' as one would say today, an 'Existentialist must.' Ultimately, it would have been almost shameful to own an apartment. They paid on a daily basis. Or did not pay...Most of the people had sizeable bills. Besides, the hotel meant Bohemian life...One was considered a bourgeois if one had an apartment."[9]

Uncomfortable little hotels—Saint-Germain-des-Prés was still a popular neighbourhood and its inhabitants were not rolling in money, far from it. Jacques Audiberti dwelled at the Hôtel Taranne; Alice Sapritch, still a student at the Conservatoire, was at the Hôtel Saint-Yves, on the rue de l'Université, just like the painter Jean Fautrier or the young Suzanne Flon; Roger Vailland stayed at the Pont-Royal, on rue de Montalembert; the guitarist Henri Crolla was at the Hôtel des Beaux-Arts, on the rue Bonaparte; Simone de Beauvoir, at the Hôtel d'Aubusson, on the rue Dauphine, Sartre, at the Hôtel Chaplain; Mouloudji, in a little hotel, on the rue Jacob, that would be replaced, after the war, by Éditions du Seuil...Until the Hôtel La Louisiane would, soon, welcome the smart set of Saint-Germain. Others preferred to find shelter in a family boarding house; there were many in the neighbourhood, set up in old, quasi-historical dwellings. On rue Servandoni, at number 20, in the shadow of the towers of Saint-Sulpice, Mme Morin-Pillière, a large woman with an imposing physique and a heart of gold, her hair retained by barrettes, accommodated a clientele of intellectuals and artists: Hélène Duc—the Mahut d'Artois of the first *Rois Maudits* (*The Accursed Kings*) of the television series—the puppeteer Frédéric O'Brady, Robert Marcy, who would appear on radio after the war, Marguerite Cassan, Jean Marsan, Yvette Étiévant...and numerous salaried actors from the Théâtre de l'Odéon. On the first floor, in a large bedroom with a high ceiling, lived a discreet couple, Nicole and François Fourcade. After the war, they would separate. Nicole would meet Gérard Philipe whom she would marry; she would become Anne Philipe.

Before committing herself to a genuine theatrical career, Hélène Duc taught French at a school in Bergerac, in Dordogne. In 1940, among her little pupils in 7th grade, she noticed one who had a passion for reading poetry by heart: "When she recited poems, her beautiful black eyes lit up, one could

---

[9] Robert Scipion, interview, in *Saint-Germain-des-Prés, 1945-1950, op. cit.*

perceive in her a veritable tragic power, but her voice could already produce inflections of sweetness and irony."[10] She was called "Toutoute." The adolescent's mother, who had quickly joined the Résistance, recommended her daughter to Hélène Duc, in case, as she said, she were to be arrested.

The young girl—she was sixteen at the time—presented herself one fine evening in the autumn of 1943 at the door of the boarding house on rue Servandoni, shuddering in her navy blue summer dress. She had just been freed from the Gestapo prisons, where her mother and older sister were still held prisoners. A poor discoloured dress, a little raffia vest, bad shoes into which water seeped, a purse of bonded fibre… All alone in the world, without a cent in her pocket. "There was a piano in the lobby, on which we used to play the hit tunes of the era, related Hélène Duc. The very evening she arrived, we heard her sing *Mon amant de Saint-Jean* (My Lover from Saint Jean)…"[11] Toutoute was set up in a little room, on the fifth floor; she became the pet of the boarding house. A notary from Bordeaux sent off to her scrupulously, every month, at the rue Servandoni address, the money to cover her room and board. "She was moreover the only one who really paid regularly. Thank God, Mme Morin-Pillière was not very demanding as concerned the rent," Hélène Duc noted. To make room for a clandestine, pursued by the Gestapo, Toutoute went up to the attic to sleep; and it was under her mattress that were hidden the 7 million francs that London had parachuted in for the use of the Résistance… The real name of this Toutoute a bit too plump, whose nose was a bit too long? Juliette Gréco.

"It mattered little to me to have one bedroom, and that it lacked charm: I had Paris, its streets, its squares, its cafés…" Simone de Beauvoir affirmed for her part in *La Force de l'âge*. The Hôtel Mistral, on rue Cels, the Welcome Hôtel, on the rue de Seine, the Hôtel du Danemark, on the rue Vavin, finally the Hôtel d'Aubusson, on the rue Dauphine, where she set herself up in the autumn of 1942… A bed, a table, two chairs, a closet, a shelf to put away her books, bad lighting, sometimes a little kitchen that also served as a bathroom. That was all.

"I had Paris, its streets…, its cafés…" Because it is at the café that they worked, at the café that they chatted with their friends; to the café that they rushed when the slightest misfortune arrived—this warm refuge, this haven… The Deux Magots, the Royal-Saint-Germain, the Rhumerie.

---

[10] Hélène Duc, *Entre cour et jardin,* Pascal, 2005.

[11] Conversation with the author, May 2006.

And the Flore. Especially the Flore. Sartre, Beauvoir—and many others—worked, indifferent to the noises. It was on the pedestal tables of the Flore and the Deux Magots, amidst the cigarette smoke, the sound of percolators, laughter and conversations that were created *L'Être et le Néant*, *Huis clos*, *Pyrrhus et Cinéas*, *Les Mouches*, *Le Sang des autres*, *Les Chemins de la liberté*, *Tous les hommes sont mortels*, *Les Bouches inutiles*. Also the first plays by Arthur Adamov, those by Audiberti, the first novel by Mouloudji, *Enrico*...

"Solitude is austere when confronting a blank page; I would raise my eyes, verify that human beings existed: this encouraged me to write words that, perhaps, one day, would affect someone," observed Simone de Beauvoir in *La Force de l'âge*. While opposite her, seated on a wall bench of red leatherette, the young Mouloudji—now eighteen years old—did not take his eyes off her: "I was waiting to catch her eye before daring to greet her discretely, a wait that was not often rewarded because she had her own unique way of lifting her head and staring into space, lost in her thoughts. I really believe she was the one who launched the fashion of earning her living in public as a writer at the Café de Flore."[12]

Did she really invent this fashion? Already, François Sentein showed us a Thierry Maulnier seated at a table at Lipp's, in 1939, in front of a pile of green sheets that he covered with a swift handwriting: "From time to time he concentrated by looking into the void (one would say that he is pissing, said Milleret). Then he would start up again while grimacing a bit because of the cigarette smoke, without any erasures."[13] Simone de Beauvoir, in any event, was one of the most assiduous in "working with her pen in public," to be imitated soon by Sartre when he returned from captivity—which would make their friend Jean-Pierre Bourla say, hovering between irony and irritation: "When they die, it will be necessary to dig a grave for them under the floor!"[14]

If it was the fashion to write in the café, it was first of all a practical one. Almost a matter of survival. Indeed, how could one remain immobile for long hours, seated at one's table, in a hotel room without heat? No coal,

---

[12] *La Fleur de l'âge, op. cit.*

[13] *Minutes d'un libertin (1938-1941), op. cit.* (dated December 30, 1939).

[14] Quoted by Simone de Beauvoir, *La Force de l'âge, op. cit.* A former student of Sartre at the Lycée Pasteur, Jean-Pierre Bourla, born in 1924, his real name being Juan Bourla-Benjamin, a Jew of Spanish origin, would be arrested with his family. Interned at Drancy, he would be deported to Auschwitz, where he would die, on April 13, 1944. In the same convoy was Simone Veil.

no gas, little electricity—and the harsh winters during the Occupation, when the thermometer was stuck below zero for days on end...At the Flore, on the contrary, it was warm. Shortly before the beginning of the hostilities, the provident owner had installed " the most imposing coal stove that had ever been seen during the Occupation. It stank, spat out flames one metre high, no matter! At the Flore, life was nice[15]." And, undoubtedly, this stove was not foreign to the Café de Flore's success, the rendezvous of the Parisian intelligentsia during those four years of occupation: "I miss my Saint-Germain-des-Prés," lamented Hélène Duc, far from Paris, "the long hours at the Flore, around the stove."[16] Robert Scipion: "We all went there to warm up";[17] Nicolas Bataille: "It was warm at the Flore and we could stay there for hours over an ersatz café or a Viandox";[18] François Sentein: "This Flore that is our welcoming centre—its stove!"[19] Simone de Beauvoir strove to arrive there as soon as it opened, " to occupy the best spot, the one where it was warmest, next to the stovepipe."[20] And did not budge from there, or almost, until the closing. To such an extent that certain pages of *La Force de l'âge* can be read as a sort of chronicle of life at the Café de Flore during the dark years.

"I enjoyed very much that moment when, in the still-empty room, Boubal, with a blue apron tied around his waist, brought his little universe back to life."[21] The boss, scolding his staff, regained possession little by little of his domain: "In his solid native-of-the-Auvergne face, his eyes were blood-shot: for one or two hours he remained in a temper. In an irritated voice, he would give orders to the dishwasher who, through a trap door open near the cash desk, sent up bottles and boxes. With the waiters, Jean and Pascal, he commented on the events of the previous day..."[22]

Paul Boubal, "Boubal," as he would be called familiarly at Saint-Germain-des-Prés, remained almost a half-century in control of the Café de Flore, a mythical boss if ever there was one. And not always

---

[15] Christophe Boubal, *Café de Flore, l'esprit d'un siècle*, Lanore, 2004.

[16] *Entre cour et jardin*, op. cit.

[17] Interview, in *Saint-Germain-des-Prés, 1945-1950*, op. cit.

[18] Conversation with the author, March 2008.

[19] *Nouvelles Minutes d'un libertin (1942-1943)*, Le Promeneur, 2002.

[20] *La Force de l'âge*, op. cit.

[21] *Ibid.*

[22] *Ibid.*

an easy one, his eyes were everywhere—especially as concerned reordering drinks, too rare an occurrence for his taste. A character. A real character. "*Literrary* café!" would exclaim the man from the Rouergue. "Can you see me telling the tax collector: I run a literary café; they come here to talk, not to drink—He will answer me: And the Deux Magots, Lipp, aren't they literary cafés, too? Nevertheless I ask you to believe that people do drink there!—And he will be right. Why?—Because, at Lipp's, after being there for a half-hour, M. Cazes will come over and say: Monsieur, won't you order something else?...You want to think? Fine: Émile, a half-glass for M. Thierry Maulnier...So M. Thierry Maulnier crosses the boulevard and comes to think here. Because here people can think the whole day long over a café crème. If M. Thierry Maulnier had drunk as many of my green chartreuses as he has filled all those little green sheets with his black scribbling...And M. Mouloudji, the whole afternoon, the other day, the whole afternoon on the first floor, with only one drink...He left at 7 o'clock. He had written a whole book. And when they know one another—M. Mouloudji, M. Sartre, Mlle de Beauvoir—each one of them takes a table, because they have to work. At M. Prévert's table, I'm not denying it, there are people; they talk, they cause an uproar, perhaps...But even M. Prévert, I can't say that he is what you would call a good customer."[23]

It's true, they did create quite a few uproars at Prévert's table. Just as they did before the war, just as they did during the period of Octobre. They talked loud, they called out to one another. In an atmosphere of fraternal warmth. All the pals were there. The old mingling with the new generation. "Prévert's Gang had grown with the years. Among the new arrivals was the young Nicolas Bataille, barely seventeen years old, a student enrolled in Solange Sicard's drama course, whom Prévert took under his wing after having noticed him at the Pathé studios, where the young man was doing a scene for his professor.

"—You're good, you have qualities. Have you been studying drama for a long time?

—A year.

—And how do you live?

—I have a little room that my father found for me. For meals, I stuff cotton in my ears and eat at his place.

---

[23] François Sentein, *Nouvelles Minutes d'un libertin (1942-1943), op. cit.* (dated December 30 1943).

—Why the cotton in your ears?

—In order not to hear his thoughts.

—What does he say?

—At your age I was working...If you had continued your studies! You could have graduated from a school, for example the School of Mining Engineers...

—Sinister-looking?

—What do you mean?

—Nothing! If it suits you, I can get you hired as an extra. Of course it's not a role, but you'll earn a bit of money."[24]

That was Prévert in a nutshell: a big heart under the trappings of revolt. And there went young Bataille up to the last row of the gods: way up on the balcony of the Théâtre des Funambules—that fragile edifice made of canvass and wood, erected by Marcel Carné on the set of Francoeur studios. A week as an extra in *Les Enfants du paradis*, for which Prévert wrote the dialogues. What a godsend for the young man! "Prévert was so kind that ultimately, even for a kid like me, he was not at all impressive. At the outset, I would call him monsieur Prévert, then Jacques, like everyone else. I very soon became one of his intimates; I was a bit like one of his children. I was part of the Prévert Gang." How proud I was!..."[25]

"Paul Boubal, he's the king of the neighbourhood," affirmed Boris Vian in his *Manuel de Saint-Germain-des-Prés,* before adding: "He is 41 years old, has plastered-down brown har, is 1,75 m. tall. He is neither fat nor thin. When he isn't clean-shaven something is going wrong in the neighbourhood." Boubal played himself in several shots in the film by Yves Allégret, La Boîte aux rêves (The Dream Box), produced in 1943, in Nice, at the Victorine studios, where the Café de Flore was reconstructed. "Handsome and serious like a Valentino, his hair coated with an impeccable gel and not at all out of place among Viviane Romance and Simone Signoret on one of her first jobs, the Boss was playing his own part, that is to say, the Great Master of the Cash Counter."[26] The cashbox...because Boubal, as a solid earthling, deaf to the siren calls of legend and of snob-

---

[24] Nicolas Bataille, *Le théâtre, c'est pas un métier,* L'Harmattan, 2006.

[25] Nicolas Bataille, conversation with the author, March 2008.

[26] Christophe Boubal, *Café de Flore, l'esprit d'un siècle, op. cit.* It is also in this film that Gérard Philipe made his début on the screen in a small role.

bishness, really believed only in the virtues of money. Moreover this is what Matthieu Galey confirmed many years later in his Diary: "Boubal, the boss of the Flore, speaks of his establishment. For him, legend boils down to good business: 'Do you realize,' he said, with his ineradicable, suitably grating Marvejols accent, 'that during the past ten years that the newspapers have been talking about us, there would be at least fifty million francs worth of publicity.'"[27] His Rouergat good sense would not prevent the owner of the Café de Flore from becoming an almost mythical character: in Émile Binet's painting, *Saint-Germain-des-Prés*, conceived in the naïve tradition of the Douanier Rousseau around 1950, Boubal—in a black vest, white shirt, bowtie and with a table napkin on his arm,–occupies an important place, among other purebred Saint-Germain denizens: Jean-Paul Sartre, Juliette Gréco, Camille Bryen, Boris Vian, Jacques Prévert and Raymond Duncan...

Paul Boubal was a server at the Boeuf sur le Toit in its heyday when it was owned by Louis Moysès, on avenue Pierre-Ier-de-Serbie, before acquiring a restaurant-café in the Halles, le Panier Fleuri. It was in 1939 that he crossed the Seine and set himself up in Saint-Germain-des-Prés. Almost by chance! He had his eye on an establishment located at the Porte de Vincennes, but as for his wife, she preferred the Café de Flore, whose owner, M. Boussigue, put up for sale at the same time. Henriette Boubal won out. For the good fortune of the couple and the good of their future customers. "The candidate owner and his wife imagined they had acquired a quiet little bar, in an agreeable neighbourhood, but they had just set foot, without realizing it, on the territory that glory would magnetize."[28] And what glory! On the title page of the copy of *L'Âge de raison* (*The Age of Reason*) belonging to Mme Boubal, Sartre wrote: "It is at the Flore that I reached the age of reason."

Here, precisely, was Mme Boubal: "Blond, curly-haired, rosy, well-groomed, his wife came down the staircase in turn and took her seat at the cash desk. The first customers were arriving."[29] Many writers were among them, regular customers, who sat down at the marble tables to read or work: "Thierry Maulnier, Dominique Aury, Audiberti, who lived opposite at the Hôtel Taranne, Adamov, with his bare and blue feet in sandals. One

---

[27] Matthieu Galey, *Journal*, t. I, *1953-1973*, Grasset, 1987 (dated October 1 1958). Paul Boubal did not come from Marvejols, but Saint-Geniest-d'Olt, in the Aveyron.

[28] Christophe Boubal, *Café de Flore, l'esprit d'un siècle, op. cit.*

[29] Simone de Beauvoir, *La Force de l'âge, op. cit.*

of the most assiduous was Mouloudji."[30] For his part, he contemplated the Castor (the Beaver)—"like all the privileged people, I called her by this nickname"—with a sort of fascination that was not necessarily sympathy: "One characteristic stuck out a mile for me, the way she isolated herself. She erected between herself and the others a wall that no one could jump over. Even her voice with its laryngitis-like timbre would remain internal; only her laughter seemed a bit natural.[31] Just as fascinated, Juliette Gréco, on the contrary, is kinder: "Her stormy sea-blue eyes shoot off barely concealed lightning bolts and when she lowers them on the paper to write without raising them for long hours, one wonders whether the white sheet is not going to burn. When she raises her eyelids, her gaze is turned towards the interior of her mind. She doesn't seem to see anyone."[32]

The morning progresses, the hall fills up; when it is time for the aperitif, there is no longer any place on the benches. Picasso comes as a neighbour, accompanied by Dora Maar who holds Kazbek, the painter's beautiful Afghan hound, on a leash; Robert Desnos, Maurice Sachs, Léon-Paul Fargue, still faithful to Saint-Germain-des-Prés, Arthur Adamov—with his bare feet, indeed, blue from the winter cold, in sandals—Maurice Merleau-Ponty, Albert Vidalie, Roger Blin, ex-member of the Groupe Octobre, Joëlle Le Feuve, the actress, Marthe Robert, the future author of *Roman des origines et origines du roman* (*The Novel of the Origins and the Origins of the Novel*), the translator of Kafka and Nietzsche: "A young woman always dressed in black aroused in me a strange desire. She impressed me, first of all because she must have been an intellectual, then because of the incessant quivering that ran through her dress and betrayed a secret body that I imagined obviously sublime and white as the moon. I was in love with her for a long time. I never dared speak to her or contemplate her for more than a few seconds. After the war, I found out her name."[33]

A strange little game, repeated from one table to the next: when a newcomer opened the door, all heads would be raised, but there was never a greeting, never a sign. That was the rule, and no one would every think of transgressing it. The new arrival went, gliding discretely, over to a table where, often, ten or so people had already congregated; "He did

---

[30] *ibid.*

[31] Mouloudji, *La Fleur de l'âge, op. cit.*

[32] *Jujube*, Stock, 1982.

[33] Mouloudji, *La Fleur de l'âge, op. cit.*

not say hello and, when he felt like it, took part quite simply in the conversation."³⁴ Returning to the Flore after a long sojourn in the free zone, Mouloudji experienced this himself: "Some regular customers, whom I recognized by their way of raising their head and registering my entrance through the glass door, sized me up with the kind of curiosity that was peculiar to the fauna of the place."³⁵ Just like the young François Sentein, whom Jean Genet introduced unexpectedly to Sartre, on a corner of the sidewalk, on the boulevard Saint-Germain. Here is the commentary: "We have been rubbing shoulders with one another for years at the Flore, having several mutual friends there. Never a word exchanged. It is true that this is the style of the house. At Lipp's one is a bench, indeed a beer pal right away; the third time we greet one another; the fifth, we no longer know how long we've known one another, each one persists in not knowing the name of the other. At the Flore, this is very rare, it is the café where they glare at you. They would change their way of carrying on if they went across the street. But the Sartre hangers-on are homebodies."³⁶ This last, rather unflattering remark was understandable, because Sentein, a supporter of the Action française, laid it on thick with irony whenever the subject of the Sartre gang cropped up. "In short, Sartre held out his hand to me with an amiable word. First of all an excellent bourgeois of the Sixth district, like Cocteau was of the First, that is to say, well brought up. The firebrand bit comes later."³⁷

As firebrands went, Genet held his own quite well! But in a style completely different from Sartre's. The "book thief," this unknown whom Sentein discovered one day in October 1942 on the terrace of Capoulade, on the rue Soufflot, seated at the table of his friend Roland Laudenbach, was Jean Genet himself.³⁸ The bard of evil, the "avowed enemy," as he called himself—the enemy of society. We know his story: he turned his life into mythology. An unknown father, a mother who abandoned him to the custody of the state, the foster family in the Morvan, the first homosexual stirrings, the accusation of robbery, the penitentiary colony in Mettray, the Foreign Legion, time in prison...Laudenbach brought him to Cocteau:

---

³⁴ Jean-Paul Sartre, interview, in Marcelle Routier, *Saint-Germain-des-Prés, op. cit.*

³⁵ *La Fleur de l'âge, op. cit.*

³⁶ François Sentein, *Minutes d'un libéré (1944)*, Le Promeneur, 2002 (dated October 26 1944).

³⁷ *Ibid.*

³⁸ Roland Laudenbach, 1921-1991, author, scriptwriter, founder in 1944 of Éditions de la Table Ronde. He was the nephew of the actor Pierre Fresnay.

"He's a jailbird character, marked by stays in prison. He has a paranoid disposition with a knotted up charm that gets unknotted quickly. He has an incredible swiftness and mischievousness. For me his poems are the only important event of the period. Besides, being protected by their eroticism and thus unpublishable, they can only be read secretly, by being passed on directly from one person to another."[39] And, indeed, it was clandestinely that the whole of Saint-Germain-des-Prés, at the Flore, would circulate the typed copy of *Notre-Dame-des-Fleurs* (*Our Lady of the Flowers*). In turn, Sartre got hold of Genet, who constituted in his eyes exactly what a writer should be: "He embodies so well all of the qualities whose realization Sartre was seeking that he can be seen as a distant relative of the family."[40] The Existentialist family, of course. And so would appear *Saint Genet, comédien and martyr*[41] (*Saint Genet, Actor and Martyr*)—at the outset a mere preface, at the end the first volume of Jean Genet's complete works.

A kind of protocol, at the Café de Flore, governed the relationships between the customers. A strict etiquette—"the Flore had its mores," noted Beauvoir. Two main principles: one did not exchange greetings there; even if one met there every day, one pretended not to know one another. On the contrary, if one's paths crossed elsewhere—at the Deux Magots, for example—one did exchange greetings: "I met there one day a girl, Nina, who was constantly at the Flore and to whom I had never spoken. We smiled at one another and talked together, exactly like two Frenchmen who had found one another abroad."[42] Customs, odd habit, ridiculous little traits of a society turned in on itself, deaf to outside noises. As though enclosed in a magic protective circle.

"The Flore really was our club at the time, and to imagine it, one must realize that, for those who lived there, the rest of Paris was a virgin forest."[43] A club, yes. And so closed that the occupier never set foot there. Neither "Fritz" nor "Jerry"... This was not the place where one could see the "grey mice" stuffing their faces unscrupulously. "No Germans. You might say that none ever came during these four years."[44] Except for one time: "A young German officer pushed the door open

---

[39] Jean Cocteau, *Journal 1942-1945, op. cit.* (dated February 15 1943).
[40] Maurice Nadeau, *Le Roman français depuis la guerre*, Gallimard, "Idées", 1963.
[41] Jean-Paul Sartre, *Saint Genet, comédien et martyr*, Gallimard, 1952.
[42] Jean-Paul Sartre, interview, in Marcelle Routier, *Saint-Germain-des-Prés, op. cit.*
[43] *Ibid.*
[44] Mouloudji, *La Fleur de l'âge, op. cit.*

and sat down in a corner with a book; no one budged, but he must have felt something because he closed his book very quickly, paid for his drink and cleared out."[45] This was confirmed by Christian Casadesus, who lived at the time at the Hôtel Pont-Royal, on rue Montalembert; as an actor, he had been leading since 1941 the Compagnie du Regain, that would mount *Hamlet*, in a staging by Pierre Bertin, at the Théâtre Hébertot in the autumn of 1942: "It's true that there was at the Café de Flore a completely distinctive atmosphere, that one could not find in any other café in the neighbourhood. And above all, the Germans never came there!"[46]

It was as though the waves of the war would just break up against its door. Moreover this is just about what a connoisseur, the painter Henri Pelletier, said. He was the one who managed to persuade Boris Vian, at the end of the 1940s, to write his famous *Manuel de Saint-Germain-des-Prés* (*The Saint-Germain-des-Prés Handbook*): "At the Flore, we traversed the Occupation as though it had been an ocean, the splashes caused by the events just smashed against the planks."

Behind its windows coloured in blue for "passive defence" purposes—according to legend Picasso himself, paintbrush in hand, took on the task of the colour washing—behind its thick curtains of the same opaque blue. The Café de Flore would thus live through the four years of war without too much damage—with its cellars, like the holds of a galleon of the high seas, crammed with two tons of "real" tea, acquired providentially by Paul Boubal before September 1939. "In this place we felt privileged, elsewhere, out of danger," Mouloudji recalled.

Out of danger? Not always. Because there were the alerts. They punctuated the days and nights. "In the afternoon, the evening, the alarm would often sound. Boubal would hurriedly chase out the customers and lock the doors; to Sartre, myself, and two or three others, he granted preferential treatment: we went up to the first floor and stayed there until the end of the alert."[47] They got used to it. Henceforth, the few privileged people Boubal allowed up to the first floor would set themselves up there—permanently, so to speak. Far from the buzz of the ground floor. "In the afternoon, I got into the habit of climbing up right away to the first floor," so noted Simone de Beauvoir in *La Force de l'âge*.

---

[45] Simone de Beauvoir, *La Force de l'âge*, op. cit.

[46] Christian Casadesus, conversation with the author, November 2006.

[47] Simone de Beauvoir, *La Force de l'âge*, op. cit.

Robert Scipion, author and scriptwriter, impartial observer of the times, has left us a precise description of that mezzanine in the Café de Flore, converted into a veritable study: "It gave us the impression of a classroom. Sartre was set up at a little table where he was writing *Les Chemins de la liberté*, Simone de Beauvoir, at another little table, was writing *Tous les homes sont mortels*, Mouloudji, at another little table, was writing *Enrico*, Jacques-Laurent Bost was writing *Le Dernier des métiers* (*The Last of the Trades*), a little further, Arthur Adamov was also writing, one of his plays no doubt, and I, too, occupied a little table where I was writing my book of pastiches: *Prête-moi ta plume* (*Lend Me your Pen*). From time to time people would talk to one another, but it was nonetheless very studious"[48]—to his list of regular customers, Robert Scipion could have added just as easily the names of François Sentein, Jacques Audiberti... This was precisely the atmosphere that Boubal deplored, because if people worked a great deal at the Flore, they ordered hardly anything there: "They unwrap their belongings, they look at one another without seeing one another, they think. There are days when you could call it a prep room..."[49]

There are several who have left us their vision, romanticized or realistic, of the Café de Flore under the Occupation. Mouloudji, Robert Scipion.[50] Or Guillaume Hanoteau: "In the dim light of the acetylene lamp— 'a saccharine light,' as a bitter humorist called it, because it replaced the brightness of electricity when the power was cut—most of the customers wrote, shrivelled up, cooped up, covered up in their mufflers. Over this studious universe hovered a sour odour of ink and blotting paper, of damp fibres..."[51] Hanoteau again: "It is the moment, at dusk, when the Flore starts to look like a dance hall in Cameroon. This metamorphosis is due to the heavy acetylene lamps, light fixtures typical of the colonies, that provide light for the café until the electric current is restored, which the newspapers foresee happening at around twenty hours thirty."[52]

---

[48] Interview, in *Saint-Germain-des-Prés, 1945-1950, op. cit.*

[49] François Sentein, *Nouvelles Minutes d'un libertin, 1942-1943, op.cit.* (dated December 30 1943).

[50] Mouloudji, in his novel *Un garcon sans importance*, Gallimard, 1971, Robert Scipion in his book of pastiches that is mentioned here: *Prête-moi ta plume*, Gallimard, 1946.

[51] *L'Âge d'or de Saint-Germain-des-Prés, op. cit.*

[52] *Ces nuits qui ont fait Paris, op. cit.*

"All that constituted the real Saint-Germain period, and it was really something," Jean-Paul Sartre affirmed for his part in an interview, in 1950. Before making himself clear: "Then, after the Liberation, came a flood of Americans, of young people wearing checked shirts, and the whole fauna that now frequents Saint-Germain. As for myself, I don't dare walk around Saint-Germain-des-Prés, so afraid am I of autograph seekers and seekers of all kinds. I was at the Flore fifteen days ago, on the terrace. It was two o'clock in the morning, and there was nobody. All the waiters came up to see me and we reminisced. It was very beautiful..."

The Saint-Germain-des-Prés of legend—the one taking in the years from 1945 to 1950—is not the one that Jean-Paul Sartre loved: besides, he would very soon stop frequenting it. As proof, this book he dedicated to Paul Boubal after the war: "In remembrance of 41 – 44 and the real Flore."

4

Sartre to Barrault: "The Flies are the work of a novice. My play does not correspond to this new art you want to create. With The Satin Slipper, you will show your worth"

Summer 1943. Occupation, year III.

Roundups, deportations, black market, line-ups in front of the food stores...In Paris, life continued. And even society life: "The Castor invited me to the first performance of a theatrical work by Sartre, *Les Mouches* (*The Flies*) mounted by Charles Dullin at the Théâtre de la Cité, ex-Sarah-Bernhardt."[1] Fearing power cuts, more and more frequent as the war went on, the show took place in the afternoon. The whole Saint-Germain-des-Prés was there: "The hall reunited friends and enemies from all sides. Even though the German board of censors had accepted the play, a compulsory procedure, rumours anticipated a scandal. The hall was filled to capacity and vibrating. People could sense that something unusual was going to happen."[2] But the play would not be forbidden for all that and would continue its career. A rather short career, however: twenty-five performances. And a short revival, alternating with another play, in the month of October.

It was during the summer of 1941, when he attended at the Roland-Garros stadium a performance of Aeschylus' *Suppliantes* (*The Supplicants*), directed by Jean-Louis Barrault, that Jean-Paul Sartre himself, in turn, felt like writing, after Giraudoux, after Cocteau, "his" Greek

---

[1] Mouloudji, *La Fleur de l'âge, op. cit.*
[2] *Ibid.*

tragedy. A large, open-air, sporting and mass event, the kind that the Vichy Regime loved, Aeschylus' tragedy found there, on the centre's hard court, a setting that showed it off to advantage. And a grandiose décor, conceived by Félix Labisse: "Stairs led up to the stage dominated by rust and blue colonnades, and three high statues of the gods Jupiter, Hermes and Poseidon; in the background, five hundred laurel and eucalyptus trees standing against a blue horizon canvass evoked a landscape of mountains and temples[3]." Under the big July sun that bore down hard, a hundred or so actors, actresses, supernumeraries and dancers, joined by athletes from the French Weightlifting Federation and firefighters from the City of Paris, executed crowd movements. There was original music by Arthur Honegger, played by the Orchestra of the Conservatory Concert Society, with Charles Munch at the podium; choirs directed by Yvonne Gougerné; costumes by Marie-Hélène Dasté and Lucien Coutaud. A real super-production.

Among the supernumeraries of the *Suppliantes*, two young women, students or ex-students of Charles Dullin's drama course, were furious over having to play bit parts: Olga Kosakiewicz and Olga Kechelievich—"the two Olgas," as "the Sartre family" called them. "Barrault liked them a lot and, during the rehearsals, they asked him what they had to do to get to play a real role: 'The best way, would be for someone to write a play for you,' he answered. And Sartre thought: 'Why not me?'"[4] A kind of wager, from which *Les Mouches* resulted.

In the Stalag, the previous year, he had already composed a play, *Bariona*, a kind of mystery of the Nativity, which he had placed in Palestine and which relates the people's revolt against the Roman occupier. This is the same direction in which he wanted to travel at present, by inventing a plot both prudent and transparent, that could nevertheless be interpreted as a veritable invitation to resist. As for the subject, he would find it in the *Orestia* of Aeschylus—adapting it to the particular situation of occupied France. Oreste, returning to Argos after a long exile, discovers that his mother, Clytemnestre, helped by her lover, Égisthe, has assassinated the King Agamemnon. He fulfills his duty of filial vengeance by killing the two lovers, with the support of his sister Électre. But, with Sartre, the idea of divine responsibility—at the very heart of the history of the Atridae—is replaced by the one centred on the responsibility of

---

[3] Paul-Louis Mignon, *Jean-Louis Barrault, le théâtre total*, Éditions du Rocher, 1999.

[4] Simone de Beauvoir, *La Force de l'âge*, op. cit.

man. No more fate, the gods have nothing to do in this matter; Oreste assumes his action entirely—a precursor of the "Existentialist" heroes who will soon come to life under the pen of the philosopher-novelist. As concerns the framework, Sartre had it already, it was the memory of a voyage in the summer of 1937: Greece, the volcanic island of Santorini, the village of Emborio, blindingly white, as though scraped to the bare bone and deserted under summer's blazing fire.

He started working on it at the beginning of October. Most often at the Café de Flore. The copy of *Les Mouches* belonging today to the Boubal family carries on the title page: "To Monsieur Paul Boubal this work that was written under his eyes in 1941-42, by a 'pillar' of the Flore." While writing it, did Sartre already know that this play would no doubt constitute his only contribution to the Résistance? This in any event is what Simone de Beauvoir herself seemed to say, in *La Force de l'âge*: "He then got down tenaciously to the play that he had started: it represented the sole form of resistance that was accessible to him." This was not for lack of having tried another form beforehand. But in vain.

When he returned from captivity, in the spring of 1941, Sartre opened his heart to Maurice Merleau-Ponty about his desire to draw closer to the opponents of the Nazis. Merleau-Ponty spoke to him at the time about a group of students at the École normale supérieure that put out more or less regularly a tract titled "Sous la botte" (Under the Boot). In this group were people preparing the Agrégation, theses, philosophers, mathematicians...All young, indeed very young. Among them: François Cuzin, Jean-Toussaint and Dominique Desanti, Simone Devouassoux...Sartre and his close friends would join them: Jean Pouillon, Jacques-Laurent Bost..." The first meeting took place in Simone de Beauvoir's bedroom, at the Hôtel Mistral, on rue Cels, which did not comply too well with the rules of caution governing underground activity[5]..." It was there that the ephemeral movement Socialisme et Liberté (Socialism and Freedom) was set up, which Beauvoir described at length in *La Force de l'âge*. "Socialisme et Liberté," was also the name the little group gave to the news sheet it would publish clandestinely. Dominique Desanti would take on the task of typing the texts on stencils that would then be fed into the duplicating machine. "We were all living at the hotel at that time, and to use a typewriter at night in a hotel room ran the risk of arousing the curiosity of certain people...We brought up to the sixth floor, an attic under the

---

[5] Dominique Desanti, conversation with the author, February 2008.

rooftops, the Underwood that I had borrowed from my father. I can still see Simone de Beauvoir, barely out of breath after climbing up six flights of stairs, bringing me Sartre's editorials: 'He said you can make cuts if it's too long.'"[6] But Sartre wanted to go further. To establish links with the non-occupied zone, to persuade, perhaps, other intellectuals to join the movement, which for the time being was vegetating. During the summer, on the occasion of a trip down to the South of France, he tried to convince Gide and Malraux. Both of them ducked out of it. From then on, the adventure of Socialisme et Liberté was condemned, all the more because one of its members, Yvonne Picard, was arrested.[7] So the group was disbanded. This would not prevent Sartre from continuing to offer texts to "Sous la botte." "I remember especially a particularly virulent editorial," relates Dominique Desanti, "that he gave us at the time of the law about the wearing of the yellow star. 'It's the lepers' rattle...' he said."

Thus it was indeed as a work of resistance that the public welcomed *Les Mouches* at its creation. When Charles Dullin, who interpreted the role of Jupiter, moved forward onto the stage and exclaimed: "Oreste knows that he is free," Cries of approval greeted his line. "*Les Mouches*," Dominique Desanti emphasizes today, "is the individual's struggle against everything that assails him. Replaced in the context of the Occupation, it is quite obviously a work of resistance. This is exactly how we received it, and we were not the only ones!..." Certainly, in this troubled period, Parisian spectators were a rather good audience, as they say, and would get enthusiastic over very little. But it was for a good cause. A phrase, even an allusion were enough to unleash applause and murmurs of contentment in the balconies. At the Comédie-Française, where Henry de Montherlant's play, *La Reine morte*, was created, certain lines would arouse, every evening, demonstrations in the audience: "The flower of the kingdom is in prison!" or "They kill and the sky brightens up!" In a muzzled Paris, the theatre was like a safety valve. "It is undoubtedly the most sought after entertainment and the one that best suits times of war. Propaganda and censure reign. Demonstrations are forbidden. A hall filled with Parisians who had braved the cold and the night, risked missing the last subway train, was ready to hear words of hope or anger that could only be spoken on stage. All it took was a word loaded with meaning, a line spoken by one of the actors to touch off applause or vengeful

---

[6] *Ibid.*

[7] She would die in deportation.

laughter... To go to the theatre was to deny the Occupation, the war and its dangers."[8]

Even today, for the specialists of that period, "Sartre's text reveals itself without any ambivalence as a work committed to the Resistance, it contains numerous critical allusions to the guilt-trip practiced by the National Revolution and a denunciation of the Pétain ideology."[9] Resistance? This is saying a bit too much. Because *Les Mouches*, in fact, had only a very weak political effectiveness to the extent that this text "was relevant only for spectators who were already convinced."[10] Nothing that could truly upset the regime in power.

Logically, it was to Jean-Louis Barrault that Sartre first proposed his play, since it was while attending the show at Roland-Garros that he felt the urge to write it. And, right away, Barrault could see far ahead. Much further ahead... Although a member of the Comédie-Française, he had only one desire: to escape from it. His own theatre, his own repertoire, his own troupe: that is what he wanted. As far as the theatre was concerned, an opportunity came along: the departure of Louis Jouvet on a long tour of South America left the hall of the Athénée vacant.[11] *Les Mouches*, plus *Hamlet*—for which he had just asked André Gide to provide a new translation—plus *Le Soulier de satin* that Paul Claudel had promised him: this already constituted the beginning of a repertoire.

But the Sartre-Barrault collaboration would scarcely go any further, since the former absolutely wanted the role of Électre to be attributed to Olga Kosakiewicz—Olga Dominique was her stage name—and the latter refuse absolutely to comply. "It would take a lot of nerve to mount a work in which the feminine starring roles were performed by debutants: Barrault backed out," noted Simone de Beauvoir in *La Force de l'âge*. A lot of nerve or, rather, recklessness.

Nevertheless, a letter from Jean-Paul Sartre, addressed to Jean-Louis Barrault, seems rather to place the affaire on a private level. At least in its first paragraphs: "You have said and repeated, in front of me, through allusions, and, in front of others, more clearly, that Olga was my mistress and that I wanted to 'push her ahead.' If you believed this, you must have

---

[8] Michel Morht, *Tombeau de la Rouërie*, Gallimard, 2000.

[9] François Noudelmann, in *Dictionnaire des pièces de théâtre françaises du XXe siècle*, under the direction of Jeanyves Guérin, Honoré Champion, 2005.

[10] *Ibid.*

[11] Jouvet and his troupe would not return to France until 1945.

had the very disagreeable impression that an author, in collusion with his sponsors, was taking advantage of your friendship to impose an actor on you. This is all my fault: I generally dislike talking about my private life, and my silence has favoured this misunderstanding. I an anxious for you to know, today, that Olga has never been and will never be my mistress: it is only her talent that I wanted to serve..."

A long letter, that went on for nine pages, where one could understand, also, little by little, when passing from the private to the artistic spheres, why Jean-Louis Barrault, disconcerted by a play which, after all, corresponded neither to his dramatic aesthetic nor to his objectives, increasingly procrastinated, dragged his feet and hesitated for that reason: "It would be better for you not to have any sympathy for me and to simply feel, as an artist, the necessity of directing my play. Now, this is what cannot be. *Les Mouches* are the work of a novice, still very imperfect; and even if my play were ten times better, it does not correspond to this new dramatic art that you wish to create: it has been written in particular circumstances, it is very well-behaved—you know why—it cannot serve as a manifesto for Jean-Louis Barrault. Another project, far greater and far bolder, has claimed all your attention. How could I hold a grudge against you? It is obvious that by mounting *Le Soulier de Satin* you will be able to show your worth..."[12]

In any event, the Athénée adventure came to a sudden end, because several theatre directors, jealously watching over their prerogatives, viewed with a jaundiced eye Barrault's arrival in their midst. Veto! And so the latter remained at the Comédie-Française, where *Le Soulier de Satin* was waiting for him, and with which, several months later, he would truly show his worth. In the meantime Charles Dullin took over the staging of *Les Mouches*: "I was able to convince myself that he liked the play and that he was interested in it. Moreover, for him, Olga is not an unknown imposed on him: he appreciates her, she was his best student and she has already performed a small role at the Théâtre de Paris..."[13]

It is not certain that the audience at the Théâtre de la Cité shared Sartre's opinion about Olga Dominique's talent. Beauvoir herself remained very reserved: "There was a considerable number of walk-on

---

[12] Jean-Paul Sartre's letter to Jean-Louis Barrault, July 9 1942, museum library of the Comédie-Française.

[13] *Ibid.* At the beginning of the war, Charles Dullin directed the Théâtre de Paris for a short time.

actors, women, children, seniors, a whole people that had to be moved around on the vast stage of the Théâtre Sarah-Bernhardt; Dullin found himself less at ease than on the stage of the Atelier. The actor who played Oreste lacked experience; Olga as well; the role of Électre was crushing; she portrayed it with accuracy but neither she nor her partner connected with the audience."[14] As for the press collaborating with the Nazi regime, it unleashed its fury, as could have been expected. Alain Laubreaux, in *Je suis partout* (*I am Everywhere*), declared: " Jean-Paul Sartre is afflicted with an absolute and total absence of dramatic sense." The others agreed: "a nauseating buzzing around a decaying carcass," "a tragedy of putrefaction," "an endeavour without air, stifling and too weighted down with obsessions..." The best disposed remembered the *Électre* by Jean Giraudoux—and the comparison, of course, was not to Sartre's advantage. In his *Nouvelles minutes d'un libertin* (*A Libertine's News to the Minute*), François Sentein is not tender either: "*Les Mouches* attract fly paper. The press that gets stuck to it is thick. We attended a remarkable end-of-the-year graduation display, the revision of a course offered to his pupils by the Parisian master of Existentialism."

Dullin himself was not spared: "People jeer at him for his incarnation of a carnival-like Jupiter, for his wrought iron hair, his limping god gait, his colonial exhibition décors and his saraband of the Erinyes compared to a wild free-for-all of savages on the warpath. They bait the unfortunate wretch, in the evening, when, leaving the stage, he gets his buskins caught between the floorboards; infuriated, he turns around to yell out three resounding "Shit" at the audience..."[15] Nevertheless, Michel Leiris, in the clandestine *Lettres françaises* praises the political significance of the text. "The public did not flock to it. We were already in June and the theatre had to close," concluded Simone de Beauvoir. "Awful box office receipts," commented Charles Dullin for his part. A failure? Yes and no. Because Sartre would make up for it—and handsomely—the following year, with *Huis clos* (*No Exit*).

There was room for everyone on the Paris stages during the Occupation: Jean-Paul Sartre or Jean de Letraz, Montherlant or Feydeau, Paul Claudel or the little naked ladies of the Concert Mayol... The theatres and cinemas enjoyed, during these years, a public that thronged to them and was crazy for them to such an extent that one would have

---

[14] *La Force de l'âge, op. cit.*

[15] Hervé Le Boterf, *La Vie parisienne sous l'Occupation*, France-Empire, 1997.

almost dared talk about a golden age if the times had not been so hard, and the Parisians so miserable.

After the debacle of June 1940, once the first moment of stupor had passed, the inhabitants returned to the capital. Admittedly, they were still quite few in number, scarcely more than a million in July.[16] On returning to the fold they found a city left to its own devices. No cars, no buses: the operation of motor vehicles was forbidden in the department of the Seine. Paris was empty. Streets deserted under the summer sun, iron curtains lowered. Cafés, brasseries and entertainment halls closed—the Café de Flore itself would not reopen until July. "It was a dead city, like a destroyed civilization," Maurice Sachs noted sorrowfully.

A dead city? Not really. Rather another city, completely different from the one they had left in haste, several weeks earlier, chased, in their exodus, down the roads by the old visceral fear of the invader. Curfew at 23 hours, daily march-pasts by the occupation troops, German time, cinemas transformed into Soldatenkino, ministries, barracks and large hotels requisitioned… On the avenue Kléber, the Majestic housed henceforth the military high command in France; at the Hôtel Meurice, on the rue de Rivoli, was set up the headquarters of the Greater Paris Command; the propaganda services found refuge on boulevard Raspail, at the Hôtel Lutétia. Finally, on the Place de la Concorde, the Crillon lodged the officers of the Kriegsmarine. All of these were in the shadow of large red flags marked with the black swastika. All the while, little by little, shortages became the rule, and collaboration, still in its infancy, became organized. "Life is broken, perhaps for twenty-five years," remarked Jean-Louis Barrault in his *Journal de bord* (*Log book*).[17]

As soon as the conditions for the armistice were applied, the occupants encouraged the resumption in Paris of a "normal life"—but could one qualify as "normal" the life that was unfolding? As a matter of priority, they wished to favour the resurgence of artistic activity, proof, according to them, of civil peace. The ulterior motive is simple: how does one win the neutrality of the Parisian population—if winning them over is impossible—if not by giving them back that in which they take most

---

[16] In October 1940, the capital had 1,867,115 inhabitants, whereas the census of 1936 listed 2,871,429 of them.

[17] *Journal de bord*, June 1940, National Library of France, Department of Performing Arts, Renaud-Barrault Collection.

pride, namely, their culture? All the more because it was just about the only thing they had left; the only possession that would not be snatched from them during these four years when the country, bled systematically, would be stripped little by little of all its wealth. French cultural life—an old glory dented, tottering, where Molière, Mistinguett, Flaubert, les Folies-Bergère, Philippe de Champaigne, Maurice Chevalier, Victor Hugo were jostling one another any old how...

The Pigalle cinema set the example by reopening its doors on June 15, that is to say, the very day after German troops entered Paris, copied, as early as the 23rd, by several establishments on the Champs-Élysées. A month later, on July 19, almost all the halls on the Grands Boulevards were projecting new films. Then it was the turn of the music-halls: the ABC, on boulevard de Bonne-Nouvelle, reopened on July 4, the Alcazar on the 6th; on the 12th, Concert Mayol revived its light revue *Paris 40*, followed soon by the Folies-Bergère with *Tous aux Folies (Everybody to the Folies)*. On rue de Clichy, the Théâtre de l'Oeuvre put on *Juliette*, by Jean Bassan, while Sacha Guitry returned to the Théâtre de la Madeleine with a revival of *Pasteur*... As a result, less than one month after signing the armistice, the "vie parisienne," as one called it, regained part of its vitality. On December 31 1940, 34 theatres, 14 music-halls, the Cirque d'Hiver and the Cirque Médrano, as well as thirty or so cinemas, resumed their regular activity. In his memoirs, published in 1953, Otto Abetz, Germany's ambassador in occupied France, affirmed: "French literary, artistic and scientific life recovered an almost normal rhythm shortly after the defeat[18]."

Even so: this return to normal was taking place under very tough surveillance—fussy censorship, rigorous monitoring of the shows' contents, constant worry about maintaining order—thanks to the unfailing vigilance of Staffel Propaganda and the Comité d'organisation des enterprises de spectacles (The Organizational Committee of Performing Arts Enterprises)[19], the veritable "eye of Berlin" bearing down without any benevolence on French artistic activities.

---

[18] *Histoire d'une politique franco-allemande, 1930-1950*, Stock, 1953.

[19] The COES, created on July 7 1941, had as its mission to reorganize—or rather "moralize"—the theatrical profession. Without, of course, losing sight of the ideas advocated by the "National Revolution." Based on this mindset it accumulated regulations, controls, restrictions: It was notably responsible for the decrees forbidding or controlling the hiring of Jews and "Negroes" by performing arts establishments. In fact, the COES, supposedly independent, would monitor in an absolute manner

Was it because pre-war leisure pursuits had become almost impossible to carry on? Was it to forget the deprivations, the black market or the cold? In any case, "this people obsessed with daily worries, vanquished and tyrannized, subjected to the risk of repression and condemned to political silence, would seek an outlet for its anguishes and uncertainties about the future in the practice of their culture which, in many respects, represents escape, compensation, indeed proof of their vitality and their existence[20]." From 220 million viewers in 1938, the cinema went up to 304 million in 1943. As for the stage, it enjoyed unprecedented attendance figures, drawing up to 800,000 spectators per month in 1943. 18 dramatic creations in Paris for the last three months of 1940, 95 in 1941, 145 in 1942...

Colette, in *Paris de ma fenêtre (Paris from my Window)*[21], a kind of day to day chronicle of the Paris of the black years, described the queues that lengthened in front of the box office of the Comédie-Française: "Expectant people of both sexes make sure they bring a newspaper and turn them into leg-warmers attached with a string against the cold. Some men, weary of standing, extend an arm over the barrier to lessen the weight of their bodies. The silent ones read, leaning at an angle, change their footing like horses at a halt." Jean-Louis Vaudoyer, the administrator of the Français, informed Paul Claudel, several days after the début of *Le Soulier de Satin,* that people got into fights at the wickets to obtain tickets. He even added that it had been necessary, on certain mornings, to get the police to intervene for the purpose of restoring order.

Le Soulier de satin was indeed the great success at the end of that year 1943. It played to sold out houses—despite the air alerts, despite the power shortages, the cold, the curfew, despite the last subway train that didn't wait... No doubt audiences saw in this drama a kind of solar image of France; an image that was exactly the opposite of the one that Vichy and the occupier had been holding up to them for more than three years, an image of transgression, of punishment, of remorse, of a necessary and harsh redemption. Here, it was only a matter of surpassing oneself, of heroic sacrifice, of lyricism: "Deliverance of captive souls," proclaimed the final words of *Le Soulier.* And it was to hear this message that every

---

and under the vigilant eye of the Germans every theatrical activity until the end of the Occupation.

[20] Serge Berstein and Pierre Milza, *Histoire de la France au XXe siècle*, Complexe, 1995.
[21] Éditions du Milieu du Monde, 1944.

evening, in the very heart of winter, in a glacial hall, audiences would throng, enveloped in blankets.

A river of a play, which was reputed to be unperformable, a five-hour-long spectacle, dozens of roles, décors, hundreds of costumes... A play that fascinated some—"We went there around five p.m., with a little sandwich in our purse since the play lasted more than five consecutive hours. And it was the most beautiful thing one could imagine: the décors, an admirable interpretation, a text! We forgot everything. I was deeply moved[22]..."—and annoyed others. A humorist, finding the time long, exclaimed: "Fortunately, it was not one of a pair!" The comment has been attributed to Sacha Guitry, Henri Jeanson, Marcel Achard, and still others... because unto those that have shall more be given.

For the walk-on parts, Barrault called upon, among others, the students in Solange Sicard's course on dramatic art, very highly frequented during those years. An actress of imposing stature, afflicted with a stiff leg, Solange Sicard enjoyed a certain prestige in artistic milieus, despite a modest career. Almost as destitute as her students, she resided at the Hôtel Saint-Yves, on the rue de l'Université. "She gave her courses at the Pathé studios, on the rue Francoeur, anyway it was rather a course on the cinema, in which one learned how to be natural. Among the students, there were Juliette Gréco, who acted out quite a few scenes from tragedies, Christian Marquand, Nico Papatakis, Henri Vidal, Nathalie Nattier[23]."

So there were twenty or so girls and boys who gathered, one fine morning, in the attic of the Comédie-Française , where Barrault would explain what he expected of them. Among those present, was Hélène Duc's little protégée, the lost child who had rung the doorbell, one evening, at the Servandoni boarding-house: Juliette Gréco. She had only one dream, the theatre. "Filled with pride, she arrived at the first rendezvous. Jean-Louis Barrault was there. Standing, lightly supporting himself on one leg, he considered the little troupe of young people, silent and holding their breath. The course began. It was about imitating the movement of the waves in one of the tableaux of *Le Soulier de satin*. By the end of a very

---

[22] Edwige Feuillère, conversation with the author, 1996.

[23] Nicolas Bataille, interview with the author, March 2008. Afterwards, Solange Sicard would give her courses at 3 rue du Pré-aux-Clercs, in the basement of the Hôtel Saint-Thomas-d'Aquin, in the beautiful vaulted cellar where Francis Claude would open the cabaret Le Quod Libet in 1948.

few days the students were all in love with their master and went all out to create a storm[24]." Alas, on the evening of the première, as the staging demanded, the stagehands unfolded a large tarpaulin, a painted canvass evoking the sea, over the unfortunate wretches. "Disappointment. They would sway anonymously while dying of heat. Underneath. But not just anywhere nor with anyone[25]." Gréco's companions in misfortune, under the tarpaulin: two other students, Michel de Ré, François Chevais. Two boys who would soon be seen again in Saint-Germain-des-Prés. While waiting, "they consoled themselves with a Viandox, exchanging their impression, and the next day re-entered through the stage door, their heads high, greeting the concierge just as a permanent member would. They were part of the show. Of the House itself [26]."

In 2001, recalling her anonymous theatrical debut, Juliette Gréco confided to Bertrand Dicale: "I got to sing by chance, my only ambition was to be an actress[27]."

---

[24] Juliette Gréco, *Jujube, op. cit.*
[25] *Ibid.*
[26] *Ibid.*
[27] Bernard Dicale, *Gréco, les vies d'une chanteuse*, Jean-Claude Lattès, 2001.

5

Jean Cocteau: "I continued Simone de Beauvoir's book, *She Came to Stay*. Threesomes. Cafés crème... An extraordinary talent. The author has the sharp eye of a Minerva in a decomposing Athens"

July 1 1943. Simone de Beauvoir to Jean-Paul Sartre: "So yesterday I completed my move." Indeed she had just settled into the Hôtel La Louisiane, at 60 rue de Seine, a modest establishment where many regular customers of the Café de Flore had already found accommodations. "There was a sofa in my room, shelves, a big massive table, on the wall was a poster representing an English horse guard. I had a kitchen at my disposal. From my window I could see a large expanse of roofs. Never had any of my shelters come so close to my dreams[1]." At the other end of the corridor, Jean-Paul Sartre would soon occupy a little room whose exiguity and bareness would astonish more than one visitor[2], while on the floor below Nathalie Sorokine and her young friend, Jean-Pierre Bourla, both belonging to the "family," also found refuge in a large round room. Four years later, Beauvoir changed her mind, the shelter of her dreams was no more than a slum in her eyes: " I am writing to you by candlelight, it's very romantic, perhaps a bit too much so. The power has gone off as usual, this hotel is really atrocious. The walls reek humidity, it is

---

[1] Simone de Beauvoir, *La Force de l'âge, op. cit.*

[2] *Samedi-Soir*, in its issue of November 17 1945, affirmed that Simone de Beauvoir occupied room no. 50 at the Hôtel La Louisiane, while Jean-Paul Sartre lived at no 17

so glacial when one gets out of bed that every winter I say to myself that I'll have to get away from there."³

It's true, the Louisiane had nothing of a palace about it. Its clients were broke and moved out without paying. Which forced the owner to impose on them a veritable surveillance strategy: "M. Alazé keeps an eye on his tenants through a bull's-eye window overlooking the staircase, and from which one cannot escape in any way. Little by little valises of stiffened cardboard and the most ill-assorted objects left as security ended up filling the cellar and emptying the unfortunate man's cash box. As a result he became very suspicious, and his clients acquired a diabolical ingeniousness."⁴

One day someone will have to write the history of this place, a kind of Chelsea Hotel à la française, through which several generations of artists passed. Writers, like Simone de Beauvoir and Jean-Paul Sartre, of course, Albert Cossery,⁵ Jean Rougeul, Ernest Hemingway, Henry Miller… Singers: Mouloudji, Juliette Gréco… Anne-Marie Cazalis, winner of the Paul-Valéry Poetry Prize; Annabel, a model and soon a writer, who would marry the painter Bernard Buffet; Michel de Ré (whose real name was Michel Gallieni, grandson of the Marshall), an actor; Wols, "the first painter of the atomic age," as an American critic described him; jazz musicians; models… In short, all of Saint-Germain-des-Prés lived, at one time or another, at the Louisiane. It was there, no doubt, in that hotel where "everyone had plans, insomnias, sometimes genius, but never any money,"⁶ that the legend of Saint-Germain was born, and prospered, through random encounters, friendships or enmities: "We knew everybody and we knew nobody. 'Hello, how are you?' That was all."⁷

After Nathalie Sorokine, gone off to seek out in America the improbable GI whom she would end up marrying, it was Juliette Gréco who moved into the round room, the one "that is at the corner of the rue de Buci, just above the vegetable merchant and next to the horsemeat butcher shop,"⁸ that she shared for several months with Anne-Marie

---

³ *Lettres à Nelson Algren, op. cit.* (dated November 15 1947).
⁴ Juliette Gréco, *Jujube, op. cit.*
⁵ Albert Cossery, who died in June 2008, lived more than sixty years at the Hôtel La Louisiane.
⁶ Juliette Gréco, *Jujube, op. cit.*
⁷ Anne-Marie Cazalis, *Les Mémoires d'une Anne, op. cit.*
⁸ *Ibid.*

Cazalis. Because Saint-Germain-des-Prés, during those years, was still an "old populous neighbourhood, frequented by housewives and lady street merchants," as *Samedi-Soir* informed its readers in its edition of November 17 1945.

This large round bedroom, the windows of which were decked out in red plush curtains... One entered it, one exited it, one found oneself there again: "The hotel owner had installed a bathroom. Jujube would leave the key permanently on the door so that the others could take advantage of the bathtub."[9] Which they did, and as a result at all hours of day and night "noisy phantoms obsessed with cleanliness traversed the room and, what is more, made the floor crack while simultaneously apologizing profusely. Sometimes one or two would remain on the tiled floor till the morning, clean, blissfully happy and fast asleep."[10]

Les Mouches did not achieve the expected success; nor did *L'Être et le Néant*, that passed almost unnoticed. On the other hand, people were talking a great deal about a novel that appeared at Gallimard during the summer: *L'Invitée (She Came to Stay)*, the first work published by Simone de Beauvoir. They were talking about it all the way to the Académie Goncourt. In vain, inasmuch as the Goncourt Prize 1943 would be attributed to Marius Grout for his novel *Passage de l'homme (Passage of Rights)*.

To say that *L'Invitée* is the story of an amorous trio, is obviously to reduce the novel to a vague bit of ribaldry and miss the philosophical crux, even though it was announced in its entirety in the epigraph borrowed from Hegel: "Every consciousness pursues the death of the other." This however is what Jean Cocteau did, whose judgments were normally more sensible: "Simone de Beauvoir's book is *Claudine à Paris (Claudine in Paris)* in 1943 (with Sartre playing the role of Willy. A Willy straight out of the Sorbonne and the Flore)."[11]

Pierre and Françoise, anxious to establish a new erotic order between them, have "invited" into their couple a graceless, young provincial girl,

---

[9] *Ibid.* Jujube was the nickname that Juliette Gréco gave herself in order to relate her memoirs. Jujube, in her eyes, was the secret Gréco whom neither glory nor age could spoil.

[10] *Ibid.*

[11] *Journal 1942-1945, op. cit.* (dated November 18 1943). Cocteau is wrong about *Claudine*... If *L'Invitée* can make us think about one of the books in that series, it is rather *Claudine en ménage* (Claudine at home). And if it is absolutely necessary to evoke Colette, it is rather with her novel *La Seconde* (The Second One) that *L'Invitée* invites a comparison.

Xavière. At the end of the narrative, by choosing to kill off the woman who has become a kind of rival, Françoise "will choose herself." Even summed up superficially, the novel appears clearly for what it is: the staging of the irreducible confrontation between consciousnesses.[12] If Jean Cocteau was blinded, it is because he, in the long run, wanted to see in *L'Invitée* only a kind of roman-a-clef: "I could place fifty names on each personage. I know their mechanism, their way of speaking, of dressing, of dragging themselves, of judging. It is the style of the Café de Flore. A veritable opium. The café crème opium."[13] Fifty names? Maybe not, but a few, at least: Pierre Labrousse is Sartre and also, in a certain way, Charles Dullin; Xavière is Olga Kosakiewicz, with traits of her sister Wanda and others belonging to Nathalie Sorokine; Gerbert is Jacques-Laurent Bost, the "little Bost"; finally, Françoise is Beauvoir herself, who, nevertheless, lends to the character the artistic activities of Simone Jollivet, Dullin's companion. The entire "family" indeed! Even the locales were inspired by reality: the Dôme, the Théâtre de l'Atelier, le Bal Nègre, the bars of Montparnasse...

No ambiguity there. And besides, as Deirdre Bair, de Beauvoir's biographer, emphasized in her work, when Olga Kosakiewicz became aware of the success the novel garnered, she flew into a violent rage.[14] No doubt the regular customers of the Café de Flore got it right when they recognized their own way of living—the cafés, the hotel rooms, the bal of the rue Blomet, alcohol, tobacco...—related with the precision of an entomologist. Jean Cocteau's diary: "Continued Simone de Beauvoir's book. Threesomes. Café crèmes. The Dôme, the Coupole, the Bal Nègre, etc. But with an extraordinary talent. As though the deepest liveliness had put itself at the disposal of sloppiness. One must believe (and in this sense the book is a document of the first rank) that the best minds are the victims of a fashion and take pleasure in it while preserving their cutting edge. The author has the sharp eye of a Minerva in a decomposing Athens. It is odious and marvellous. But strength will consist in escaping from this dead zone."

That *L'Invitée* had as its background Montparnasse, that the novel was written on the pedestal tables of the Dôme, is nothing more than a

---

[12] The expression comes from Éliane Lecarme-Tabone in *Encyclopédie thématique*, I, note "Simone de Beauvoir", Encylopaedia Universalis, 2004.

[13] Jean Cocteau, *Journal 1942-45, op. cit.* (dated October 30 1943).

[14] Deirdre Bair, *Simone de Beauvoir*, Fayard, 1990. It is to be noted that *L'Invitée* is dedicated to Olga Kosakiewicz.

detail, basically a mere question of dates: Saint-Germain-des-Prés had no trouble recognizing itself. Where Cocteau saw only "sloppiness" (he would not be the only one), what counted was the reinvention of our relationship to others. Saint-Germain-des-Prés would be the human and literary laboratory of this experiment. For example, Anne-Marie Cazalis affirmed that she decided to move into the neighbourhood after having read *L'Invitée*: she wanted to live that kind of life.

Because the literature had changed, was changing, would change again. Relationships with others—"hell is other people," Sartre would soon say—but also man's responsibility, individual freedom... The literature of the Occupation—just like its theatre, in fact—while giving the impression of blandly prolonging the aesthetic of the 1930s, was really preparing the one that would triumph soon after the Liberation. So it didn't matter what Jean Cocteau said, this time he was preaching in the desert: "I am reading Simone de Beauvoir's book, *L'Invitée*, about which everybody is talking. Is this what you call living? Then I am not alive. It is the life of a she-dog who relates stories about dogs that gnaw at bones, piss one after another against the same streetlamp, bite one another or smell each other's rear ends. Can one drink to such a degree and drag oneself around to such a degree, never sleep and if one does sleep, never sleep alone[15]?" For his part, Gabriel Marcel, charmed by the vivacity of the rejoinders that the characters exchange, advised the young woman to write for the theatre: "Your dialogues are remarkable, you must write for the stage[16]." His advice would be heeded.

On the evening of the dress rehearsal for *Les Mouches*, while he was standing in the foyer of the Theatre de la Cité, near the ticket booth, Jean-Paul Sartre was approached by a stranger. A dark, handsome young man who extended his hand when introducing himself: "Albert Camus." Between the two men, the empathy was immediate.

A journalist at *Alger républicain* (*The Algiers Republican*), the organ close to the Algerian Communist Party, Camus had to leave the city in 1940, after a grave disagreement with Algeria's governing body. He moved to Paris, where he became the secretary of the editorial board at the newspaper *Paris-Soir*. It was then that he published one after the other, in 1942, *L'Étranger* (*The Stranger*) and *Le Mythe de Sisyphe* (*The*

---

[15] *Journal 1942-1945, op. cit.* (dated October 30 1943). Cocteau would write Simone de Beauvoir a letter of praise.

[16] *Les Nouvelles littéraires*, November 8 1945.

Myth of Sisyphus), the first titles of a body of works he would call "The Cycle of the Absurd," soon to be completed by two plays, *Le Malentendu* (*The Misunderstanding*) and *Caligula*. "Like us, Camus had moved from individualism to engagement; we knew, without his ever having alluded to this, that he held important responsibilities in the "Combat" movement. He had an appetite for success, notoriety, and he made no bones about it."[17] Camus soon became an intimate. They were seen together at the Flore or in the neighbourhood restaurants. And even more often at the home of the Leiris.

It was at this time, in fact, that the Sartre-Beavoir couple became friends with Michel Leiris and his wife Louise—who was known as "Zette" in the artistic circles. Ethnologist, writer, formerly close to the Surrealist group, Michel Leiris—who attained notoriety in 1939 with the publication of *L'Âge d'homme* (Manhood)—worked at the Musée de l'Homme (The Museum of Man); As for Zette, she directed the art gallery of her brother-in-law, Daniel-Henry Kahnweiler, the famous merchant who launched most of the cubist painters.[18]

As big art collectors, the Leiris possessed among others an impressive array of Picassos. They lived at the frontier of Saint-Germain-des-Prés, at 53bis Quai des Grands-Augustins, on the fourth floor of a beautiful old building from which one could survey, in the same quick glance, the Seine and the Île de la Cité. There lived as well—in secret, once the racial laws were promulgated—Daniel-Henry Kahnweiler. He would soon leave Paris and take refuge in the southwest of France. It was a vast abode, furnished in bourgeois fashion, crammed with precious objects, books and modern paintings: Picasso, Masson, Mirò... During her first visit, Simone de Beauvoir remarked in amazement that the office chairs were covered in upholstery based on cartoons by Juan Gris.

During the harsh winter of 1941—the first winter of the Occupation—Picasso tried his hand at concocting a sort of late post-Surrealist humorous piece, conceived according to the procedures of automatic writing, *Le Désir attrapé par la queue* (*Desire caught by its tail*). A wild farce, in six acts, the action of which unfolded in a place called Sordid's Hôtel. In Act

---

[17] Simone de Beavoir, *La Force de l'âge, op. cit.*

[18] Actually, Kahnweiler is the father-in-law of Louise Leiris, née Gordon. The Gordon family, for inheritance purposes, passed off Louise as the sister of the person who was in reality her mother. By marrying the two "sisters", Kahnweiler and Leiris in actual fact married the mother and the daughter.

II, the setting is a corridor of the Sordid's Hôtel: "The two feet of each guest are in front of the doors to their rooms, twisted in pain;" transformation in Act IV: "The sewer-bedroom-kitchen-bathroom of the villa of Anguishes." In short, unplayable on a real stage.[19]

As soon as he heard about this text, published in the glossy revue *L'Arbalète*, Michel Leiris, a great admirer of the painter, took it into his head to organize a public reading at his home; a simple reading, without décors or costumes. And he rounded up straight away at the Quai des Augustins all the important personalities , intellectuals, and artists residing in Paris...

On March 19 1944, then, around 19 hours, in the Leiris' large salon, whose windows looked upon "the most beautiful landscape in Paris, framed by the masterpieces of modern painting, the most regal expanse of the river, surrounded by admirable Picassos and sublime Juan Gris,"[20] there was the typical crush of big Parisian evenings. "Several rows of chairs had been arranged, but so many people came that many listeners remained standing at the far end of the room and in the anteroom."[21] Georges Bataille, Jean-Louis Barrault and Madeleine Renaud, Armand Salacrou and Lucienne, his wife, Georges Braque, Mouloudji, Maria Casarès, the psychoanalyst Jacques Lacan and his wife, the actress Sylvia Bataille, Pierre Reverdy, Valentine Hugo, Georges Limbour... And let's not forget that Argentinian millionaire couple, Marcello and Hortensia Anchorena, who chose to entrust the decoration of their home on the avenue Foch to the finest artists of the moment: Braque painted a door, Chirico another, Picasso was to paint a third... As for Cocteau, he considered decorating a piano.[22]

Laughter, buzz of conversations, social chatter... There was a sudden silence when Picasso rose and piously placed on the mantelpiece of the salon the portrait of Max Jacob, who had died at the camp of Drancy several days earlier. The performers, chosen by Michel Leiris himself, holding their booklets, formed a group in front of the audience. Performers? Rather readers of good will who had rehearsed conscientiously, several afternoons in succession, under the direction of the master of the house.

---

[19] The play would nevertheless be performed in 1952, in New York, by the troupe Living Theatre. Then in 1967, in France, in a staging by Jean-Jacques Lebel. Finally, Jean-Christophe Averty would produce a televised adaptation of it in 1988.

[20] Guillaume Hanoteau, *Ces nuits qui ont fait Paris, op. cit.*

[21] Simone de Beauvoir, *La Force de l'âge.*

[22] See *Journal 1942-1945, op. cit.*, especially on the date of September 17 1942.

The cast of *Le Désir attrapé par la queue*, was, with a few exceptions, the Gallimard publishing house catalogue for the year 1944:

Jean Aubier: The Curtains;
Simone de Beauvoir: The Cousin;
Jacques-Laurent Bost: Silence;
Zanie Campan : The Pie;
Germaine Hugnet: Scrawny Anguish;
Louise Leiris: The Two Doggies;
Michel Leiris; The Big Foot;
Dora Maar: The Fat Anguish;
Raymond Queneau: The Onion;
Jean-Paul Sartre: The Round End.

Next to them, Albert Camus, armed with a "brigadier," the stick used in the theatre to strike the three blows that signal the start of a performance, was the master of ceremonies, announcing the changes of acts and tableaux, describing the décors, presenting the characters. In this role, as they say, he knew his stuff. Because he was enamoured of the theatre. Almost a professional. In Algiers, he directed a troupe, the Théâtre de l'Équipe, and, beforehand, another called the Théâtre du Travail. When they met, Sartre spoke to him about his new play; he suggested Camus take on the principal role as well as direct it[23]. Albert Camus accepted.

At the Quai des Grands-Augustins, the performance was ending. Loud applause, exclamations, flattering murmurs. "In that milieu, they took seriously—at least superficially—all of Picasso's actions. Everyone congratulated him," Simone de Beauvoir noted somewhat mischievously, who, by her own admission, spent a lot of money on her outfit: a red angora sweater, a necklace of big blue pearls. And who received with pleasure the painter's compliments.[24] Certainly, *Le Désir attrapé par la queue* was a bit dated. Or rather, it came upon the scene too late, with its false airs of Jarry or Apollinaire—the Apollinaire of *Les Mamelles*

---

[23] The play is *Huis clos*.

[24] Three months later, on June 16 1944, Picasso reassembled his impromptu actors in his workshop, in order to thank them. Photos done by Brassaï, taken that day, testify to the event. One important person was absent from the negatives: Dora Maar. A quarrel had indeed broken out between the two lovers in the month of April.

de Térésias (*The Breasts of Teresias*). Which prompted some malevolent minds to say, in a low voice: "That desire has neither—tail nor head!"

"We didn't dance, in order not to scandalize the tenants living below, but Leiris put on some jazz recordings softly. Mouloudji sang *Les Petits Pavés* (The Little Cobblestones) in a lovely voice that was still childlike; we requested of Sartre *Les Papillons de la nuit* (*The Night Butterflies*) and *J'ai vendu mon âme au diable* (*I sold my soul to the devil*); Leiris and Camus read a scene from a melodrama they chose; as for the others, I don't know how they expended their energy."[25] Because the performers in the play—and several close friends—chose not to depart at the time of the curfew. In other words, they were forced, all together, to wait for the liberating dawn. "Eating and drinking together, in the heart of the shadows, was such a fleeting pleasure that it seemed to us illicit; it had something of the charm of clandestine joys."[26]

And Heaven knew that the only joys during those times were the clandestine ones... Even if one could glimpse the end of the tunnel, the war appeared to go on forever in that spring of 1944. And bore down more and more heavily on the French, as though incarcerated, despite themselves, "within the heart of darkness." Prisoners, deported as part of the STO program (Service de travail obligatoire/Compulsory Work Service), volunteers, requisitioned workers: this was a labour force estimated at 2,600,000 men whose absence was cruelly felt in the country, where industrial production had not stopped dropping since the armistice[27]. There were fewer workers in the factories, but also fewer peasants working the land, whereas the removals from agricultural production—meat, cereals, milk products—became heavier and heavier: about one fifth of the production was thus diverted to Germany. During this period, France had become a kind of horn of plenty—alas not inexhaustible—from which Germany was drawing by the armfuls. In Paris, for example, the food supply diminished by 40%. The Construction and automobile industries, the cement works, to name only these, were working up to 75% for Germany.

---

[25] Simone de Beauvoir, *La Force de l'âge*, op. cit.

[26] *Ibid.*

[27] In relationship to the figure 100 in 1939, the index of industrial production evolved in the following manner: 68 in 1941, 62 in 1942, 56 in 1943, 43 in 1944. From this production, the occupiers took away 34% (sources: Serge Berstein and Pierre Milza, *Histoire de la France au XXe siècle, op. cit.*

Hence a very strict rationing of the food supplies. In 1942, the Parisian received barely 8 kilos of bread per month, whereas he would consume 13.5 in 1939, 3.5 kilos of potatoes instead of 15 before the war, and 720 grams of meat versus 3.5 kilos. Two years later, rations were reduced to the point of shrinking away: 250 monthly grams of meat, 200 grams of fat content. As for coffee, the sale of which was forbidden since 1940, a bad mixture replaced it, a sort of ersatz sold under the name of National Coffee and composed of one third coffee and two thirds substitute.

The well stocked buffet to which the Leiris' guests joyfully did justice after the reading of *Le Désir attrapé par la queue* is an exception; an enormous chocolate cake, brought in by Marcello and Hortensia Anchorena, occupied the place of honour in the midst of the victuals. Paid for no doubt at the heaviest price: the black market one, whose rates reached heights inaccessible to most. During the period from April to June 1944, the kilo of roasting beef, the legal cost of which was 70 francs, was bargained for between 150 and 200 francs, the litre of milk, which normally cost 4.60 francs, went up to 12 and sometimes even 30 francs, while the dozen of eggs would sell for 120 francs (value: 43 francs) and the kilo of butter for 450 francs (legal price: 77 francs)[28]. In reality, there were no limits.

There would be other nights like the one that continued after *Le Désir attrapé par la queue*. White nights, entirely devoted to drinking, laughing, privileged ones, flamboyant apotheoses of a moment in time saved from the atmosphere of unhappiness, that would acquire, in the Saint-Germain mythology, a henceforth famous name: the "fiestas."[29] And so much the worse if, later on, under the pen of malevolent columnists, these parties would become synonymous with debauchery. In actual fact, they were more noisy and wine-saturated than scandalous.

Just like the one that Mouloudji organized, in April 1944, right after winning the Prix de la Pléiade.[30] And which unfolded according to the usual scenario: the revellers forgot curfew time and thus found themselves, by force of circumstances, constrained to wait until early morning before going home. "It took place in Taverny in a house lent by someone or other. I made the rounds of the seedy joints to find bottles of wine and edible tri-

---

[28] Source: INSEE.
[29] The word comes from Michel Leiris.
[30] For his novel *Enrico*.

fles. The merrymaking ended at dawn[31]." The Kosakiewicz sisters, Sartre, Beauvoir, Camus, Bost, the Leirises, Queneau, Merleau-Ponty... The regulars. Plus several comrades from Saint-Germain. They were heavy drinkers, especially of red wine, spirits being rare. They danced as well: rumbas, tangos—and those beguines that were in fashion, before the war, at the Bal Nègre on rue Blomet. "While I was admiring Olga, relates Mouloudji, I was struck for the hundredth time by the contrast between her face, normally pallid, a bit blurred, a bit lunar, and her body that was swaying."[32]

But Olga, suddenly, stopped dancing; she wondered aloud: Where is Bost?" A kind of intuition... Bost, "a very handsome young man, highly successful in winning ladies' hearts," according to Vian; Bost with whom Olga formed an improbable couple. And so she darted off looking for him, dragging along Mouloudji through the house. In some spots people were sleeping, elsewhere others were in conversation... At the door to the winter garden, Olga perceived whispers, something like fabrics rustling... Mouloudji, sensing an impending drama, wanted to prevent her from entering. She pushed him aside. Bost appeared, sheepish like a character in a farce caught in the closet. Howls, insults, vociferations... Several sleepers, waking up with a start, came to see what was happening. "We were closer to Feydeau than to Hegel," concluded Mouloudji. Fortunately, the guests' attention was diverted by a squadron of Allied bombers that were passing, on their way to Germany. All lights being turned off, people rushed to the windows: "A superb spectacle with searchlights scanning a sky streaked with blazing gunfire. The whole atmosphere was enveloped in the fireworks of multicoloured shells that would tear through the night as though it were flesh[33]." Then the evening got back to normal again: "I had the honour of seeing Sartre dance the parody of a tango. Many of the guests were drunk and were having a whale of a time. In the air floated a perfume of freedom coming from the West and everyone in his heart of hearts dreamt of the troop landing that was so longed for."[34]

The landing? On the morning of June 6, on leaving a fiesta washed down with plenty of wine, that one organized at Charles Dullin's place,

---

[31] Mouloudji, *La Fleur de l'âge, op. cit.* The house in question here belonged to the family of J.-L. Bost.

[32] *Ibid.*

[33] *Ibid.*

[34] *Ibid.*

on the rue de la Tour-d'Auvergne, Sartre, Beauvoir, Camus, Maria Casarès and their friends learned the news: the Allies were on French soil.

"I will never forget that stifling dress rehearsal, under a summer-like temperature. In the tiny and full house, everyone was drenched in sweat and was sponging himself... They were invading Sainte-Mère-Église and the fighters were falling en masse at the foot of the Normandy cliffs, but the event of the month was the play by Jean-Paul Sartre."[35] On June 10, indeed, at the Théâtre du Vieux-Colombier, Jean-Paul Sartre introduced *Huis clos*, his second play, to the press.[36] A Second Empire salon, a mantelpiece and a bronze object, three couches—and "hell is other people"...

At that moment, hell was rather the Normandy coast, where for four days the Allies were fighting relentlessly to gain a foothold on the continent. The operation launched against Sicily, in July 1943, by the Anglo-American troops, was only the first phase of a vast plan to re-conquer the European space. The Quebec Conference, organized a month later, from August 17 to the 24th, would lay the foundations for the next stage. Despite opposition from Churchill, who was an advocate of a landing in the Balkans, it was the American solution of an invasion of Europe from the west, already envisioned in May, during the Washington conference, that was chosen. The code name for the operation: *Overlord*. The initial landing date foreseen: May 1 1944. By the end of 1943, General Eisenhower was named Supreme Commander of the Allied Forces. As a result, within barely several months, Staff Headquarters would have to solve problems that seemed insoluble in such a time frame: equipment, arms, gasoline... They would all receive their solution. A pipeline, submerged under the Channel, would supply the troops on the ground; two artificial ports, at Saint-Laurent-sur-Mer and especially at Arromanches, would allow the transmission of weaponry. And on June 6, at 6 hours 20, jumping from flat-bottomed barges under German fire, the attacking infantry poured over the Normandy beaches, renamed in the American way "Omaha Beach," "Utah Beach"... A sea front of 17 kilometres, with a boat every seventy metres: the greatest landing of all time had begun. That evening, five American divisions, three British and two Canadian ones were anchored between the mouths of the Orne and the Vire rivers.

---

[35] André Roussin, *Rideau gris et Habit vert*, Albin Michel, 1983.

[36] June 10 is the date of the dress rehearsal. The play had been running since May 27.

Saint Germain des Prés

The operations continued till June 12. 80,000 men in total, of whom more than 2000 would fall dead on the pebbled shores of Normandy.

Now back to *Huis clos*. At the outset, it was supposed to be a story about a family. The "family." Jean-Paul Sartre had written a play, *Les Trois Autres* (*The Three Others*), whose feminine roles he intended to give to his young friends Wanda Kosakiewicz—who would take in the theatre the pseudonym of Marie-Olivier—and Olga Kechelievich, called "Olga la Brune" (The Dark Olga), who had become Olga Barbezat after her marriage to Marc Barbezat, the owner, in Lyon, of a laboratory of pharmaceutical products and, especially, the editor of the sumptuous magazine *L'Arbalète*.[37]

Huis clos: a play for the occasion, in short. To such an extent that, in the first typed draft of the manuscript, the characters are only designated by the names of the actors.[38] Sartre made himself clear on this matter: "At the time I wrote *Huis clos*, in 1943 and at the beginning of 1944, I had three friends and I wanted them to perform the play, a play of mine, without favouring any of them. That is to say that I wanted them to remain together on stage all the time."[39] The third friend was, of course, Albert Camus. We saw how, at Sartre's own request, he had agreed to stage the play that was not yet called *Huis clos*, and to play the masculine part.[40] The objective was to arrange a tour in the provinces.

The first rehearsals took place at the Hôtel La Louisiane, in Simone de Beauvoir's bedroom: "With Wanda, Olga Barbezat and Chauffard as the bellhop: he was a former student of Sartre, who wrote, but wanted above all to become an actor. The swiftness with which Camus threw himself into this adventure, the readiness that it revealed about him ensured our friendship for him."[41] But Olga Barbezat was arrested by the Gestapo.[42] And the project was abandoned. All the more because the Allied Air

---

[37] Marc Barbezat had tried, in vain, to mount *Les Trois Autres* at the Théâtre des Célestins, in Lyon.

[38] Jean-Paul Sartre, *Les Trois Autres*, typed copy, French National Library, Department of Performing Arts, Charles Dullin Collectioin.

[39] Jean-Paul Sartre, "La Naissance de *Huis clos*", a text recorded by the author as an introduction to the phonograph recording of the play, Deutsche Grammophon Gesellschaft, 1965.

[40] Nevertheless, at first, Sartre had sounded out the actor Sylvain Itkine.

[41] Simone de Beauvoir, *La Force de l'âge, op.cit.*

[42] Imprisoned in Fresnes, she would be liberated in June.

Force's heavy shelling of roads and railway stations made it difficult, if not impossible, to organize a tour.

That is when a newcomer entered the scene: the very recently appointed director of the Théâtre du Vieux-Colombier, an ex-lawyer converted to dramatic art. Alerted by Gaston Gallimard, Sartre's editor, he in turn expressed an interest in the play. He, at the same time, would find its definitive name. "Sartre told us he was not satisfied with the title. He explained that he would have liked a title that synthesized the situation of three guilty individuals tearing into one another for all eternity in a hotel room in hell. Each one brought forward suggestions. Suddenly Chauffard called out: *Huis clos!* That was exactly what was suitable, and Sartre approved that stroke of inspiration."[43]

When he picked up the lease on the Vieux-Colombier, in 1943, Paul Annet-Badel, a skilful businessman, perhaps too skilful—it was said that he succeeded in selling a good chunk of the forest of Fontainebleau to the Germans!—"who tried out all trades and did not wish to ply any of them,"[44] Paul Annet-Badel, then, wanted to restore to Jacques Copeau's hall the lustre that had been rather dimmed by the years and some rather rash theatrical experiments. The building had hardly changed, despite transformations and modernizations; at first glance, the regular performers found their bearings again. Valentine Tessier, for example, who had returned to create in the theatre of her youth the play by Marcel Aymé *Lucienne et le Boucher* (*Lucienne and the Butcher*), was astonished to discover the old décors of yesteryear, stocked in the courtyard: "Filled with emotion like a big girl who has just seen again the house of her childhood, she went into the corridors, looked around everywhere, said, 'over there, that was my dressing room,' and recognized the concierge who had not changed since Copeau."[45] After the latter had left, in 1924, the movie director Jean Tedesco opened, as he called it, the "avant-garde" cinema hall: Griffith, Abel Gance, Marcel L'Herbier, Chaplin, Jean Epstein... Among others were presented there *Le Sang d'un poète* (*The Blood of a poet*) by Jean Cocteau and *La Petite Marchande d'allumettes* (*The Little Match Girl*), that Jean Renoir produced in 1928 in collaboration with Tedesco himself. Then the Vieux-Colombier

---

[43] Mouloudji, *La Fleur de l'âge, op. cit.*

[44] The expression comes from Boris Vian. Paul Annet-Badel, at one time nicknamed "The Six Million Scoundrel", would die in Switzerland in 1986, where he sought refuge after being ruined.

[45] Georges Douking, in Marcelle Routier, *Saint-Germain-des-Prés, op. cit.*

was given back to the theatre, with the Compagnie des Quinze, directed by Michel Saint-Denis and composed of some of Copeau's former colleagues. Sacha Pitoëff and his troop presented Ibsen's *Le Canard sauvage* (The Wild Duck) and *Maison de poupée* (*The Doll House*). In 1935, René Rocher, whom we would find several years later, during the Occupation, at the head of the Théâtre de l'Odéon and, especially, of the redoubtable Comité d'organisation des enterprises de spectacles (COES), assumed control of it; in a hall completely renovated by the decorator André Boll, he created a play by Pierre Brasseur, *Grisou* (*Firedamp*). What followed was an uncertain period, during which boulevard comedies and so-called "serious" plays followed one another on the stage of the Vieux-Colombier.

In the meantime, Camus withdrew from the project, judging, no doubt correctly, that he was not qualified either to direct an important production or to perform in the company of professional actors. Raymond Rouleau, ex-collaborator of Antonin Artaud and Charles Dullin, who was now a movie star, would take charge of the staging. Then came up the thorny question of casting—thorny because, in the circumstances, private lives and artistic demands would find themselves inextricably intertwined in a veritable battle involving several women... Guillaume Hanoteau has left us a picturesque account of the negotiations: "Discussions began on the first floor of the Flore, between the author, the theatre director and the new stage director. For the man's role, there was no debate, they agreed on Michel Vitold. There was no wrangling either about Chauffard. For a long time Sartre dug in his heels to save Wanda, a novice actress. At the end of these disputes, the ravishing Gaby Sylvia—the author of *L'Être et le Néant* supposedly went so far as to compare the intoxicating beauty of that redhead to the tired-looking, pretty little face of his protégée—finally won out."[46]

Gaby Sylvia, who found herself entrusted with the role of Estelle, possessed a considerable asset: she was the wife of Paul Annet-Badel. Whereas Tania Balachova, who would play Inès, was the ex-companion of Raymond Rouleau. Thus, despite Sartre's laudable efforts and the laborious negotiations at the Café de Flore, none of the actors originally approached—except for Chauffard—would remain in the definitive cast. And one can easily imagine the recriminations, tears and reproaches that Sartre must have endured, in the corridors of the Hôtel La Louisiane, when Wanda Kosakiewicz found out that she would not be Inès...

---

[46] *Ces nuits qui ont fait Paris, op. cit.*

"A Second Empire-style salon. A bronze object on the mantelpiece:" Sartre, on the first page of *Huis clos*, does not burden himself with explanations. When the curtain rises, on this June 10th 1944, the spectators do indeed discover a banal Second Empire-style salon. But designed by Max Douy[47] At the back, a fireplace and, on the shelf, a Barbedienne fake bronze statue. Above the fireplace, the glass overmantel has been taken down; in its place, an opaque wall, the very image of nothingness. Stage right, a brick partition marks the space where a window has been sealed up. A chandelier—"a concierge's chandelier," said Guillaume Hanoteau. And three hideous, uncomfortable sofas: yellow, spinach green, burgundy. This prompted the critic of *Combat*, Pierre Chapuis, to say, on the occasion of the play's revival in the autumn of 1944: "Max Douy's décor uses genuine talent to deliberately create ugliness."[48] Stage left, a door opens up onto an invisible corridor. The bellhop, wearing a white apron and a striped vest, ushers Garcin in—shirt, tie and dark suit, fedora.

GARCIN, *he enters and looks around him*
So this is it.

THE BELLHOP
This is it.

GARCIN
That's the way it is.

THE BELLHOP
That's the way it is

GARCIN
I guess that sooner or later one gets used to the furniture.

THE BELLHOP
That depends on the people…

---

[47] Max Douy would be one of the most active cinema set designers in the 1950s, collaborating particularly with Claude Autant-Lara.

[48] *Combat*, September 20 1944.

Tania Balachova entered the stage in turn, hard, tense, aggressive—in a dark dress, a high turban fashionable in the forties, tied in the front. Then came Gaby Sylvia, with her arms uncovered, supple in a long light-coloured dress.

INÈS
Well, they have saved the cost of staffing. That's all. The clients provide the service themselves, like in self-service restaurants.

ESTELLE
What do you mean?

INÈS
The executioner is each one of us for the two others.

GARCIN, *in a soft voice*
I won't be your executioner. I don't wish you any harm and I have nothing to debate with you. Nothing…

In the overheated hall, the spectators were holding their breath. Sartre was in the wings, where he watched the performance. Annet-Badel was jubilant: it was a success. One line, however, unleashed unexpected laughter in the audience:

GARCIN
Where is the light switch?

THE BELLHOP
There is none.

GARCIN
So? You can't turn it off?

THE BELLHOP
The administration can cut off the power. But I don't remember them ever having done it on this floor. We have as much electricity as we want.

Now a power outage, several moments before the start of the performance, had plunged the hall in darkness, according to Guillaume Hanoteau.

"And the play unfolded, diabolical, fatal, implacable," recalled Daniel Gélin who would pick up the role of Garcin, in September, before playing it hundreds of times, in Paris and on tours. "I point to the Barbedienne bronze on the mantelpiece and slowly, livid with lucidity, almost tenderly, almost happy[49] [say]:

GARCIN
...They had foreseen that I would stand in front of this fireplace, pressing my hand on this bronze, with all those eyes fixed on me. All those eyes that are eating me up. (*He swerves sharply*). Ha! There are only two of you? I though you were many more. (*He laughs*). So, this is what hell is all about. I would never have believed it...You remember: the sulphur, the stake, the grill...Ah! What a joke. No need for a grill; hell is other people.

"Hell is other people." Without a doubt, there is not, in the whole of contemporary theatre, a line on which people have rambled as much. Yet Sartre had made himself clear on the matter: "People thought that I meant by it that our relationships with others were always poisoned, that they would always be infernal relationships. But what I mean is entirely different. I mean that if relationships with the other are twisted, contaminated, then the other can only be hell. Why? Because the others are basically what is most important in ourselves for our own self-knowledge."[50]

However, the most subtle analysis of the play remains the one made by Francis Jeanson, when he compared *Huis clos* to *L'Être et le Néant*. Explaining, in a way, one in terms of the other. "You are a coward Garcin, a coward because that's the way I want it. I want it, do you understand, I want it...I am nothing more than these eyes that see you, than this colourless thought that reflects you...Come on, you have no choice: You must convince me. I have you nailed," Inès cries out. "The Other has power over me," replies *L'Être et le Néant*, "my original downfall is the existence of the other," "conflict is the original meaning of being-for-the

---

[49] Daniel Gélin, *Deux ou trios vies qui sont les miennes*, Julliard, 1977.
[50] *Un theatre de situations*, Gallimard, 1992.

other"[51] ... Francis Jeanson's conclusion: "No doubt it appears sufficiently obvious that the hell in *Huis clos*—at a certain level of interpretation—is a hell fully alive, that it is inscribed in the human condition as the latter's natural way of being alive."[52]

Parisian audiences were themselves also aware of the coherence of a body of works where *Huis clos* appeared as the clear illustration of the massive tome *L'Être et le Néant*. Because the play was a real success, durable, constant, that erased the semi-failure of *Les Mouches*; the public that came to the Vieux-Colombier was young and enthusiastic. The press itself was, on the whole, laudatory: "The skilful demonstration of a philosophy professor. This does not prevent the work from being perfectly valid and containing dramatic moments of admirable theatrical power";[53] as for the review *Comoedia*, it compared the dramatic force of Sartre to that of Strindberg. On the other hand, as usual, the Collaboration journalists, like André Castelot in *La Gerbe* on June 8, flew into a rage: "When M. Jean-Paul Sartre, while writing one of his plays, finds a detail saturated with human ugliness, one easily imagines him rubbing his hands. This time, with *Huis clos,* one's disgust is total."

Nevertheless, victory was changing sides. The wind, henceforth, was blowing from the west, and everyone knew it. And many, as one would say, were putting water in their wine. Starting with a conciliatory Robert Brasillach, who recognized: "A talent who purifies what could appear unwholesome"; whereas Drieu la Rochelle noted subtly in his Diary: "Once again, we are dealing with a man who cannot escape the Christianity of his birth, who can only present it as a caricature."[54] "The article by Laubreaux was even full of praise, with a touch of melancholy," relates Guillaume Hanoteau. "And a discreet confession. The polemicist no longer believed in what he was doing. Sartre's drama announced a new era of which he would not be part."[55] Indeed, for once, Laubreaux toned down his discourse. Under the title "Hell and Damnation," his column, published in *Je suis partout*, merely reproached Sartre for having

---

[51] We can also compare this expression to Hegel's statement, quoted by Simone de Beauvoir at the beginning of *L'Invitée*: "Every consciousness pursues the death of the other."

[52] *Sartre*, Seuil, 2000.

[53] Jean Turlais, *La Revue du monde*, July 1944.

[54] *Journal 1939-1945*, Gallimard, 1992.

[55] *L'Âge d'or de Saint-Germain-des-Prés, op. cit.*

been inspired by illustrious predecessors. Among others, Dostoïevski and Édouard Bourdet. Peccadillos. Really, this time around, his heart was no longer in it!

A new era? Definitely. *Huis clos* marked a major date. Something like the charter founding Saint-Germain-des-Prés. The post-war Saint-Germain-des-Prés; the one belonging to legend. Because *Huis clos*, to a certain extent, closed a cycle, that of the Occupation. And opened another: the golden age of Saint-Germain-des-Prés.

Ever since they landed, the Allies did not stop progressing on French territory: Bayeux, Isigny were among the first to be liberated. On June 26, it was Cherbourg's turn, on July 9 it was Caen's. The breakthrough at Avranches, at the end of the month, opened up the road to Brittany to the Allied troops, then, after a vast encircling movement, the road to Paris. "On August 11, the newspapers and the radio announced that the Americans were approaching Chartres," noted Simone de Beauvoir on the last pages of *La Force de l'âge*. But the impatient Parisians were faster. As General von Choltitz, the Commander in Chief of the Whermacht, was preparing to repulse the assault of the Anglo-American troops, it was the Parisians who attacked him. From within. Because, on this point, the orders coming from the Résistance were irreversible: Paris had to liberate itself.

As of August 17, the CGT and CFTC labour unions—forbidden by Vichy—appealed to the Parisians to stage a complete strike. Everything stopped. The capital was at a standstill. Neither metro nor gas, electricity was delivered in dribs and drabs, at the rate of thirty minutes per day. Banks, post offices, theatres and cinemas were closed. No funeral services. Even the state-owned pawnshop closed its doors.

The French Forces of the Interior, created in March to bring together the Résistance fighters, were the instigators of a vast insurrectional drive that developed at that time in the capital. On August 19, their leader, Colonel Rol-Tanguy, ordered his troops in Île-de-France "to attack the isolated Germans or the light detachments, to create a permanent state of insecurity in the enemy and to block its movements." Nevertheless, the means the insurgents had at their disposal were derisory in the face of the German forces that occupied the terrain with 16,000 men: 29 mines, 4 machine guns, 83 repeating rifles and barely as many submachine guns, 562 rifles, 825 revolvers. To which would be added, on the following days, the arms snatched from the enemy. Courage and audacity would take care of the rest... 1,500 volunteers heard Rol-Tanguy's call—they would very quickly become thousands more. Among them were two young, almost unknown actors, Gérard Philipe and Michel Auclair, who turned up, on the morning of August 20, at the doors of the Hôtel de Ville, in order to come to the assistance of the FFI which gained control of the building, under the military command of Roger Stéphane.

"From Saturday 19 till Friday August 25, the battles waged in Paris against the Germans, first by Rol's FFI troops, then by the soldiers of the 2nd DB (Division Blindée/Armoured Division), helped by the first, would be as sporadic as they were violent in nature, as dispersed in space as they were variable in intensity. Some neighbourhoods would be exempt from fighting, whereas certain flashpoints saw frequent skirmishes[56]." Fighting went on at police headquarters, at the Hôtel de Ville, in front of Notre-Dame, of which a door was torn off by a German shell, at the Théâtre de l'Odéon, where the Nazis, entrenched in the public foyer, were firing on the Résistance combatants; on rue de la Huchette they [Parisians] had set up barricades... In the evening of August 20, "a hesitant crowd was loitering on Saint-Germain-des-Prés Square. Some people, however, said that there was gunfire near the Gobelins, at the Place d'Italie and in other parts of the city..."[57]

On August 23, the 2nd Armoured Division of the Forces françaises libres (Free French Forces), commanded by General Leclerc, swooped down on Paris: 16,000 men in 4000 vehicles covered 200 kilometres during the day. Because time was of the essence. The Parisian FFI let it be known that they feared not being able to resist a serious attack from the Germans. On the 24th, the French troops were in Meudon, in the Parisian suburbs. In Paris, the fever was at its peak. "They are at Antony!... They are on the heights of Châtillon... No, they are still fighting... They are repairing the road in order for the tanks to pass... They have entered... They are entering..."[58] In the afternoon of the 25th, General Leclerc received the surrender from General von Choltitz.

Paris was free.

Combat, the clandestine organ of the Résistance, could at last appear in broad daylight. The newspaper set itself up on the premises of *L'Intransigeant* (*The Intransigent*), at 100 rue de Réaumur. An enor-

---

[56] Pierre Bourget, *Paris 1940-1944*, Plon, 1979.
[57] Simone de Beauvoir, *La Force de l'âge, op. cit.*
[58] Colette, *L'Étoile Vesper*, Éditions du Milieu du Monde, 1946.

mous disorder reigned in the building from top to bottom: the disorder of freedom. People were congratulating one another, laughing, sifting through the news—the false and the true—articles were being written in haste, on table corners; no one was sleeping, they would eat anything in any way... Everything had to be invented. Or rather reinvented. Albert Camus, who assumed control of the daily, was exultant. And asked Sartre to write a series of on-the-spot articles on those insurrectional days.

The coverage appeared in serialized form, from August 28 till September 4, under the title "A Stroller in an insurgent Paris." This work, chronicling the efforts of the ordinary people of Paris to cast off the Nazi yoke, sketching flash portraits of the fighters as the skirmishes unfolded, has often been criticized. On September 12, François Sentein expressed his indignation: "I am reading the current issues of *Combat*. This is a first in the press: Sartre and Beauvoir are writing up their reports indoors[59]. Watching history from one's window. We have seen them seated every day for four years on these wall seats[60] that were not the earth armrest the French soldiers in the trenches during the First World War leaned on to fire. They really waged war. Now that the "liberation" has opened up infinite horizons for them, *Combat* is making Sartre and Beauvoir its great reporters. This has put them at risk from the crossroad of Saint-Germain-des-Prés to the crossroad of rue de Bucci, where their hotel is[61]."

It's true, this coverage does not bear the mark of an authentic war correspondent. And one scarcely senses danger in it: For example, it does not have the breathless aspect of the account that Claude Roy drew up, in *Nous* (Us), of the liberation of Paris. The things they saw were seen, for the most part, from the window of the Leiris' dwelling, on the Quai des Grands-Augustins. And, more than the genuine work of a journalist, we have here a more or less skilful montage of testimonies and remarks picked up elsewhere. Moreover, Sartre warned his readers: "Today, I will talk to you about battles as I saw them myself, on the Quai des Grands-Augustins, while completing my information with the testimony of friends worthy of trust[62]." Whether on foot or on bicycle, Jean-Paul Sartre did not venture forth very much outside of his preserve: the Vavin crossroad, Pont-

---

[59] It does indeed appear that Simone de Beauvoir collaborated closely on this coverage. One finds in *La Force de l'âge* a number of anecdotes already related in *Combat*.

[60] These were, of course, the wall seats of the Café de Flore.

[61] François Sentein, *Minutes d'un libéré (1944), op. cit.*

[62] Jean-Paul Sartre, "Un promeneur dans Paris insurgé. IV", *Combat*, August 31 1944.

Neuf—never any further. But this is, paradoxically, what constitutes the value of his work. Because as they stand, written as the ideas came to his head, these columns show daily life during the battles for the liberation of Paris. And, more precisely, during the battles in Saint-Germain-des-Prés. Even if it is the Liberation seen through the short end of the opera glasses—because Sartre had a fondness for detail. Snatches of dialogue, overheard on approaching Pont-Neuf: "A strapping, peaceful fellow holds a bottle of gasoline, a grenade and a rifle: he is a tank attacker. 'And with what are you going to take them?' 'With that. You throw the bottle on the tank and the gasoline catches fire. The tank burns, the occupants come out of it and you take your rifle to snipe at them'[63]."

In his work *Paris 1940-1944*, Pierre Bourget, a historian of the Second World War, defined the insurrection as "a succession of skirmishes, brief assaults, born of a temporary situation; have the Germans abandoned a depot? The FFI occupy it. Is a patrol moving away? It is attacked."[64] This supports the manner in which Sartre related the event. An excerpt from *Combat*, dated August 31 1944: "The truck appears, like a bull who comes out of the bullpen. The Résistance fighters take aim at the tires, this time. The truck is hit, it stops dead. The Germans begin to fire; the FFI move forward without protection and fire as well. A German throws a grenade that doesn't explode; an FFI runs under the gunfire, seizes the grenade at the risk of getting blown up with it and throws it in the Seine. A volley of shots. The onlookers return prudently to their rooms; already bullets are whizzing past their ears. After five minutes of silence, heads reappear at the windows, and then there is an immense clamour: the Germans are all dead. From all the doors, from the corner of the rue Dauphine, of the rue des Grands-Augustins, a crowd of women and children rush towards the immobile vehicle. But the FFI contain them, forbidding them from pillaging. They themselves take only the munitions. But the action is a fruitful one. There are rifles, submachine guns…"

---

[63] *Ibid.*
[64] Op. cit.

6

"Man, as Existentialism conceives him, if he is not definable, it is because he is nothing at the outset. He will only be afterwards, and he will be as he will have made himself"

Paris was free. The war was not over, certainly, it would require several more months—a whole winter, a whole spring. Fighting was still going on in the east. But the danger had subsided. And the capital, in convalescence, renewed its acquaintance with itself, rediscovered itself... And one noticed that, in Saint-Germain-des-Prés, nothing or almost nothing had changed. Four years had passed like a bad dream.

Except that there were all those who would never come back: "I often think of you, my dead little girls. Sonia, her blond hair, quivering and draped in her beauty, you disappeared overnight and we never saw you again. It is said that you were put in a brothel—you were so beautiful—and were used as a whore by the German officers before dying. I often think of you, Sylvain Itkine. I imagine you, tortured after the interrogation at Fort Montluc. I think of you, Desnos. And Bella, arrested on leaving the Flore, and all these darling little Jewish girls fallen into the traps during the roundups... I think of you, poor Bourla[1]..." War had thinned out the ranks. On the wall seats of the Café de Flore and the Café des Deux Magots, phantoms occupied the places where formerly sat Sonia Mossé, Max Jacob, Jean Prévost...

Paris free... Sweet autumn evenings, of which we had lost even the sensation; once again we wander, after midnight, on the boule-

---
[1] Mouloudji, *La Fleur de l'âge, op. cit.*

vard Saint-Germain. We linger on the terraces of the Rhumerie, of the Flore... No more curfews, no more patrols in army boots or the clicking sound of rifles. And he who might have fallen asleep in 1939, on waking up in the present, would recognize his village. Intact. Here, the war did not leave any traces, except in memories and hearts. There were the same narrow little streets, the same faded façades, the same shops. And the same inhabitants who hadn't changed either—the genuine ones, the old stock Saint-Germain denizens. Even if, already, Saint-Germain-des-Prés was not quite any longer the "village of the 40s, the big market town under its square church tower, with its courtyards resounding with artisans' tools, its ordinary people plying the trades of genial fellows."[2]

There remained several of them, however. Like old man Roussel, one of the old brigade; a character of the neighbourhood, for whom the trip up to the slopes of Montmartre—he was the one who said it—was quite a palaver... In his dark smithy on the rue Gozlin, at the back of the courtyard, where a little furnace gave off a red glow, old man Roussel, seventy years of age, was still fashioning by hand knives for painters. Just like before the war. And he took pride in considering André Dunoyer de Segonzac and Henri Matisse among his faithful customers. "Dear Monsieur Roussel," the latter wrote to him from Vence where he resided, "would you be kind enough to make this knife as good as new again? I believe you will be willing to take on this work for a customer of 50 years, because it is already 50 years since I came to you to get some of your good painting knives that I still have." With his cap screwed onto his cranium, his moustache, his hand-knit vest, his scarf, Roussel, in his way, was an expert; he grasped delicately in his pincers a rod of heated steel and, on the anvil, fashioned a painting knife in a few minutes. An expert and a survivor. Because he knew that his days were numbered. As were numbered the days of the bookbinder Gaucher, on 30 rue Jacob, a lover of books and of leather. The same applied to the printer in the courtyard of the Vieux-Colombier who turned his hand-driven press—for how much more time?... "I am the only one in Paris," said old man Roussel, "who makes by hand tools for artists, but I am not the only artisan in Saint-Germain-des-Prés, there are still a few of us, but we are all old."[3]

---

[2] Claude Roy, *Nous*, Gallimard, 1972.

[3] Quoted in Marcelle Routier, *Saint-Germain-des-Prés, op. cit.*

It is true that they were not young. Neither the printer nor the bookbinder. Nor old man Riffault, behind his counter, at the Sauvignon de Quincy, at the corner of the rue des Saints-Pères and the rue de Sèvres. Nor old man Quillet—a former wine grower, born in 1876—who served in his bistro, one of the last real cabarets in Paris, at the corner of the rue Bonaparte and the rue du Four, two—only two, but admirable—Anjou wines: a white pinot de Savennières, a red cabernet. And if you pushed open the door at the Hôtel d'Alsace et de Lorraine, on the rue des Canettes, a middle-aged lady would welcome you: Mme Albaret—"Céleste" in literature. Albaret would relate to anyone willing to listen the final moments of Marcel Proust, as she was his last housekeeper.

All of these little trades were there, as well as the oldest in the world... But not for very much longer: Marthe Richard would see to that! Her law would be voted in April 1946. A last glance at the first floor of the rue Saint-Placide—a salon decked out in velvet, like a candy box, and, within, completely naked, the girls, like sugared almonds in their box, that the customer would chose gluttonously through a bull's eye window: "Houses of all houses, the most foreign to untruthfulness, although—or because—they were devoted to pleasure, may peace be with you!"[4]

In the Saint-Germain-des-Prés of the Liberation there survived, like a village atmosphere of yesteryears, the humble soul of a big market town in one of the French provinces, where all the inhabitants knew one another, spoke to one another, esteemed one another—or hated one another. Maurice Fombeure, who resided at 6 rue du Vieux-Colombier, affirmed this: "I still know well almost all the merchants of the neighbourhood, as though I were in Châtellerault, in Poitiers, in Mirecourt. In Saint-Germain-des-Prés, I feel I'm at home. I lead there a quiet life in the midst of good-natured people."[5] For how long?...

Because a new generation had arrived in Saint-Germain-des-Prés. The generation of 1920. As though drawn by a magnet. Noisy, eager to take revenge on the four black years that it had just endured. Future painters, future musicians, future singers, future actors... "At the same time that I was taking Solange Sicard's courses in dramatic art, I was enrolled in the ones Tania Balachova was giving at the Théâtre du Vieux-Colombier. Once the course was finished, students and teachers would gather at

---

[4] François Sentein, *Minutes d'un libertin (1938-1941)*, op. cit.
[5] Quoted in Marcelle Routier, *Saint-Germain-des-Prés*, op. cit.

the neighbourhood bistros. And we would talk for hours[6]." There were young actors determined to make their mark in the movie studio and on the stage: "So they produced proof that in a period bogged down in inextricable and paralysing financial hardships, young adults, often destitute, managed to put on plays, make astonishing 16 mm films, in conditions that defied analysis[7]."

Just like the *Ulysse ou les Mauvaises Rencontres* (*Ulysses or Bad Encounters*) that Alexandre Astruc—at 25 years old—did indeed film in 16mm. At the Théâtre du Vieux-Colombier, at Annet-Badet's place, who financed the venture. On stage, in the hall, in the cellars... It was a film made by pals. *Combat* was there, to help out as soon as the cameras began rolling: "A projector collapsed over a row of seats, shadows were moving around noisily, a man leaned over the prompter's box[8]." The script? It was *L'Odyssée* (*The Odyssey*), in a reduced and updated version by Anne-Marie Cazalis and Jean Cau. "It is the story of a man who comes home after a long voyage, the latter informed journalists. He meets a whore, which is very sad. Then a good girl, which is even sadder. Who has his cards read. Who makes the acquaintance of two women of doubtful morals and then of a man whose morals are no better[9]." Then they filmed a scene where Neptune appeared, whom Christian Bérard brought to life. A long-haired, bearded Neptune. To depict the underwater universe of the god of the Oceans, Astruc had the idea of filming Bérard through the frosted glass portholes set in the doors leading to the foyer; a sponge saturated with water, squeezed on the glass, completed the illusion. Christian Bérard as Neptune, Jean Cocteau as Homer; Juliette Gréco played Circé, Yvonne de Bray was the Pythia, Simone Signoret Penelope, Gaby Sylvia a siren; Boris Vian and Anne-Marie Cazalis made up the ancient chorus; the cinema critics France Roche and François Chalais incarnated Helen and Paris; Marc Doelnitz was Ulysses and Daniel Gélin Telemachus. Everyone who counted in Saint-Germain-dés-Prés answered present to Astruc's roll call. Alas... badly put together, full of false link shots, never mounted, do the film's rushes still exist somewhere? One would hope so. If only

---

[6] Nicolas Bataille, interview with the author, March 2008.

[7] Colin-Simard, "Saint-Germain-des-Prés, terre de poussière et de feu", *Combat*, August 17 1948.

[8] *Combat*, November 4 1948.

[9] *Ibid.*

for this fabulous cast. This was a kind of *Who's who* from Saint-Germain-des-Prés' grand era[10].

Daniel Gélin lived two steps away, on rue de Sèvres; Simone Signoret and her husband, the film director Yves Allégret, had been regular customers of the Café de Flore for a long time; Gérard Philipe, who triumphed at the Théâtre Hébertot in *Sodom et Gomorrhe*, by Jean Giraudoux, moved into two small rooms at 7 rue du Dragon. And that is where the movie critic Georges Sadoul met him one evening for the first time: "A rather timid young man, with not an ounce of the ham actor in him, glimpsed for five minutes during one of those Paris nights, soon after the Liberation. There was not one car on the streets, it was a macadam desert where the first leaves were beginning to bud, on the boulevard Saint-Germain, under the still dim light of the electric street lamps[11]."

Neither cars, in fact, nor great illuminations...During these years immediately following the end of the Second World War, Paris, its freedom restored, was still an impoverished city: nights without lighting, extremely reduced automobile traffic, difficulty in obtaining supplies... "We are still in a state of terrible poverty, in France," Simone de Beauvoir wrote to Nelson Algren. Saint-Germain-des-Prés was no exception to the rule. After describing the intellectual effervescence in this little perimeter represented by the square and the two or three neighbouring streets, Beauvoir added: "Outside of this pocket, all is darkness and death[12]."

A famous photo, taken by Robert Doisneau, shows a group of young people, seated in an old car decorated with big squares, the "chequered car," the old and celebrated Renault 6CV, the 1922 model, designed by the painter Yves Corbassière, parked right in front of the Tabou. Behind these figures of the "Existentialist" Saint-Germain-des-Prés—Corbassière, the actress Catherine Pré, Tarzan, the bouncer of the Tabou, Michel de Ré and his companion, the American Eddie Einstein, the designer Dropy—the rue Dauphine was deserted, neither cars nor passers-by, so was the rue Christine. Both streets were lined with cracked, blackened, fissured façades. With its dark front, the Tabou looked like a gloomy bar. Sad, poor. The Liberation left the capital in the same state in which the occupiers had found it, in 1940. Except that in the meanwhile

---

[10] The print of the film seems now to be definitively lost.

[11] Georges Sadoul, *Gérard Philipe*, Lherminier, 1984.

[12] Simone de Beauvoir, *Lettres à Nelson Algren, op. cit.* (letter dated July 26 1948).

five years passed. Without maintenance, without repairs. Yes, "darkness and death"... On rue Jacob, rue des Saints-Pères, behind a fence covered with posters, the enormous concrete and steel carcass of the new Faculty of Medicine was awaiting better days... Begun in 1936, on the terrain of the former Hôpital de la Charité, the building project was interrupted in 1940 on the orders of the Germans. They immediately converted the basements into a garage. Since their departure, "two caretakers lived in a little cabin, decorated with potted plants, overwhelmed by the huge skeleton of the uncompleted building."[13] Behind its enclosure of rough-hewn boards, the abandoned work site resembled a wasteland.

So it was a city bled white, the capital of a country out of breath, that barely emerged from an unprecedented conflict, from a humiliation—that of the Occupation—itself unparalleled in the history of modern France. During more than four years, the occupier extracted a heavy tithe—human, financial, agricultural and industrial—from a population already weakened by deprivations of all kinds. In 1944, the war indemnity, earmarked to finance the maintenance of occupation troops, which France paid out to Germany by virtue of the armistice agreement signed in 1940, amounted to 700 million francs per day.[14] A considerable sum, given the country's reduced capacities. In their *Histoire de la France au XXe siècle (History of France in the 20th Century)*, the historians Serge Berstein and Pierre Milza calculated that the total of the sums extracted during the black years was 700 billion francs. This gives one an idea of the dilapidated state of the French economic system in 1945. The France where peace was restored was a France of shortages. And she would remain so for several more years.

The harsh winter of 1945–46 would bring this crisis out into the open. The Liberation did not change much for the French as far as living conditions were concerned. They were still subjected to restrictions: a poorly fed, poorly heated, poorly housed, poorly dressed population. The economic machine was broken down. Ration tickets were still in force. The daily bread ration, which was 350 grams in September 1940, went down to 250 grams in 1947. Moreover it was not until 1949 that the rationing of bread and coal would come to an end, thanks to the increase

---

[13] *Combat*, April 3 1947.

[14] This indemnity never stopped increasing during the whole Occupation: 440 million francs per day in 1940; 500 million after the Germans had invaded the free zone in November 1942 and 700 million following the Allied landing in Normandy.

in French production that would then only reach a level more or less equal to the one in 1938.

On August 6 1945, an American aircraft dropped on the city of Hiroshima, in Japan, the first atomic bomb ever used in a conflict. The official goal: to force the Nippon Empire, that persisted in pursuing the war despite Germany's capitulation on the preceding May 7, to give back ill-gotten gains.[15] The event—75,000 deaths at the time, tens of thousands later on, as the consequence of sharp radiations that the population underwent—caused a considerable fright in the world. All the more because the American army repeated the operation on Nagasaki three days later.

In France, Albert Camus was one of the first to protest against what he called "the lowest level of savagery" in an editorial that would stand out: "It will be necessary to choose, in the more or less near future, between collective suicide or the intelligent use of scientific conquests. In the meantime, one is justified in thinking that there is something indecent about thus celebrating a discovery that is placed in the service of the most formidable destructive rage that man has shown in centuries. That in a world abandoned to the heartbreaking consequences of violence, incapable of any control, indifferent to justice and the simple happiness of mankind, science is committing itself to organized murder, no one, undoubtedly, unless he is an impenitent idealist, will think of being astonished by it.... In the face of the terrifying perspectives that are opening up to humanity, we realize even more strongly that peace is the only war that is worth waging..."[16]

These perspectives, terrifying indeed, to which would be added the revelations, just as terrifying, about the Nazi extermination camps, ask of the human conscience a question both simple and almost insoluble: how can one live after all that? How can one live with this indelible blot? How can one live after Dachau, after Auschwitz, after Hiroshima, after these millions of deaths?... A questioning that acquired its full meaning in a neighbourhood like Saint-Germain-des-Prés, frequented by intellectuals and artists—for whom, to the mere fact of being alive, was added the act of creating. And it was of them, first and foremost, that this ques-

---

[15] Historians question this official version. It would appear that in the mind of the Americans what counted was rather to impress the Soviets and stop their advance. In a way, these were the beginnings of the Cold War.

[16] *Combat*, August 8 1945.

tion was asked, bluntly. How does one live and how does one create? On writing a review of the paintings exhibited at the Salon d'automne, Jean Grenier noted: "This era is perfectly inhuman and artists are depicting it very well since they are sterile when facing figures and landscapes. Picasso himself, the greatest, presents a very inhuman art—this time as much out of solitude and despair, as out of technical virtuosity."[17]

The painter Georges Brunon was, during those years, a student at the National School of Fine Arts: "Each one of us had lived through the war alone with his own history. We were striving to understand what had happened to us. We talked about it in the cafés, at the Mabillon, at the Rhumerie… The question was not political, but existential: 'What are we doing in this world? The camps, Hiroshima… This world where one has the impression that those who won the war are not the resistance fighters, but rather the traffickers on the black market…' Art did not offer any response to this questioning. Perhaps Existentialism did."[18] Existentialism, yes. Even if it frightened some people, because of the dizzying sense of freedom of choice it left man. And because of the responsibility it entailed.

This is practically the same point of view that Simone de Beauvoir defended when she tried to explain, *a posteriori*, the relationship between Sartre and his readers in 1945: "They had discovered History under its most hideous face. They needed an ideology that integrated these revelations, without obliging them, however, to throw overboard their former justifications. Existentialism, endeavouring to reconcile history and moral standards, authorized them to assume their transitory condition without renouncing a certain absolute, to confront the horror and absurdity while at the same time preserving their human dignity, to safeguard their singularity. It seemed to provide them with the solution they dreamed of."[19]

But this was a delusion. The novels, the philosophical writings of Sartre—Existentialism, since we must call it by its name—reflected back to the readers an image that they refused outright: "They were inclined to hear some kind truths about themselves, not to look squarely at themselves. Opposed to the Marxist dialectic, they demanded their freedom; but Sartre exaggerated: the freedom he offered them implied

---

[17] *Combat*, October 6 1944.

[18] Georges Brunon, interview with the author, January 2007.

[19] *La Force des choses*, op. cit.

tiring responsibilities; it went against institutions, morals; it destroyed their sense of security."[20]

And yet, Sartre affirmed at the very outset: Existentialism is a humanism. This is even the title he gave to his famous lecture in October 1945, a kind of defence and illustration of his philosophy, already so disparaged. And he added: "We mean by Existentialism a doctrine which makes human life possible and which, moreover, declares that all truth and all action imply a context and a human subjectivity[21]." The first principal of Existentialism, according to Sartre, is contained in several words: man is nothing other than what he makes of himself. Only then, is he this or that. In other words: existence precedes essence—according to the formula that would be all the rage in Paris after the war, and that was repeated indiscriminately, out of its philosophical context (just like, in the preceding year, were repeated the words "hell is other people"). Besides, this formula would inspire a kind of "Existentialist hymn" written in order to provoke laughter, a few verses put together one evening, among the initiated, on the corner of a table at the Le Catalan restaurant, on rue des Grands-Augustins. The authors? A sharp crew: Boris Vian, Anne-Marie Cazalis, Maurice Merleau-Ponty, René Leibowitz. And Juliette Gréco, who hummed the first measure of it that very evening, in "her rasping voice and on a jazz melody composed that very instant[22]." *Samedi-Soir*, really in the know about everything that happened in Saint-Germain-des-Prés, whether the events were big or small, affirmed for its part: "This hymn begins like a Beethoven allegro and ends in a samba[23]."

> *I have nothing more in my existence*
> *Than this essence that defines me*
> *Because existence precedes essence*
> *And for that reason money shuns me*
> *I've read the books of Jean-Paul Sartre*
> *Simone de Beauvoir and Merleau-Ponty*
> *But all the time it's the same disaster*
> *Even poor you're free, you choose yourself*

---

[20] *Ibid.*

[21] Jean-Paul Sartre, *L'Existentialisme est un humanisme*, Gallimard, 1996 (first printing : Nagel, 1946).

[22] *Jujube, op. cit.*

[23] *Samedi-Soir,* May 15 1948.

> *I've really tried other things*
> *Maurice Blanchot and Albert Camus*
> *Absurd faux pas! It's the same thing*
> *Life is nothing but a vast misunderstanding*
> *Tomorrow Sisyphus, anguish, morals*
> *Aminadab, Nausea and company*
> *All the time it's the same disaster*
> *For even at Flore's, there's no more credit!*[24]

"Even poor you're free, you choose yourself." According to Sartre, man's responsibility roots itself in this choice—"you choose yourself"—that the authors of these verses mock amusingly. The corollary of choosing oneself is, of course, subjectivity: "When we say that man is responsible for himself, we do not mean that man is responsible for his strict individuality, but that he is responsible for all men. There are two meanings in the word Subjectivism. Subjectivism means on the one hand the choosing of the individual subject by himself and, on the other hand, the impossibility for man to go beyond human subjectivity. This second case contains the profound meaning of Existentialism. When we say that man chooses himself, we imply that each one of us chooses himself, but by that we also mean that by choosing himself he chooses all men."[25] This justifies, *a posteriori*, the phrase often quoted from *L'Être et le Néant*: "As profoundly responsible for war as if I had myself declared it." It should be compared to the quotation from Dostoïevski by which Sartre began his presentation before the first session of Unesco's General Conference held in Paris, in November 1946: "Every man is responsible for every other one in the eyes of all."

In the 19th century, the Danish philosopher, Sören Kierkegaard, was the first to use the word "existence" in its philosophical connotation. He did this by affirming "the irreducibility of existence to concept and the necessity to start from existence as it is lived subjectively."[26] In its wake, a Christian Existentialist movement was created, represented notably by

---

[24] Quoted by Juliette Gréco, *Jujube, op. cit. Aminadab*: a novel by Maurice Blanchot published by Éditions Gallimard in 1942; *La Nausée* is of course the novel by Sartre published in 1938 by the same editor.

[25] Jean-Paul Sartre, *L'Existentialisme est un humanisme, op. cit.*

[26] Sophie Bilemdjian, *Premières Leçons sur "L'existentialisme est un humanisme" de Jean-Paul Sartre*, PUF, 2000.

the German Karl Jaspers or the French Gabriel Marcel: "They have in common the determination not to separate thought from the flow of real life, to propose a dramatic conception of human existence, to attribute a metaphysical importance to the encounter as well as to the relationship with God based on the model of interpersonal relations, and finally to bet on people's ability to tear themselves from their dereliction and the disorder of the modern world in order to rebuild authentic communities."[27]

More coherent, Sartre emphasized, is atheistic Existentialism: "What does the statement 'Existence precedes essence' signify? It signifies that man exists first of all, gets to know himself, appears suddenly in the world, and defines himself afterwards. If man, as Existentialism conceives him, is not definable, it is because he is nothing at the outset. He will be something only later on, and he will be just as he will have constructed himself. Thus, there is no human nature, since there is no God to conceive it."[28]

Would Existentialism then answer the questions that youth was asking after the war? Perhaps. In any case it arrived in the nick of time: as though everybody was waiting for it. To condemn it or to adopt it. And it sent a libertarian breath of fresh air over Saint-Germain-des-Prés. To the great displeasure of the Communists and conservative Catholics, for once in agreement: Existentialism was drawing youth away from true values...

The conference of October 1945, a kind of session devoted to practical studies of *L'Être et le Néant*, "an essay on phenomenological ontology," as its sub-title indicates, the end result of research and reflection carried out by the philosopher over ten or so years, did not resolve the ambiguities that surrounded the movement. The very contrary was true: the mundane event would take precedence over the clarification. In the Salle des Centraux, on rue Jean-Goujon, where the Club Maintenant, "a club

---

[27] *Ibid.* Karl Jaspers, nevertheless, in a letter of 1937, told the French philosopher Jean Wahl: "Existentialism is the death of the philosophy of existence."

[28] *L'existentialism est un humanisme, op. cit.* Some people have at times reproached Sartre for declaring the non-existence of God without even trying to demonstrate it. Nevertheless, he takes pains to specify: "Existentialism is not so much an atheism in the sense that it would exhaust all of its resources to demonstrate that God does not exist. It declares rather: even if God existed, that would not change anything; this is our point of view. Not that we believe that God exists, but we think that the problem is not that of his existence; man must get hold of himself and persuade himself that nothing can save him from himself, not even a valid proof of God's existence."

for literary and intellectual activities," created after the Liberation by Jacques Calmy and Marc Beigbeder, invited Sartre to speak on October 29 1945, there was a stampede. Three hundred people attempted to enter a room that could scarcely hold half that number. Intellectuals, high society ladies, snobs, students... Shoving, exchanges of blows, chairs broken, women fainting.

Standing in front of his audience, Sartre spoke without notes. But his ideas, intentionally simplified, dulled and blurred the themes and the theses he developed in *L'Être et le Néant*, and at times twisted them out of context. The complexity and novelty of the analyses he had developed in his work were only vaguely represented. By wanting to justify himself in the face of the campaign of disparagement of which he was the target, as much in the newspapers as in the Christian and Communist milieus, Sartre did the very opposite: he underscored the malaise. Thus he very quickly regretted having authorized the publication of the typed and barely corrected text of his lecture, which appeared at the beginning of 1946 at the éditions Nagel. Moreover he was not the only one. His admirers, his earliest readers, all those who were dazzled as of 1943 by *L'Être et le Néant*, could not understand—when they didn't reprove it violently—this sudden return to a humanism that they judged devalued. Like Michel Tournier, a philosophy student at the time: "We were crestfallen. So our master picked up from the trashcan where we had buried it this worn out duffer, reeking of sweat and inner life, humanism..."[29]

Why the devil did Sartre choose to defend his philosophy at the risk of misrepresenting it, by means of a humanism which in the past he had been the first to call into question—in *La Nausée* for example, in the character of the Autodidact? The answer: "Humanism, because we remind man that there is no other legislator except himself, and that in his state of abandonment he will decide for himself; and because we show that it is not by withdrawing into himself, but by constantly looking outside of himself for a goal which is a certain liberation, a certain specific achievement, that man will fulfill himself precisely as a human being."[30] The demonstration would not dissipate the confusion of his audience nor, later on, that of his readers. "How does one interpret this sudden

---

[29] *Le Vent Paraclet, op. cit.* Certain critics, however, and by no means the least, appeared rather favourable towards the work when it was published. For example, Maurice Nadeau, who reviewed it in *Combat* on March 22 1946.

[30] Jean-Paul Sartre, *L'existentialism est un humanisme, op. cit.*

allegiance to humanism?" asked Sophie Bilemdjian.[31] Before suggesting several leads. Is it the strategy of an ambitious thinker, concerned about carving out for himself a key niche within intellectual milieus already very glutted by the two major Christian and Marxist movements? Did he view it rather as a political approach, destined to favour closer ties with the Communists? Or are we already in the presence of this ethical preoccupation that we will find again and again throughout Sartre's works? It is not certain, even today, that we can give a clear answer to all these questions.

---

[31] *Premières Leçons sur "L'existentialisme est un humanisme" de Jean-Paul Sartre, op. cit.*

7

After Huis *Clos, Caligula, Les Bouches inutiles,*
critics snort : "A high dose of intellectuality. A
theatre of ideas. Less theatre than ideas …"

In 1945, Existentialism was Saint-Germain-des-Prés; and Saint-Germain-des-Prés was Existentialism; and Jean-Paul Sartre was the great corruptor of youth. There, it was said! Once and for all. No way of getting around it. And, no matter what Sartre and his friends said or did, public opinion would never reconsider this issue. Because in a France wounded to its very core, subjected to restrictions of all kinds, shaken by the dramas of the political purges, engaged in an immense reconstruction effort, the indulgent account of mischief in St-Germain-des-Prés, spread daily by the press, had definitively discredited the neighbourhood and the man who was, in a way, in the eyes of the general public, its spiritual leader. Who could have guessed, at the time, that this "party" was only a façade? The reverse side of anguish, of aching distress? "Saint-Germain-des-Prés must also be understood as the manifestation of a feeling of helplessness, as the resolutely joyous face of a profound despair, as the living expression of the absolute need to laugh and to forget, but also, at the same time, to search for all possible ways out of this helplessness, this despair."[1] In the letters to the editor section of the review *Les Temps Modernes*, Simone de Beauvoir discovered one day a poem sent by a young man of seventeen that began with the words: "Emptiness tends towards fullness." If post-war France had to be reconstructed, so too did her youth.

---

[1] Vincent Gille, *Saint-Germain-des-Prés 1945-1950*, Éditions Pavillon des Arts, 1989 (exhibition catalogue).

The country applied itself to the task to the best of its ability. In his book of recollections, *Deux ou trois vies qui sont les miennes* (*Two or Three Lives that Are Mine*), the actor Daniel Gélin, who was twenty-three or twenty-four years old at the time, remembers these moments: "After the frustrating presence of the occupier, after the derisory settling of scores that followed, everything that unfolded around this church tower, in these streets, theses cellars and these hotel rooms, seemed to me altogether deserved. The young people who knew the neighbourhood later on could not appreciate it in the same spirit of happiness; they had not undergone the turmoil of the war and had not felt this need to let off steam that was ours." Living it up? Yes and no. Rather a kind of intimate jubilation, of permanent rejoicing: "Nothing, no victory to celebrate, just our youth. Each instant had a flavour of tenderness and renewal. It was mechanically, in a state of delight and receptiveness, that I found myself seated again at the Flore, at the Carrefour, at the Montana."[2]

"It was the dance craze, the jazz craze, the cinema craze, we talked enormously about the cinema[3]..." Youth took hold of the artistic controls. The wavy and brilliantine haired pre-war seducers no longer enjoyed the public's favour. The latter demanded new faces, on the stage and on the screen. Gérard Philipe—twenty-three years old—snatched away from Henri Rollan—fifty-seven years old—the role of Caligula, hero of the eponymous play by Albert Camus that the Théâtre Hébertot mounted in the autumn of 1945.

Camus was inspired by the story of the young Roman tyrant to illustrate one of the aspects of his conception of absurdity: the human questioning in the face of the world's silence. Just like in *L'Étranger* and *Le Mythe de Sisyphe*. He hoped to publish these three works, that he called familiarly his "three absurd ones," as he had written them, that is to say, simultaneously. At the beginning of 1941, all three were completed. As soon as March arrived, the author sent on *L'Étranger* and *Caligula* to Jean Grenier, his former philosophy professor in Algiers, who since then had become his friend. Grenier found the novel very well written, even though he admitted to being troubled by the Kafkaesque atmosphere that imbued it.[4] On the other hand, he remained puzzled by

---

[2] Daniel Gélin, *Deux ou trios vies qui sont les miennes, op. cit.*

[3] Dominique Desanti, interview with the author, February 2008.

[4] Jean-Paul Sartre would have the same reproach levelled at him after the presentation of *Huis-clos*, in June 1944.

the play, "a bit too romantic" for his taste. And he asked: how effective would it be on stage? This is undoubtedly why Albert Camus started, in 1943, a second version in which, according to certain commentators, he deliberately placed the emphasis on the political aspect of the tragedy. According to others, the accent was placed on its philosophical content.

Caligula, on the death of his sister Drusilla who was also his mistress, sank into a murderous madness. As Camus himself explained to his Anglo-Saxon readers, in 1958, in the preface to the American edition: "From then on, obsessed by the quest for the absolute... he attempts to exercise, through murder, a freedom which, he will discover in the end, is not the right one. He rejects friendship and love, simple human solidarity, good and evil.... But, if truth for him means revolting against destiny, his error consists in negating mankind. One cannot destroy everything without destroying oneself. This is why Caligula depopulates the world around him and, faithful to his logic, does what is necessary to arm against him those who will end up killing him."

Without delay, enticed no doubt by Albert Camus' growing fame, Jacques Hébertot picked up *Caligula* for his theatre on the boulevard des Batignolles. Paul Oettly was in charge of the staging,[5] under the watchful eye of the author who entrusted the décors to Louis Miquel and the costumes to Marie Viton, two Algerian friends who used to belong with him, in 1935, to the troupe of the Théâtre du Travail, then, in 1936, to the Théâtre de l'Équipe. There remained the big question: who would play Caligula? One can follow the progression of a choice that would prove to be difficult, if not strategic, through the letters that Jacques Hébertot and Albert Camus exchanged at the time. An exchange of letters that shows, if proof were needed, to what extent Camus, himself a man of the theatre, monitored the production of his play.

On February 27 1945, in a pneumatic letter addressed to the author, at 1bis rue Vaneau, Hébertot did an update: "I have introduced Oettly to the actor about whom I had spoken to you and who is quite fearful at the idea of an audition. Oettly is going to make him work, and will introduce him to you. Obviously, it is very difficult to judge an actor on the basis of a first impression. Nevertheless, I can tell you that Vidal performed, in December and January, the role of Camille in *Je vivrai un*

---

[5] Paul Oettly (1890-1959) was in the cast of *Les Mouches*. He played the role of the old servant, in the preceding year, in *Le Malentendu*. He would also stage at the Théâtre Hébertot, in 1949, another play by Camus, *Les Justes*.

grand amour (I will Live a Great Love), a role that is far from easy, and I have had nothing but praise, just like the author and the audience, for his interpretation.[6] Vidal is free and your assent would allow us to begin immediately rehearsals for the play.... I hope, then, after so many alternatives, that we are nearing our goal..."[7]

No doubt Henri Vidal's audition was not conclusive, because, a few days later, another letter from Hébertot arrived at the rue Vaneau. This one, very official, mentioned the name of a new actor: "It is understood that you accept M. Georges Marchal as the interpreter of the role of Caligula. The décors, costumes, as well as the rest of the cast will be submitted for your approval..."[8]

But the movies were clamouring for the handsome Georges Marchal, who abandoned the role. And so again the question arose: who would play Caligula? Oddly, they fixed their choice on Henri Rollan—certainly an experienced actor, but already fifty-seven years old.... The rest of the cast was then established: Margo Lion, Georges Vitaly, etc. This time, no doubt, Jacques Hébertot could imagine that his troubles were over. Error. Ever since his friend the scriptwriter Jacques Sigurd made him read the play, Gérard Philipe, whose career had taken off, dreamed of playing this role—"the Prince of Evil," as he said. One evening, on leaving the studio where he was filming *Le Pays sans étoiles* (*The Starless Country*), a film by Georges Lacombe, and heeding only his nerve, he introduced himself at Hébertot's place. And explained to him the reason for his visit.

"—But my child," he told me, "don't even think about it! Who would you like to be in this play?

—Caligula.

He exclaimed:

—But you are an angel, not a demon!

—Let me try at least.

—I'm sorry, it's not possible. Caligula is taken. It will be Henri Rollan.

---

[6] The actor in question is Henri Vidal (1919-1959), who would later on enjoy a brilliant career in the movies. *Je vivrai un grand amour*, by Steve Passeur, created in 1935 by Geores and Ludmilla Pitoëff, had just been revived at the time at the Théâtre Hébertot.

[7] National Library of France, Department of Performing Arts, Jacques Hébertot Collection. Albert Camus occupied Gide's apartment at the time, on rue Vaneau.

[8] *Ibid*. Georges Marchal (1920-1997), engaged by the Comédie-Française in 1940, was at the time a fashionable young leading man, whose attractive physical appearance ensured his success.

—All right. But if the need arises, keep me in mind nevertheless. If you do a tour, for example.

Four days later, Henri Rollan got sunstroke in Africa and had to give up the role. I went to see Camus who came out in favour of my taking up the part. And Hébertot hired me."[9]

Hébertot hastened to write to Camus, as of the following August 13: "I confirm to you that the reading of *Caligula* that you are willing to give will take place on the stage of the Théâtre Hébertot, the day after tomorrow, on Wednesday August 15 at 2:30 p.m.. That M. Henri Rollan is absolutely incapable, for health reasons, of creating the role of Caligula. That consequently and following your agreement, I have engaged M. Gérard Philipe."[10]

An engagement that Jacques Hébertot would not have to regret. Two hundred consecutive performances testify to the play's success. Simone de Beauvoir, however, saved her enthusiasm for the principal actor: "I had attended Camus' *Caligula* which, when I read it, left me cold. Gérard Philipe transfigured the play."[11] Indeed, on September 26, when the actor made his entrance on stage, a kind of admiring stupor gripped the audience. This tall silhouette, draped in the ochre tunic, timeless, designed by Marie Viton—faithful in this respect to Camus' instructions: "Everything is allowed except the Roman genre"—this storm of dark hair, this rebellious air, this moral fracture, here was the demon in person, the angel of Evil…And perhaps Hébertot, on that evening, behind the lowered curtain, whispered to him: "You are a demon, not an angel…" From a promising beginner, suddenly Gérard Philipe rose directly to the rank of star. And, above all, to that of young people's idol. Simone de Beauvoir's precious letters to Nelson Algren inform us on that matter: "A famous young actor of the stage and cinema, the darling of little girls and old French ladies, and I must say he deserves it, he is charm itself."[12]

---

[9] Remarks transcribed by Jean Nery in *Ciné Révélations*, March 24 1955. In this same theatre, Gérard Philipe created, two years earlier, the role of the Angel in *Sodome and Gomorrhe* by Jean Giraudoux. This explains Jacques Hébertot's retort: "But you are an angel, not a demon!"

[10] National Library of France, Department of Performing Arts, Jacques Hébertot Collection.

[11] *La Force des choses, op. cit.* It is interesting to compare Beauvoir's judgement with that of Gabriel Marcel (see *infra*, p. 110).

[12] *Lettres à Nelson Algren, op. cit.* (letter of February 17 1948).

Caligula, a philosophical play? Albert Camus denied this: "Naturally, it is inspired by anxieties that were mine at that time. To my great astonishment, French critics, who received the play very well, have often referred to it as a philosophical play. But I search in vain for philosophy in these four acts..."[13]

A Philosophical play: this, on the other hand, is an acknowledgement that Simone de Beauvoir could not avoid. Indeed, barely a month after Camus, she in turn confronted the Parisian critics with *Les Bouches inutiles.* Her first—and only—play. A kind of historical drama in two acts whose flaws she would recognize *a posteriori*: "The mistake was to formulate a poltical problem in terms of abstract ethics. The idealism with which *Les Bouches inutiles* is saturated embarrasses me and I deplore its didacticism."[14] This was not everyone's opinion. On reviewing the two plays within a two-week interval, Gabriel Marcel, for his part, unhesitatingly gave *Les Bouches inutiles* full marks: "[...] The work is nonetheless first rate. It seems clearly superior to *Caligula* as far as its construction is concerned. But Mlle de Beauvoir was not fortunate enough, like M. Camus, to find an outstanding interpreter like M. Gérard Philipe."[15]

It was after attending the rehearsals of *Les Mouches*, two years earlier, and then listening to the applause that greeted *Huis clos*, that Simone de Beauvoir, by her own admission, also felt the desire to write for the theatre: "The roar of the applause had affected me: it was more present, more inebriating than the scattered sounds produced by a book."[16] She found the subject of her play, that she completed in July 1944, in the voluminous *Histoire des Républiques italiennes du Moyen Âge* (*History of the Italian Republics in the Middle Ages*), by Jean-Charles de Sismondi, a historian and economist from Geneva. On reading it, a detail—but was it really only a detail?—struck her: in many besieged cities, the fighters, in order to save supplies, had to make the decision to drive the old people, the sickly, the women and children outside of the city walls. In other words, the useless mouths. And often, these unfortunate wretches died in the ditches because the enemy would not allow them to pass.

---

[13] Preface to the American edition of *Caligula*, followed by *Le Malentendu*, NTC Publishing Group, 1958.

[14] *La Force de l'âge, op. cit.*

[15] *Les Nouvelles littéraires,* November 8 1945. Albert Camus did not especially relish the comparison.

[16] *La Force des choses, op. cit.*

This could have been the theme of a strong novel, at least the plot of an episode (which moreover she would use in *Tous les hommes sont mortels*). But she could see beyond, already: "I had just, it seemed to me, discovered an imminently dramatic situation; I remained immobile for a long moment, my gaze intent, in the grip of a sharp agitation."[17] Now she had her subject: the relationship between those who are hunted and those who hunt them. "This is what I wished to show first and foremost: the metamorphosis of loved ones into people living under a death sentence, the relations of men of flesh with these irritated phantoms."[18] Instead of Italy, she would substitute Flanders of the 14th century: Vaucelles, a city besieged by the Burgundians. Not without enriching the action with a good dose of themes borrowed from the Existentialist panoply: engagement, choice, freedom... Even if it meant regretting her decision later on: "It is a work in the same vein as *Le Sang des autres* and *Pyrrhus et Cinéas*, but their common flaws are less tolerable in the theatre than elsewhere."[19] On writing these lines, Simone de Beauvoir could have just as easily replaced the word "vein" by the word "period," so steeped indeed was the era, at least in her circle, in a kind of diffuse Existentialism. Moreover, the serious critics got it right: "The central subject of *Les Bouches inutiles* is exactly the same as the one in *Le Sang des autres*";[20] "The themes treated in the play are exactly the ones we find in *Le Sang des autres*."[21]

The town of Vaucelles, that had resigned itself to outlawing its "useless mouths" in the hope of ensuring its security, soon discovers on the contrary that it is in the process of losing all the riches for which it was fighting: "How do we accede to a higher life if we first kill all our reasons for living?" cries out one of the characters in the play. Tyranny exercised against the weak authorizes all the other tyrannies, the ones of passion or ambition. As Georges d'Avesnes, the son of the mayor, shouts out brutally: "There is no more good or evil; force alone commands." But a young man, Jean-Pierre Gauthier, the real Existentialist "hero," will strive to overturn the situation by engaging his freedom in this struggle. Little by little, the mayor and the town councillors discover that by sac-

---

[17] Simone de Beauvoir, *La Force de l'âge, op. cit.*
[18] *Ibid.*
[19] *Ibid.*
[20] René Lalou, *Gavroche*, November 9 1945.
[21] Gabriel Marcel, *Les Nouvelles littéraires*, November 8 1945.

rificing defenceless human beings to the city, it is the city itself that they are sacrificing, that they are negating its essence. One cannot, for the good of the town, trample on the organic laws of life, because this gift then loses its true nature, becomes a kind of fascism, accompanied by its cortege of horrors. Is it then necessary to capitulate? No. The inhabitants of Vaucelles will attempt a sortie. At the risk of dying together... The play stops at the moment when the main gate of the city opens to allow the passage of this motley crew where mingle fighters, unarmed women, old people and children.

Will they succeed? "It is not certain and it is not basically what matters," noted Gabriel Marcel, who grasped perfectly what was at stake in the drama. "The event is unknown; risk and anguish, this is our lot. Even if death, even if total destruction occurs, it will be the triumph of a freedom that will have willed itself to endure till the very end[22]."

Les Bouches inutiles was supposed to be mounted at the Théâtre du Vieux-Colombier, but Raymond Rouleau, who hardly liked the play, refused to take charge of the staging. It was then accepted at the Théâtre des Carrefours by Jean Serge and his wife, Jacqueline Morane, who wished to interpret the principal feminine role, Catherine d'Avesnes, the wife of the mayor. The staging was entrusted to Michel Vitold. During the Occupation, under the artistic direction of Jean Serge, "Théâtre des Carrefours" was the name given to the old Théâtre des Bouffes du Nord, the former preserve of melodrama, on the boulevard de la Chapelle. This would prompt Jacques Hébertot, never at a loss for savoury comments as long as they were cruel, to declare, while the unfortunate Jean Serge was having one flop after another: "Théâtre des Carrefours? Why Carre?..."[23]

Camus at the boulevard des Batignolles, Beauvoir at the boulevard de la Chapelle: Saint-Germain-des-Prés really knew how to export its products! Then there arose a more or less farcical episode, the kind that the press, always on the lookout for the slightest faux pas the Existentialists could make, would capitalize on. It happened that Jean Serge ran out of money during the rehearsals. He spoke to Simone de Beauvoir about it,

---

[22] *Ibid*.

[23] This is a play on words. "Carrefours" means crossroads. "Four" is the theatrical term for "flop." Consequently, by asking "Why Carre"? Hébertot was implying that the theatre should have been renamed "Le Théâtre des Fours", meaning "The Theatre of Flops." [Translator's note]

confessing to her that it would be necessary to shelve *Les Bouches inutiles* unless he could find the indispensable sum to pay the actors and suppliers. "I thought the game was over," said the latter, "when, unexpectedly, a fortune plopped into my lap."[24] 100,000 francs. In cash. Which one morning, at the Café de Flore, a man put on her table. The man—he answered to the imperial name of Néron—was not an unknown. Two years earlier, while Dullin was getting ready to mount *Les Mouches*, Néron, passing himself off as a rich patron of the arts, had committed himself to paying her one million francs in order to help her produce Sartre's play. They had even made an appointment at the notary's. In vain. Because, during the night preceding the meeting, Néron, a corrupt little employee disguised as a rich protector of the arts, unable to find a way out of his lie, had thrown himself in the lake in the Bois de Boulogne, from which a German officer had fished him out, crestfallen and repentant. For the con man, the affair had ended in the Fresnes prison, while Charles Dullin went looking elsewhere for financial backing.

100,000 francs. "Earned honestly," Néron hastened to explain, appearing completely sincere as he put the thick bundle of bills on the pedestal table. "By financing *Les Bouches inutiles*," Beauvoir relates, "he would redeem somewhat, he hoped, the nasty trick he had played on Sartre. I brought the money to Serge right away."[25] But the next morning, at first light, the police knocked at Simone de Beauvoir's door: She was accused of receiving stolen goods; Néron had obtained the money by falsifying deposit slips at the Ministry of Reconstruction...

The story quickly made the rounds of Saint-Germain-des-Prés. A daily, giving an account of the affair, ran as a headline, not devoid of humour: "As cruel as his homonym, Néron delivers the Existentialists to the cops." Of course, *Samedi-Soir* did not fail to relate the event. In its fashion: "When she had composed *Les Bouches inutiles* that is playing right now in Paris, an unknown person, named Néron, came and offered her 100,000 francs to mount the work. Mme de Beauvoir had confidence in M. Néron and accepted. Several days later the police knocked at the door of room no. 50 at the La Louisiane. M. Néron was a swindler and the author of *Les Bouches inutiles* had just been arrested. At that moment a sheet was seen

---

[24] *La Force des choses, op. cit.*

[25] *La Force des choses, op. cit.*

to be moving. The sheet was lifted and, strangely enough, they discovered M. Sartre underneath it. The adventure ended at the police station..."[26]

Gallimard lent Simone de Beauvoir, against her future royalties, the sum embezzled by Néron, which she gave back immediately to the Ministry, and everything returned to normal again. The rehearsals could continue. The première took place on October 30. The décors were by Max Douy, Jean-Roger Caussimon performed the role of Georges d'Avesnes, Jacqueline Morane played Catherine, whereas one of the two inevitable Kosakiewicz sisters—Olga, this time, assumed the role of Clarisse. The young actor Jean Berger, just back from captivity, made his Paris début there, in the important part of Jean-Pierre Gauthier: "Vitold directed us by making us push our acting towards a paroxysm. Everything unfolded in a state of permanent intensity. Caussimon, Jacqueline Morane, and myself tried to warn him against this exaggeration. But to no avail. Simone de Beauvoir often came to the rehearsals. I have the memory of a beautiful, amiable young woman, with a charming smile."[27]

Les Bouches inutiles brought to life a whole city on the stage—thirty-six characters played by thirty-three actors, among whom was Sacha Pitoëff in a small role. But the Théâtre des Carrefours lacked equipment and stagehands; there were long pauses between each tableau; during the silence that fell into place between the actors' lines, one could hear the overhead metro clank on the viaduct, near the boulevard de la Chapelle. The acoustics of the hall were bad, as most of the critics emphasized, the voices got lost; the actors in charge of secondary roles were often awkward.

In *Le Figaro*, the day after the dress rehearsal, Jean-Jacques Gautier treated the play in an offhand manner, pretending to see in it nothing more than an epiphenomenon of the Existentialist fad: "A high dose of intellectuality. A theatre of ideas. Less theatre than ideas... I think that this play, if it were not by Mlle de Beauvoir, would enjoy only a rather short career; but we will be able to gage the strength of the Existentialist school by the number of performances given." Yvon Navy, in *Cité-Soir*, was of the same mind: "Art gets mixed up with teaching. Well, no, this is not acceptable. The theatre is something else entirely."

Something else... This was what Jean Genet was already saying, bluntly, on the evening of the première; and Simone de Beauvoir, seated

---

[26] *Samedi-Soir, November 17 1945.*

[27] Jean Berger, interview with the author, November 2007.

near him in the penumbra of the theatre, heard it. And perhaps she grit her teeth. "The theatre is not that! Not that at all!"[28]

It mattered little, in the end, whether it was theatre or not. Because *Les Bouches inutiles*, today, from the historical and philosophical point of view, brings up for us, exactly, the Existential questions that all those who had lived through the years of the Occupation were asking themselves at the time, "the tragic choices individuals have to make when confronting death just like the anti-Nazi fighters had done."[29]

---

[28] Jean Genet, quoted by Simone de Beauvoir, *La Force des choses, op. cit.*

[29] François Noudelmann, in *Dictionnaire des pièces de théâtre françaises du XXe siècle, op. cit.*

In Saint-Germain-des-Prés, political life was a permanent combat: Existentialists and Communists were fighting for priority of place

The Provisional Government of the French Republic, instituted on June 2 1944, did not last long. General de Gaulle left the Presidency on Sunday January 20 1946. This was the commentary in the newspaper *Le Monde* the next day: "General de Gaulle resigns from his duties, the political crisis takes on an exceptional gravity." This departure was not really a surprise. Indeed, the daily continued, "the French are not unaware that between the three major parties of the majority there was a struggle being carried on, sometimes hidden, sometimes open, under the cover of a surface unanimity."

From the polling stations emerged, on October 21 1945, a National Assembly where indeed reigned three principal parties: the Communist Party, with 160 seats; the MRP (Mouvement Républicain Populaire), the Gaullist Party, that held 152 seats; the SFIO (Section française de l'Internationale ouvrière), the Socialist Party, with 142 seats. Hence these words that the General spoke to his ministers when taking his leave: "The exclusive regime of parties has reappeared. I reprove it."[1]

On November 13, de Gaulle was elected unanimously as head of the government by the Constituent Assembly, and immediately formed a MRP-Socialist-Communist government. It was only an outward show of unanimity: "I am obliged to govern with the ministers that the parties have given me. These ministers, alas, for the most part, allow themselves

---
[1] *Le Monde*, January 22 1946.

to be guided by the orders they receive from their parties rather than by the true interests of France.... This is something I cannot endure."[2] The only outcome: to resign. And de Gaulle withdrew into his ivory tower at Colombey-les-Deux-Églises, from which he wrote to his son, on February 21 1946: "One must choose, and one cannot be both the man handling earth-shaking events and the man involved in the lowest of shady schemes."

Yet it was under this double keynote of "earth-shaking events" and "the lowest of shady schemes" that French political life—and undoubtedly international life as well—of the five years following the end of the Second World War, could be defined. With, as a kind of apotheosis, the famous "Stockholm Appeal" launched solemnly on March 19 1950: "We demand the absolute ban of the atomic weapon, a weapon of dread and massive extermination of populations. We demand the establishment of a rigorous international monitoring system to ensure that this banning measure is applied. We consider that the government that would be the first to use the atomic weapon against any other country, would commit a crime against humanity and would be treated as a war criminal. We call on all men of good will around the world to sign this appeal."

The first ones to sign would be heard. In France alone, in the space of several months, 12 million men and women would sign this text. And 600 million around the world. In their eyes, this "Stockholm Appeal" was nothing less than the ultimate bastion against a Third World War that was perhaps imminent, or in any event threatening. How did we get to that point?

The Allies did not wait until the end of the conflict to allow their disagreements, relegated to the background under the pressures of armed struggle, to break out. Winston Churchill himself provided the proof of this, as of October 1944, when he went to Moscow for the purpose of negotiating a secret arrangement concerning the dividing up of zones of influence in the Balkans: as long as Great-Britain was allowed a free hand in Greece, where her troops were supporting the monarchy threatened by the uprising of the Communist underground, it would consent, in return, to grant Stalin complete freedom in Romania and Bulgaria. Eighteen months later, however, Churchill publicly denounced, in a speech pronounced in Fulton (Missouri), the political regimes of Eastern Europe, and declared himself convinced that the USSR "only respected

---

[2] Speech by General de Gaulle to the Commissioners of the Republic, on January 19 1946.

force." Consequently, he urged "the English-language peoples to united in order to remove any temptation from ambition or adventurousness." The Cold War had begun[3]. The utopia of Yalta—a world at peace under the benevolent gaze of the three great powers—had just blown apart, barely one year after the agreements had been signed.

Stalin, in fact, did not keep the promises he made at Yalta. Instead of the elections that he was supposed to organize in the countries liberated by the Red Army, he substituted riggings and systematic pressures, with the end result that the non Marxist parties found themselves marginalized before being purely and simply eliminated. Notably in Bulgaria and Romania. While the Americans were indignant over such behaviour, the Soviets, for their part, saw in these protests a kind of meddling in the sphere of influence that Churchill had conceded to them. As a result, by way of reprisals, they supported a new uprising in Greece. To which the United States responded by the "Truman Doctrine": They would henceforth help all free peoples who resisted attempts to enslave them.

The machine was set in motion. "Two camps have come into being in the world: on the one hand, the imperialist and anti-democratic camp, whose essential goals are the establishment of American imperialism and the crushing of democracy; and, on the other hand, the anti-imperialist and democratic camp, whose essential goal consists in undermining imperialism," declared Andrei Jdanov in a report he presented in September 1947, during the Constitutive Conference of the Kominform (the Information Bureau of Communist Parties).

Korea with its future still uncertain; Indochina torn apart by colonial war and China by civil war; the conflict in Greece, Turkey, Palestine; the satellite state status imposed on Hungary, Bulgaria, Romania, Poland; in Western Europe, the setting up of the Marshall Plan; the "Prague coup," at the beginning of 1948, veritable takeover of Czechoslovakia by the Communists, and, one year later, the Atlantic Pact... Jdanov was right: two camps—soon they would be called two "blocks"—came into being in the world, no doubt ready to divide it up at the cost of a bitter struggle. That is to say, a Third World War.

French intellectuals dreaded this war that everyone knew would be worse than the preceding ones. All the more because they believed it was

---

[3] The expression "Cold War" would be popularized by the American journalist Walter Lippmann as of 1947.

inevitable. That was the opinion of Sartre and his friends; it was also Simone de Beauvoir's, who, in her daily letters written to Nelson Algren, paints an alarming picture of the state of mind that reigned at the time among the intellectuals. On December 14 1950: "Peace will perhaps continue for several years, but nothing is less sure. Moreover it will possibly be peace for you and for us a Russian occupation. It may be that war will not break out, even with Russians in Paris, but it will not be much better here. To believe that the Communist Party will strike Sartre and his friends immediately is not a vain illusion, all our acquaintances without exception are in agreement here, he is mortally hated and certainly, among the intellectuals, he is the number one enemy." On December 22: "Most non–Communist intellectuals believe that declarations and acts contrary to their convictions will be demanded of them if the Russians arrive here, and that it is thus preferable to leave beforehand. All agree that Sartre will be promptly liquidated, and I will be in great danger." On December 31: "No, we don't think that war is for tomorrow, but that it is not so far off."

Haunted by this fear of a major conflict, French intellectuals would thus attempt, by all means, to oppose a division among the democrats. These are the ones who took part in a world Conference of intellectuals for peace that unfolded during the summer of 1948 in Wroclaw, in Poland. Writers like Vercors, the author of the famous *Silence de la mer* (*The Silence of the Sea*), Julien Benda, Maurice Bedel, President of the Société des gens de letters; poets: Paul Éluard, Aimé Césaire, Pierre Seghers; painters: Picasso, Fernand Léger; Irène Joliot-Curie, the daughter of Pierre and Marie Curie, Nobel Prize winners, Under-Secretary of State for Scientific Research in 1936, in the government of Léon Blum; finally a "red" ecclesiastic, the abbé Boulier, Professor at the Catholic Institute, leader of the Christian Workers Youth Movement, whom the Holy Office would suspend *a divinis* in 1950, before reducing him to a layman status in 1953.[4]

Historians now consider this large gathering, where delegations from the two blocks found themselves side by side, to be the founding event of the Movement for Peace, which would remain, "even in the period of its greatest strength, a relay-association, devoted exclusively to diffus-

---

[4] The Soviet novelist Alexandre Fadeïev, at the time Secretary of the Writers' Union, took advantage of a speech he was presenting at the rostrum of the conference to violently attack Sartre, Malraux, Camus, etc., branded, among other things, as "bourgeois writers."

ing the big Soviet diplomatic watchwords among the non-Communists."⁵ Watchwords of which the essential can be summarized in a few formulas: defence of peace, struggle against the use of the atomic weapon... Who could declare himself hostile to such a program?

Therein lay all of Stalin's skilfulness: presenting the USSR as the camp of peace. Most French intellectuals, Communists or fellow travelers, would allow themselves to be taken in. In fact, at the time of the Kominform's creation, in 1947, when the world was already divided in half, the people around Stalin, notably in the Political Bureau of the Communist Party, were worried about the disastrous situation of the Soviet Union, ravaged by war, whereas the United States, at the same time, already had the atomic bomb. The race towards nuclear armaments had thus begun, and the USSR was behind... It was then that an idea germinated in the officials' minds. Taking advantage of the presence in Crimea of Communist leaders who had come to spend the summer months there, Stalin organized a series of meetings. During which, little by little, the Kremlin's strategy fell into place.

It was about convincing all of the Communist Parties that the world was in the process of crystallizing into two blocks, that the old alliances were broken or overturned. In short, that we were moving towards a confrontation likely to prepare the Third World War and, consequently, that it was necessary to strengthen the camp's unity. According to this plan, perfectly logical on the surface, defending peace meant defending the Soviet Union. Because the latter dreaded two things. First of all, being overtaken by the United States in the race towards armaments. Secondly, being pushed out of its European glacis. "As a result, commented Pierre Juquin, the former high official of the French Communist Party, "we would sincerely defend peace and sincerely defend the USSR."⁶

It was in this spirit that the French delegation embarked for Wroclaw—a most symbolic place, re-conquered from Germany—on August 25 1948. And that the entire group was present, in Paris, in April 1949, for the first National Congress of Partisans for Peace, during the course of which, for five days, two thousand delegates, assembled in the Salle Pleyel under the presidency of Frédéric Joliot-Curie, would loudly and in all conscience celebrate the pacifist virtues of the USSR. On

---

⁵ Pascal Ory et Jean-François Sirinelli, *Les Intellectuels en France, de l'affaire Dreyfus à nos jours*, Armand Collin, 1986.

⁶ Conversation with the author, 1991.

that occasion, Picasso would draw his famous dove which thus became the emblem of the congress.

What was necessary was to gain time, while waiting for the Soviet Union to possess the bomb as well. So, at the Kravchenko trial, before the 18th Magistrates' Court in the Seine district, in January 1949, the Communist Party sent in the guards: Emmanuel d'Astier de la Vigerie, Jean Cassou, Vercors, Joliot-Curie... In such a way that the Communist weekly *Les Lettres françaises* would turn a lost trial into a propaganda success.

Victor Andreïevitch Kravchenko was a Soviet engineer who took advantage of a mission in the United States, in 1944, to cross over to the Western camp. Two years later, he published an account that appeared in France under the title *J'ai choisi la liberté* (I Chose Freedom), where he spoke notably of the Soviet concentration camps. *Les Lettres françaises* accused him immediately of having falsified his testimony, made up from start to finish, it said, by the American services. Kravchenko made a formal complaint, obtained redress. But did not convince anyone within the ranks of the Peace Movement, so great was its blindness. It was blind to such an extent that, despite the newspaper being condemned on appeal, the affair would leave the impression in the mind of the public of a clear victory for the Communists and their traveling companion friends. All of them, as one man, in the spring of 1950, would sign the Stockholm Appeal of the Peace Movement. Because all feared war. And very few, among the signatories, questioned the true meaning of the movement. Would not accusing one camp alone of all violations against peace allow the other to quietly prepare for war?

"There will be a history to be written about blindness in the 20th century," said Pierre Juquin in 1991.[7] "We were mistaken. But it is too easy, today, to condemn in total the struggles of all those years. We come from another world." Another world, indeed. Who at the time could suspect the Soviet Union, completely ennobled by the glory of Stalingrad, of harbouring such intentions? With which voices other than the Communist ones could one rise up against the war in Indochina, German rearmament, the bomb? Commenting on the famous phrase by Jean-Paul Sartre, "An anti-Communist is a dog," Ory and Sirinelli observed: "It was difficult in that period not to be a Communist without being seen as an anti-Communist, and to be an anti-Communist without being seen as

---

[7] Interview with the author.

a Fascist."[8] The golden age of Saint-Germain-des-Prés was not the age of unconcern.

The Communist Party, that was achieving important scores at each election (160 deputy seats, in the legislative elections of 1945: more than the Gaullists), was at that time at the centre of all the debates. Discredited for having unreservedly approved the Germano-Soviet pact of August 1939, its strong participation in the Résistance movement more or less washed its sin away. "Whatever the ulterior motives of its leaders might be, the Communist Party largely succeeded in foisting on public opinion the image of itself that it intended to project."[9]

Thus it is in relationship to the Communist Party—the famous "party of the 75,000 martyrs shot to death," as it proclaimed itself—that intellectuals would define themselves. With the result that they sometimes found themselves trapped in a kind of net: "Impossible to be a Communist, impossible to be an anti-Communist," affirmed at the time Maurice Merleau-Ponty.[10] And Claude Roy: "The friends of Prévert had been Communist sympathizers (without being Communists). They got over it. The Sartre groupies would be Communist sympathizers (without being Communists) during the 50s and 60s. They would get over it too."[11]

Of course they would get over it, but not right away. "Sartre and his friends," as Michel-Antoine Burnier shows in his study on the relationships between Existentialists and politics, would strive, during those years, through the stands they took or through their writings, to be as it were Communism's bad conscience. And only its bad conscience. With more or less success, many controversies and quite a lot of ambiguities: "One must note that if Existentialism, in the years following the Liberation, did not always have recourse to the concept of class as to a fundamental operational one, it never considered it [that concept] to be unrealistic or old-fashioned."[12] Thus Maurice Merleau-Ponty, in *Les Temps Modernes*, would not be afraid of severely condemning the work of Arthur Koestler, *Le Yogi et le Commissaire* (*The Yogi and the Commissar*), a collection of essays that demonstrated the Stalinist totalitarian mechanism. Also "Sartre and his

---

[8] *Les intellectuals en France, de l'affaire Dreyfus à nos jours, op. cit.*
[9] Serge Berstein and Pierre Milza, *Histoire de la France au XXe siècle, op. cit.*
[10] *Humanisme et Terreur. Essais sur le problème communiste*, Gallimard, 1947.
[11] *Nous, op. cit.*
[12] Michel-Antoine Burnier, *Les Existentialistes et la Politique*, Gallimard, "Idées", 1966.

friends" cold-shouldered the same Koestler, considering that *Le Zéro et l'infini* (*Zero and Infinity*) played into the hands of the Fascists. All these things, however, did not enhance their standing in the eyes of the Communists. On the contrary. Several months later, the Party would launch an offensive against "Sartre and his friends" and throw its best writers into the battle: Henri Lefebvre, Henri Mongin and Jean Kanapa—the latter, an intransigent Marxist, a kind of Robespierre, an "incorruptible" of Stalinism.[13] All three were, of course, aided and abetted by [the newspaper] *L'Humanité*: "Kanapa describes for us very clearly the clever use that the reactionary and decadent bourgeoisie makes of its philosophers (yesterday Bergson, today Sartre). And what Existentialist 'Freedom,' 'Choice' 'Engagement' are really worth. And the claims of Gabriel Marcel, Sartre and Co. with regards to 'humanism'.... There is no such thing as pure philosophy. There are only philosophers of flesh and blood who live, speak and preach. Every philosophy has its frighteningly present, real consequences, for which the philosopher is responsible. Directly responsible, Kanapa asserts. That is why he moved the debate from the theoretical to the political plane and ruthlessly unmasked the monstrous imposture of the pseudo-humanists, showing, at the same time, that the Communists were the only consistent defenders of man."[14] These *ad hominem* attacks didn't surprise Sartre, who had always viewed political life as a combat. He was used to it: "As soon as the calm of 1945 was over, they attacked me. My political thinking was confused, my ideas could do harm."[15]

Faced with the Communists, the Existentialist intellectual lived in a permanent state of malaise. A malaise that Simone de Beauvoir would express perfectly in *Les Mandarins* (*The Mandarins*), in 1954. This novel, that has often been considered, rightly or wrongly, as a roman a clef, inasmuch as it imposed on the masculine characters the names of Sartre and Camus, is first and foremost a kind of chronicle of post-war Saint-Germain-des-Prés and, more generally, of its intellectual life. The book puts its finger on the real political problem that non-Communist left-wing intellectuals faced at the time: could they, without scruples, be content with their sta-

---

[13] Henri Lefebvre, *L'Existentialisme*, Le Sagittaire, 1946; Henri Mougin, *La Sainte-Famille existentialiste*, Éditions sociales, 1947; Jean Kanapa, *L'existentialisme n'est pas un humanisme*, Éditions sociales, 1947.

[14] Guy Leclerc, *L'Humanité*, January 9 1948.

[15] Jean-Paul Sartre, "Merleau-Ponty vivant ", *Les Temps Modernes*, no. 184-185, 1961. "They", of course, indicates the Communists.

tus as intellectuals? And, if they chose political engagement by the side of the Communists, could they still declare themselves intellectuals? "It is normal for a worker—the kind who was born in the proletariat—to be a Communist: the Party is made for him; it is his only way to fight alienation and achieve freedom. On the other hand, an intellectual coming from the bourgeoisie will never be able to adhere to it fully. He will always be in the way there, he will always be able to leave. His engagement lacks weight: the proletarian, on the contrary, is hard. Communism is his way of reaching a state of existence, of freedom. It is not the path for the intellectual. It is his impossible salvation: the intellectual, the enlightened bourgeois is therefore nothing but this 'useless passion' which re-assesses itself eternally to compensate for his inability to become a Communist."[16]

"Prévert's Gang," "Sartre and his friends"... And, already, "the friends of Duras." Marguerite Duras. The one readily called "Meg," in that period, if one is to believe Simone de Beauvoir.[17] Meg at whose place was held a kind of permanent Communist cell meeting. Claude Roy, Robert Antelme, Dyonis Mascolo, twenty others. In this apartment on 5 rue Saint-Benoît, the session was never over; as a result, it was not necessary to open it... It was one of these homes, affirmed Claude Roy, such as existed in the Russian novels at the time of the intelligentsia, "where, come and go, at every instant, three ideas, five friends, twenty newspapers, three fits of indignation, two jokes, ten books and a samovar of boiling water."[18] A kind of beehive of which Duras was the queen. Even if the general public still did not know of her—in 1945, she had published only two works: *Les Impudents* (*The Impudents*) and *La Vie tranquille* (*The Quiet Life*).

As Vincent Gille emphasized: "If the Communist Party is at the centre of very many polemics, it is because, as the party of the working class, it embodies, for many, the Revolution, the only possible way of changing society in depth. One can hardly imagine today the violence of the exchanges between Communist intellectuals and non- Communists, that could go as far as personal attacks."[19] Sartre knew a thing or two about

---

[16] Michel-Antoine Burnier, *Les Existentialistes et la Politique, op. cit.*

[17] This is how she designates her in her letters to Nelson Algren.

[18] *Nous, op. cit.*

[19] *Saint-Germain-des-Prés 1945-1950, op. cit.* For example, Pierre Hervé, a staunch Communist, had nicknamed François Mauriac "the feminine elegiac Corneille." [Corneille, the 17th century playwright, was know for his depictions of strong-willed, virile heros. Hence the insult. Translator's note]

this, he whom the Communists called "a jackal with his typewriter," "a hyena wielding a pen," etc. And the insults often came from on high. Directly from Moscow. Like this article appearing in the Moscow weekly *Soviet Art*: "Jean-Paul Sartre is one of the most reactionary among Western writers taking their orders from American imperialism. *Les Mains sales* is a play in which Sartre, with a bestial hatred of the proletariat, basely slanders the working class in its vanguard, the Communist Party. The political and literary activity of Sartre can only be considered with the most profound contempt by all progressive humanity."[20] A tissue of lies and falsehoods that the press related indulgently. And that the members of the Party swallowed without blinking...

A little anthology: "Sartre just like the bourgeois Simone de Beauvoir and the old fornicator André Gide are vagabonds of humanity without passports and spend their time spreading the toxic bacteria of cosmopolitism";[21] "This lamentable reactionary hack [Sartre, of course] prides himself on knowing everything, but in actual fact enjoys only the universalism of a dilettante";[22] "The characters in *Les Chemins de la liberté* are aboulic individualists on whom Sartre confers a decadent Hamlet complex by way of psychology."[23] Visiting Paris, in January 1949, where he gave a series of lectures at the Sorbonne, Georges Lukacs, considered in Hungary as one of the best theoreticians of Marxism, happily gave his little anti-Sartre speech: "Existentialism, this unthinkable third path between materialism and idealism, indirectly praises capitalism."[24] Because, he explained, it turns away from Marxism a part of the youth who, without him, would accept the Marxist doctrine. Here at least was something that had the virtue of being clear...

Because this is really the question one had a right to ask: why did the Stalinists, in Moscow just as in Paris, keep barking at Sartre's heels with such violence? Was it the violence of a watchdog, on too short a leash, defending his territory? Certainly. Dominique Desanti, a committed Communist during those years, is convinced of it today: "After the Liberation, many young people who had participated in the Résistance, often by the side of the Communists, were also close to the Existentialists.

---

[20] Quoted in *Combat*, July 25 1949.
[21] In *Literatournaïa Gazeta*, November 1949.
[22] In *Soviet Art*; quoted in *Combat*, July 25 1949.
[23] In *Novy Mir*; ibid.
[24] *Combat*, December 13 1949.

Communists by conviction, that is to say, agreeing that France needed a change of regime, but, at the same time, in complete support of Existentialist ideas. This did not make for a good household... On the one hand the individual chooses his destiny, on the other it is the group that commands[25]." The Existentialist man, in fact, was permanently facing the demands of his freedom, standing in front of his choices. In the Communist Party, it was the exact opposite: once the line is decided, all one does is follow it; those who experienced scruples are asked to remain silent. "So there was a choice to be made by these hundreds of young people who had resisted, but who read *L'Être et le Néant* with passion and who had made of Sartre a kind of Socrates, or intellectual master. The Communists saw the danger. Between Communism and Existentialism, it was necessary to choose. Sartre became the man to knock off. And since they could not knock him off, slander was pressed into service. Not being inspired by Marxism, Existentialism was thus inevitably a philosophy for petit-bourgeois minds; at Wroclaw, during the summer of 1948, during the World Congress of Intellectuals for Peace, the secretary of the Writers' Union, standing at the rostrum, took the liberty of insulting Sartre in front of delegates from all over the world;[26] *Les Main sales*, which presented the dilemma of a militant, became a vehemently anti-communist play."[27]

Slander, Slander, there will always be something left... This is what, without excessive scruples, the editor in chief of the review *Soviet Art* did: "Sartre's career, this spiritual director of all the worshippers of the depraved ideology of imperialism, has developed with a dizzying swiftness. Today, Sartre is particularly useful to his imperialist masters and above all to the imperialists in the USA, because the amorality of the human personality that he preaches constitutes the surest ideological arm of contemporary reactionary forces..."[28]

Real violence, which, beyond the personal attack, sometimes went even as far as physical confrontation. Proof of which was this scene that took place in a cellar nightclub of Saint-Germain-des-Prés: "At the end of the evening the Fascists made in a loud voice a nauseating comment on Jews, a Communist shot back: 'What's wrong with the Jews'?, and

---

[25] Interview with the author, February 2008.

[26] See *Supra,* note 1, page 128.

[27] Dominique Desanti, interview with the author, February 2008.

[28] Quoted in *Combat*, December 15 1949.

some Existentialists came up to the Communists and proposed that they form a temporary alliance to lay into the Fascists and beat them up. The Communists refused and started talking harshly to the Existentialists, each of the two groups brandishing their banner aggressively in the wind. Then the Communists left, thereby infuriating the Existentialists, one of whom advanced against the Fascist to tread on his toes. The latter said: 'You've crushed my foot,' and they began trading insults. Everyone there formed groups around the two clans, except for three or four guy who were lying stone drunk in the red armchairs, and went out to smash each other's face in. This kind of incident happens every night, I was told, in this elegant intellectual basement night club."[29]

This "elegant intellectual basement nightclub," was the Méphisto, an establishment at the corner of the rue de Seine and the boulevard Saint-Germain. And that Albert Camus and the young journalists of *Combat* readily visited. "Last year it was a private club frequented by West Indians, now the whole intellectual set of Saint-Germain-des-Prés meets there night after night. Towards 11 pm they knock at the door of a café in the most mysterious manner, a woman with black hair ushers them in, they descend the stairs till they reach a most elegant basement: carpets, deep red armchairs, a bar, a piano, records…"[30] Juliette Gréco liked the Méphisto, "a relatively clandestine place, because it's necessary to ring the doorbell and be recognized to obtain the right to enter. You can eat Creole sausage there and dance and drink, drink and dance as the spirit moves you, but most important, you talk a lot there…"[31]

Talking is not the kind of thing one could do at the Tabou! Nor be seated, for that matter, nor even enjoy a quiet drink. Dancing? Not for sure either. Entering the Tabou after leaving the Méphisto was like leaving Purgatory to enter Hell. This at least was what Boris Vian maintained…

---

[29] Simone de Beauvoir, *Lettre à Nelson Algren, op. cit.* (letter date June 20 1947).
[30] *Ibid.*
[31] *Jujube, op. cit.*

9

"A long vaulted cellar, filled with tables and empty stools, meets her gaze: Fascinated, she walks to the very end of it..."
Juliette Gréco had just discovered the Tabou

Too much noise, too many people, too much music, too much smoke... Opened on April 11 1947, the Club du Tabou met with almost immediate success. Success: the word is inadequate. It was much more a triumph, the echo of which, like a ground swell, quickly reached Europe and America. In barely two months, the name of the Tabou was known on five continents. There was not one foreign personality passing through Paris who failed to go down into the most famous cellar in the world—Greta Garbo, Gary Cooper, Marlene Dietrich... Its founders—all young, all broke at the time—did not entertain such an ambition, far from it. What they wanted was a place where they could get together. Period.

At the beginning, there was a little restaurant, Chéramy, on 10 rue Jacob, that Prévert and his friends from the Groupe Octobre readily frequented at the end of the 1930s. A kind of almost family-style canteen, whose owner, Augustin Chéramy, prided himself on offering unlimited credit to his guests: "You're not going to contract debts elsewhere, at least?" he asked in a worried tone.[1] In 1944, Chéramy sold his business to a certain Henri Leduc who, in place of the restaurant, soon opened one of the first real American bars in Paris; in any event the first in the neighbourhood. Henri Leduc himself was close to the ex-Groupe Octobre. A

---

[1] Remark made by Maurice Baquet, interview with the author, 1998. Later on the cabaret L'Échelle de Jacob opened on the site of Chéramy.

native of Montmartre, with the smile of a Parisian street urchin on his round mug, Leduc had plied all the trades: worker, actor, stage manager, street peddler... Now he was a barman. "But Leduc was so lazy," related Boris Vian, "that at six o'clock in the evening, when his first customers would arrive, he would say to them: 'I'm not yet open, let's go get a little drink next door instead.' Next door was the Bar Vert, run first by a Breton named Madec. So, Leduc launched his competitor[2]." Very soon, in fact, the whole smart set of Saint-Germain-des-Prés rushed to the Bar Vert, set up in a former butcher shop, at two street numbers from the place, at no. 14—the very building Richard Wagner inhabited during his sojourn in Paris, from October 1841 to April 1842. Roger Vailland, Maurice Merleau-Ponty, Raymond Queneau, Roger Vadim, Juliette Gréco, Anne-Marie Cazalis, Alexandre Astruc, Henri Pichette, the painter Matta, Nicole Védrès, Christian Casadesus, Jacques de Beaumont, Sartre of course... For her part, Simone de Beauvoir was much more reserved as to the charms of the spot: "I drink a glass with Bost and Rolland at the Bar Vert which competes awkwardly with Chéramy, with attractive posters, but ugly red tables and walls that are too green."[3] A photographic reportage, dated at the end of the 1940s and done by Michel Brodsky, shows a very ordinary bistro: a counter, some bottles on the shelves, on the walls posters of art galleries, a cast-iron stove, a door partially opening onto the kitchen where, in the stingy light of a naked light bulb, a woman turns the handle of a coffee mill; on certain negatives, one sees a toothless violinist playing on a fiddle, a guitarist...

What was not ordinary, on the other hand, was the barman: Bernard Lucas. A quite unusual model for his profession. Barely twenty years old and he had already, under his belt, the editorship-in-chief of the review *Arts et Lettres*, the publication of a novel, *Le Journal d'un déserteur* (*The Diary of a Deserter*). A specialist in classical music, of which he possessed a rich record library, a bibliophile, "Lucas was tall, thin, dark, active."[4] And he succeeded in creating a circle of friends around him.

The Bar Vert had only one flaw: it closed around one o'clock in the morning. Just like the metro. That is really early when people have

---

[2] *Manuel de Saint-Germain-des-Prés, op. cit.*

[3] *La Force des choses, op. cit.* (dated May 1 1946). Beauvoir still called Henri Leduc's American bar by the name of Chéramy, out of habit no doubt.

[4] Boris Vian, *Manuel de Saint-Germain-des-Prés, op. cit.* Bernard Lucas would write the musical column of the newspaper *Combat* until 1950.

the whole night ahead of them. And when one is young—because they were all very young, all those people who would put le Tabou on the map: Gréco was born in 1927, Vian in 1920, Bernard Lucas in 1924, the same for Cazalis... When one is young and emerging from four years of occupation, of bans, of curfews... Where to go? They all lived in hotels, in rooms that were gloomy, badly heated, tiny. And, once the Bar Vert closed, lively conversations continued on the sidewalk, between the garbage cans. Not for very long, inasmuch as the inhabitants of the rue Jacob protested vigorously. One can almost hear them, these upright, angry workers: "Will this racket be over soon? Go have fun somewhere else! We guys, we get up early, tomorrow morning!..."

Elsewhere, but where? "Ah, if only we had a place for ourselves..." sighed the young people. Forced to adhere to a strict schedule by order of the police prefecture, all the bistros were closed at that hour, in the neighbourhood and elsewhere. There was of course the Bar Bac, in the street of the same name. It was open all night, and the typographers of the *Journal Officiel* would go there to quench their thirst, but it was miles from anywhere. Here, there was nothing but lowered metal shutters. Except for a run down joint, at the corner of the rue Dauphine and the rue Christine. With a bizarre name: Le Tabou. Where would congregate, during their break, the workers and truck drivers of the Press Delivery Services, whose premises were located on rue Christine. The "nocturnal people," as Bernard Lucas called them, quickly zeroed in on the spot. And mingled with this hard-working clientele, itself very happy to welcome "intellectuals..." Every night, after the Bar Vert closed, it was like a migration, a kind of daily transhumance that was set in motion, through the dark and cold streets of Saint-Germain-des-Prés, till it ended at the rue Dauphine.

There it was: 33 rue Dauphine. During the terrible winter of 1946 ("Paris is freezing, the hotel is not heated, we have absolutely nothing to wolf down, we have no electricity; all the bars close at 10 p.m.," noted Simone de Beauvoir in a letter addressed to Jean-Paul Sartre, who at the time was in the United States), the Tabou, open all night by special dispensation, was a haven of warmth and friendship, a veritable *querencia*, as Beavoir would say. They were all there, all the ones from the Bar Vert as well as the others, Lucas, Alexandre Astruc, Camille Bryen, Pierre Desseau, Wols, Léo Sauvage...

Behind the counter: Louis and Marcelle Guionnet, a couple from Toulouse who had come up to Paris after the war, having made their fortune on the black market selling sausages. Could the Guionnets imagine that by investing in the drink business this money so ill-acquired in the delicatessen trade, they would make their modest drinking establishment world-famous? "Loulou" Guionnet "has the accent of Toulouse and the height of a dwarf. Only his head, surrealistically, rises above the counter."[5] Madame was equal in height and proportions; but she had in the past sung in the choir of the Capitole, which, she thought, allowed her to feel she was in connivance with the artists who came to rest their elbows at her bar.

The poet Alexandre Toursky, who directed in Marseille the Club des Amis du Vieux-Port (The Club of the Friends of the Old Port), suggested one evening to Bernard Lucas that he open a similar club in Paris. And why not here, at the Tabou, since the place boasted a cellar that would do perfectly? A dry cellar, besides, despite the proximity of the river. Bloody Guionnets! It was: "no." They forgot the cellar, they forgot the club.

One fine day, or rather morning, more of a glacial little dawn, Juliette Gréco—she is the one who related this—opened the door of the Tabou, of which she was at present a regular customer. She placed her coat near the entrance, on a kind of guardrail that was used as a cloakroom. Her precious, her only coat that she owed to the generosity of her friend François Bamberger, whose family possessed a coat-manufacturing factory in the North. Because people were poor in Saint-Germain-des-Prés. Flat broke. And it was certainly not the play by Roger Vitrac, *Victor ou les Enfants au pouvoir* (Victor or the Children Take Power) she performed at the Agnès-Capri Theatre that was going to make her rich.[6] The Compagnie du Thyaze, that Michel de Ré directed and that received, several months earlier, the prize of the Jeunes Compagnies, had neither the means to have printed the poster designed by Bernard Quentin nor the possibility of getting costumes for the actors; Gréco herself had to provide her own: the dress worn by her grandmother the day after her wedding. Something black, a brilliant silk that gave her the respectable appearance demanded by her role: Thérèse Magneau, housewife. For

---

[5] Juliette Gréco, *Jujube, op. cit.*

[6] This was the Gaîté-Montparnasse that Agnès Capri directed after the war. The première of *Victor ou les Enfants au pouvoir* took place on November 12 1946. Juliette Gréco would find herself on stage again with Michel de Ré many years later, in the play by Françoise Sagan, *Bonheur, Impair et passé*, at the Théâtre Édouard-VII in 1964.

her coiffure, she brought up her long brown hair in a kind of strict Belle Époque chignon. She was 19 years old then.

Created by Antonin Artaud in 1928, *Victor* came onto the French stage like a lightening bolt. Or rather like a wet firecracker, so doggedly determined were critics and audiences alike to understand nothing about the harshness in this text with Surrealist tendencies that they mistook no doubt for a kind of over-heated light comedy. It was with a little haughty, vaguely disgusted air that the columnist of *Paris-Soir* at the time declared: "We listened to all of this in silence, with a somewhat sad smile conveying pity, the kind one would have when visiting the insane asylums of Sainte-Anne and Bicêtre." Victor is nine years old, he is already one metre eighty tall. It is his birthday. His first act is to smash a vase. Then to smash everything. Absolutely everything. Reputations, lies, shams. "Who is Victor? A myth. The myth of precocious childhood. The caricatured promise of the child genius. Victor dies quite simply on the day of his ninth birthday. In the most foolish manner—like a petit-bourgeois—but intact, at the very moment when he becomes acutely conscious of life, of life the way it is."[7] Because Victor knows that the beautiful lady covered in pearls and precious clothes who arrives solemnly in the second act, blasting out like mad her foul-smelling farts, Ida Mortemart, the compulsive farter, the improbable childhood friend of his mother, Victor knows that she carries another shorter and more terrible name…And he confidently puts his hand in the gloved hand of the beautiful visitor.[8]

Journalists in 1946 were not much more tender than those of 1928. Did Roger Vitrac foresee this, when, in his article for the *Figaro* he asked the question: "I can hear it said already: 'Was this revival necessary? Has the work aged?'"[9] "Yes," replied the critics rashly as one man.[10] Without understanding, once again, that *Victor* was a tragedy disguised as a boulevard light comedy: the total refusal of any compromise, and "thus the radical impossibility of living in this world."[11]

---

[7] Roger Vitrac, in *Le Figaro*, November 11 1946.

[8] This "shorter and more terrible name" is "Morte", which in French is the feminine form of the word "dead." [Translator's note]

[9] *Ibid.*

[10] It would be necessary to wait for Jean Anouilh's staging and the portrayal of the role by Claude Rich, at the theatre de l'Ambigu, in Paris, in 1962, for the play to be really rediscovered.

[11] Henri Béhar, in *Dictionnaire des pièces de théâtre françaises du 20ᵉ siècle, op. cit.*

Was it not from the same sickness that post-war youth was suffering? From the equally radical impossibility of making do with this dilapidated world that peace had given back to them, after four years of confiscation—deportations, camps, millions of deaths, Hiroshima and Bikini, the Soviet block, the American block, the Cold War... In its way, *Victor ou les Enfants au pouvoir* attests to the difficulties French society was experiencing in digesting not only the war and the Occupation, but also their consequences and the upheavals they engendered. It is not a coincidence that this project was born in Saint-Germain-des-Prés, and that a troupe of very young people was its prime mover: "We chose to revive this play," declared Michel de Ré in an interview granted to *Combat*, "because it has for us the value of a manifesto." Duly acknowledged.

Perhaps, that morning, on arriving at the Tabou, Juliette Gréco had come from a rehearsal of *Victor*? Several days before the dress rehearsal, it was not rare, in fact, for the troupe to work all night. So, she put her famous coat on the railing, sat down at the bar, began a conversation with the people who surrounded her. The regular customers. Jean Witold, who was putting the final touches to the musical broadcast he would present on the radio within a few moments; Alexandre Astruc, who took a break, to come to the Tabou, from the mounting of the film *Aller et Retour* (*Round Trip*) that he has just shot; Anne-Marie Cazalis, who was never very far from her friends—"Anne–Marie, that big rusty needle," as the dark Gréco said facetiously about the redhead Cazalis, "as different as day and night," asserted Vian; Marc Doelnitz, a redhead as well... Marc Doelnitz—d'Oelsnitz was his real name—after a few little roles with no glory in the movies and in the theatre, had enlisted in 1945 in the French Forces; on his return, after having vainly attempted to make his career in the fashion world, following in Christian Dior's wake, he returned to Saint-Germain-des-Prés. He would become the great organizer of its festivities, rounding up duchesses and highnesses of all types in the neighbourhood. Vian said of him: "He is an actor, mime, varieties entertainer, imitator, always moving about, red-haired like an Englishman (and just as much of a drinker), as fresh as Bacchus[12]..."

When she was ready to leave, no more coat. Juliette Gréco feverishly tossed around the pile of rags, thrown higgledy-piggledy on the guardrail. Nothing. Panic: she already imagined herself without a coat, in the

---

[12] *Manuel de Saint-Germain-des-Prés, op. cit.*

heart of winter... She then leaned over the banister, to determine if the coat did not slide over to the other side. And just then she discovered a staircase, precisely on the other side... A staircase whose very existence she was unaware of, stone stairs, rough hewn, that plunged into the darkness. She went down, gropingly. At the bottom, her hand encountered a switch. Light. The article of clothing was there all right, rolled up in a ball, "as round as a sleeping cat, leaning against a door that she pushed open. A long vaulted cellar, filled with tables and empty stools, lit by small electric bulbs of lively colours that threw the African masks into relief, met her gaze. Fascinated, she went to the very back of the cellar to touch a metal grate.[13] It opened up onto a sandy spot, like a prison in the reign of Louis XI. She returned to her departure point, and along the way, well hidden, near the entrance door, there was a bar."[14] With, as a bonus, a mass of empty bottles, of barrels, of old metal scraps and wooden crates, all lying under a thick velvet of dust; in an odour of mustiness and bitter, cheap wine.

Juliette Gréco had just discovered the Tabou.

The young woman raced up the stairs, as enthusiastic as if she had just uncovered a gold mine, and told her comrades about her discovery. They didn't believe their ears. And rushed in turn down the staircase. So there, under their feet, a treasure lay asleep... Here at last was the spot they were all dreaming about, this "spot belonging to us," as they said. "The ideal refuge was found, now it had to be theirs."[15] The Guionnets, who had vaguely heard about the success of the Lorientais, the cellar night club on the rue des Carmes, where Claude Luter was playing, really had to be coaxed a bit. But only as a matter of form; drawn by the lure of gain, four months later they yielded to everyone's entreaties. Headed by Bernard Lucas. And Alexandre Toursky's idea came back up for discussion: to create here a kind of circle, based on the model of the Club des Amis du Vieux-Port. An association of friends united under the label "Club du Tabou."

The first stage: cleaning and tidying up. And it was not a small matter: "In actual fact we needed a professional mover's courage to clear out this absolute dump," related Marc Doelnitz.[16] Bernard Lucas took charge,

---

[13] This grate separated the cellar of the Tabou from the basements of the Hôtel d'Aubusson.
[14] Juliette Gréco, *Jujube*, op. cit.
[15] *Ibid.*
[16] *La Fête à Saint-Germain-des-Prés*, Robert Laffont, 1979.

helped by several brawny guys. Second stage: music. A piano and phonograph found their way to the basement. The Club du Tabou was officially born. Founding members: the writer Roger Vailland, Frédéric Chauvelot, a diplomat in defiance of the accepted code of conduct, Jean Domarchi, an academic, professor at the Law Faculty of Dijon, soon-to-be collaborator of *Les Temps Modernes*. Without forgetting Bernard Lucas himself.

Tabou. Why this name, right smack in the 6th district? The previous owners had opened here, during the Occupation, a rather "special" night club, as people said, closed quickly moreover by order of the police. There was nudity, under the pretext of ethnology. Hence this décor of African masks, hung up on the walls, and this name of "Tabou," that entered our daily language, designating in the Polynesian religion that which is forbidden—and so much the worse if one mixed up thus, light-heartedly, Africa and Oceania... The Guionnets, not seeing any harm in it, retained the name of the establishment. It would no doubt go a long way in explaining the sulphurous reputation of the place.

The inauguration of the Club Tabou took place, then, on April 11 1947. Just as they had all dreamed it: "We are at home! We pay for our drinks, but we are at home."[17] They would play jazz recordings, they would dance, they would have passionate discussions, among friends. About theatre, cinema, music. Thirty-five years later, Juliette Gréco, in *Jujube*, wondered about this infatuation for the "underground," as she called it: "Did it come from the habit acquired during the war when alerts were called? From our desire to remain outside of life, at the margins? From our need to create a kind of distance between adults and young people? From the comforting feeling of knowing whom we could find at what time and where? Undoubtedly all that simultaneously and yet there were other reasons, like fear of solitude. A certain idea of the community, of the family home we dreamed about, filled with people we chose and loved... The cellar represented a safe investment indispensable for their happiness. Their idea of freedom."

This was the moment when the general public, astounded, discovered "Existentialism" through the pens of the editors of *Samedi-Soir*. Whose words were immediately picked up by the international press. The black legend of Saint-Germain-des-Prés was launched. It would no longer stop. "We are at home! At home!" said the club's young founders. Not for very much longer.

---

[17] Juliette Gréco, *Jujube, op. cit.*

Indeed, at the beginning of June, Bernard Lucas, called to direct the Bar Vert, which he would convert into a kind of space for encounters and exhibits for young painters, was replaced by Frédéric Chauvelot at the head of the Tabou. Chauvelot—Fred or Frédy, as his friends called him, a tall blond young man of good family, with an attractive moustache of the Errol Flynn type—scented a good business, and the sustained zeal that the press manifested towards his establishments strengthened him in this idea: "Chauvelot possessed the great art of giving a form to what had been only an idea or the very beginning of a project," declared, not without dishonesty, Anne-Marie Cazalis.[18] Who was not uninvolved either in the arrival of the "Françamedimanchesoir" clique, as Boris Vian called it, in Saint-Germain-des-Prés.

Quickly, the décor was repaired. The club of friends became a private club. The nasal-sounding phonograph was put into storage, and replaced by a little jazz band: Guy Longon on the trumpet, Timsy Pimsy on the guitar. They were rapidly followed by the orchestra that Boris Vian put together around himself. Boris played the trumpet; his two brothers, Lélio, played the guitar, Alain was at the drum kit; Guy Montassut was on the tenor sax; Henri Renaud at the piano; the trombonist was Christian Vienot... Joined sometimes by Yves Corbassière, who did not consider it beneath him to scratch the double bass. "All the friends would come there for a jam session or rather 'to jam,' according to the accepted expression."[19]

An engineer by profession (École centrale, class of 1942, 54th out of 72), Boris Vian was "a false nonchalant who works on a production line. He is on his sixth professional activity: engineer, novelist, translator, lyric writer, trumpeter: at present he sings. He wrote *J'irai cracher sur vos tombes* (*I Will Spit on Your Graves*) in twelve days, and translated Bradley's memoirs in nineteen. Ironic in his manners and the attitude he takes, he is in reality very attentive. A soft heart. Almost a sentimental person carefully concealed."[20] To this long *curriculum vitae* one must add yet a seventh activity: jazz critic.[21] And a particular sign that was not devoid of

---

[18] *Les Mémoires d'une Anne, op. cit.*

[19] Boris Vian, *Manuel de Saint-Germain-des-Prés, op. cit.*

[20] Mathieu Galey, *Journal 1953-1973, op. cit.* (dated December 14 1955).

[21] As a jazz critic, Vian collaborated notably with *Combat* and *Jazz Hot*. His best articles have been published by Lucien Malson, at the Éditions Jean-Jacques Pauvert, under the title *Chroniques de Jazz*.

importance: the author of *Le Manuel de Saint-Germain-des-Prés* never lived in Saint-Germain-des-Prés! It was only his place of work. Ville-d'Avray, where he was born, in 1920, la cité Véron, in the 18th district... But never Saint-Germain-des-Prés. This did not prevent him from knowing the neighbourhood inside out. It was thanks to Raymond Queneau, who as early as 1945 was interested in the manuscript of *Vercoquin et le Plancton* (Vercoquin and the Plankton), his first novel, that Vian became a regular visitor to the neighbourhood, of which he soon was one of the leading lights. "Flashing teeth, pale pink lips, almost violet coloured, blue eyes, a long head like a melancholic horse," this is how Jean Cau, Sartre's secretary at that period, saw him. Simone de Beauvoir met him at the bar of the Hôtel Pont-Royal, in March 1946. The first encounter was without warmth: "He listens to himself talk,"[22] was her irrevocable judgement. Two months later, a change of heart: "I am reading *L'Écume des jours* (Froth on the Daydream) by Vian, that I like very much, especially the sad story of Chloé who dies with a water lily in her lungs; he has created his own world; this is rare and this always moves me."[23]

"A world of his own," said Beauvoir. This strangeness in the tone and the behaviour of the man is what also struck Dominique Desanti. After the war, she was working for newspapers that grew out of the Résistance, one of which was named precisely *Résistance*: "The nights when I was putting the newspaper to bed, when I left, there was no more public transportation. I lived far, at the Porte d'Ivry. So, often, I would join the "Sartres." It was with them that I met Boris Vian for the first time. It was at the Club des Lorientais. All the girls had a soft spot for him, it was obvious; he had the elegance to pretend not to notice it. Handsome? Yes. Scintillating yet at the same time far away, because he knew how to keep his distance. He would play in the orchestra; but at every pause, he would come back to our table. I remember him saying: "To dance the be-bop well, you must have jumped over a serpent!" In order to make us understand, no doubt, the liveliness this dance required. His conversation was like this: a collage of diverse and heterogeneous images, a poetic humour, an irony that today I think announced *L'Écume des jours*. Even if all this, of course, had not been structured at all."[24]

---

[22] Simone de Beauvoir, *La Force des choses, op. cit.*

[23] *Ibid.*

[24] Dominique Desanti, interview with the author, February 2008.

Within a few months, as his biographer, Philippe Boggio emphasizes, "after Queneau, Sartre, thanks to jazz, Boris acquired a perfect mastery of Saint-Germain, to the point of knowing, sometimes simply by sight, all those who mattered there."[25] And whom we soon found, filed away tenderly or slammed without much mercy—he could be very biting—in his *Manuel de Saint-Germain-des-Prés*.

Vian would never be one of Sartre's intimates. A good friend at most. A good friend whom the collaborators of *Les Temps Moderne* mistrusted, unable to appreciate the humour of a man who signed his columns, in the review, with the flippant pseudonym—"The Liar"—impermeable to a form of wit that was closer to the College of Pataphysics[26] than to Existentialism. As usual, Vian extricated himself with a pirouette. "I am not an Existentialist. Indeed, for an Existentialist, existence precedes essence. For me, there is no essence."[27] This prompted Philippe Boggio to declare: "A Sartrian iconoclast, but a Sartrian nonetheless."[28] Sartrian and loyal: because Vian, without hesitating, would take up the philosopher's defence against the denigrators of Existentialism, the army of politically correct parrots who reproached Sartre, in the interminable columns of their newspapers, for his "fetid and unwholesome universe." In a long, brilliant, jovial and brutal text, "Sartre et la..." (the word to be filled in is "shit"), that Léo Sauvage had the courage to publish, on July 12 1946, in the sixth issue of his review *La Rue*, which had already been subjected to plenty of snubs during the few months of its existence:[29] "[...] It seems to us that these superficial exegetes are committing a gross error by attributing to the author, by an abusive extension, their own exclusively latrine-like preferences. They never have reproached him for

---

[25] *Boris Vian*, Flammarion, 1993.

[26] The "Collège de pataphysique" or College of Pataphysics was a humoristic term coined by the 19th century French Poet, Alfred Jarry. It means the science of imaginary solutions. [Translator's note]

[27] *La Rue*, n. 6, July 12 1946.

[28] *Boris Via, op. cit.*

[29] Léo Sauvage reused the title of the newspaper founded in 1867 by Jules Vallès. The review, authorized to appear on September 10 1944, saw the light on April 13 1945. Banned as of April 23, it published as a replacement a special issue on freedom of the press on June 3 1945, before being again authorized, on December 5 1945. *La Rue* ceased publication with issue number 12, in November 1947. For lack of supporters, of readers and of money. One notes in the table of contents the names of Jacques Lemarchand, Jacques-Laurent Bost, Léo Mallet, Jacques Prévert, Jacques Debu-Bridel, Jean Vilar, Albert Camus...Léo Sauvage would later direct, for many years, *Le Figaro*'s bureau in New York.

liking the blue sky. Now, Sartre also talks about it sometimes... Let us praise, gentlemen, let us praise Sartre! He is in psychoanalytical terms an unmistakable sign: only the degenerate, the repressed, the jerks of all kinds are afraid to touch it. The good people knead it up by the handfuls, without being any more embarrassed than if it were any other kind of filth, and once they have recognized it, they hasten to fertilize their lands with it. We suspect that these disgusted people making a terrible fuss love it secretly... They are the same ones whose fathers buried Jarry under the bile of Chassé and the students of Rennes' Polytechnic School. They have twisted the necks of the large bronze serpents, but let them beware: the day will soon come when, in a rumble of thunder, the statue of a naked Jarry, in full erection mode, dressed like a semi-god, will emerge from the earth at Saint-Sulpice Square. He will hold the world by its neck, in order to rub its nose in that chamber pot he'll hide under his black robe. May the disgusted ones perish! They have denied the evidence. There is lots of it on all the sidewalks. Sartre sees it and tries to find a use for it. They, raising their eyes to the heavens, walk into it on purpose and keep it on their heels."[30]

---

[30] The author thanks Pierre Sauvage, the son of Léo Sauvage, for having transmitted this text to him.

10

Seen in the newspapers:
"Le Tabou cellar nightclub, around two o'clock
in the morning, is a den of hell"

Who will ever know how reputations are made and unmade? How rumours arise? Within a few weeks, by word of mouth, the whole of Paris knew that something was happening at the Tabou. And rushed to the rue Dauphine. The little rendezvous for Existentialist pals, the club furnished with odds and ends, became a profitable business. And when *Life* got involved, through an article that alerted the rest of the planet, each evening there was a compact crowd pushing at the top of the staircase that Juliette Gréco had discovered by chance. "Ten o'clock struck when we showed up at the Tabou. A real crowd, eager to dance the be-bop, poured down the steps in our wake," remembered Marc Doelnitz,[1] who, helped by Gréco and Anne-Marie Cazalis, was passing out rum and Coca Colas, the only drink sold in the place.

Because Frédéric Chauvelot, no doubt overwhelmed by its success, proposed to the three friends that they take charge of the destiny of the Tabou; unless he saw in this three-member team, about whom the press was beginning to talk—the dark one, the redhead and the entertainer— a supplementary opportunity to attract the curious. And it was at his request that Christian Bérard, the famous set designer, conceived for the young women a Scottish pant style, trimmed with mink at the ankle. A kind of uniform.

"—What kind of fur is this? inquired Juliette Gréco, who had never seen mink.

---

[1] *La Fête à Saint-Germain-des-Prés, op. cit.*

—Mink, replied Bérard.

—A mink, how is it made? she asked innocently.

—You will soon find out, replied Bérard, laughing up his sleeve.

It was true," Gréco concluded simply, relating the anecdote in her book of memories, *Jujube*.

The task with which the three young adults were entrusted was simple: "It meant sorting out the people, and excluding the curious. We would remain among ourselves."[2] The three friends would execute their mission beyond all expectations: "Naturally, after several days everyone was in the know, everyone wanted to go down into the cellar and see what was going on."[3] Here is Boris Vian's comment: "The real reason why the cellar broke all attendance records, was the clever team of Gréco-Cazalis-Doelnitz. It was up to me to organize the pandemonium; Annie, Gréco and Marc were the ones who brought in the victims ready to get down to the job."[4] Completely willing victims. Anonymous small fry and big sharks of the Paris smart set whom Marc Doelnitz, a pilot fish of the first magnitude, guided towards the blue-green waters of the Tabou's aquarium. Witness this scene that Jean Éparvier described:[5] "I remember an evening when Maurice Chevalier, about to leave for America, came to make a royal visit to this Tabou, and, in the blazing light of the Vacublitz lamps, shook hands with Jean-Paul Sartre who had gone down exceptionally into this place of which, legend has it, he was a regular client. A historic minute."

Once the victims were ready to get down to the job, as Vian stated, Gréco took care of them. In her way, sometimes vigorously. A forceful way which was perhaps also her way of defending herself. Because, as she herself admitted, she felt as ill at ease on the staircase of the Tabou as a monkey sitting on his rock in the zoo: "She stations herself at the top of the staircase and chases away the visitors. She insults them. She will even slap them. What she will learn later on is that such tactics excited even more the noisy, fashionable and scent-wearing race. She pinches the rear ends of the women in Dior creations, the "New Look"

---

[2] Anne-Marie Cazalis, *Les Mémoires d'une Anne, op. cit.*

[3] *Ibid.*

[4] *Manuel de Saint-Germain-des-Prés, op. cit.*

[5] Quoted in Marcelle Routier, *Saint-Germain-des-Prés, op. cit.* Jean Éparvier is notably the author of *Médecins de campagne*, Julliard, 1953.

ladies, yet not one turns around. Gréco concludes from this that they are used to it."⁶

But one did not enter the Tabou just as one wished. Many were called, certainly, but few were chosen: "Connections were needed!" Boris remembered in his *Manuel*. Yet the reddish brown façade against which stood out, painted in yellow, the five letters of the word "Tabou" was not much to look at. Nothing very chic. But everybody wanted to be part of it. And anyone who thought he could access the holy of holies by pushing open a simple glass door was not out of the woods yet. He drew back a thick curtain…And there, twenty, thirty people, sometimes more, waiting anxiously, stamped their feet in front of the man whom Vian called "the grand master of the staircase," Robert Auboyneau, barely twenty years old, the son of a diplomat, the nephew of the Admiral who commanded the Free French Forces and was made a Companion of the Liberation by General de Gaulle. His role: to verify the cards of the club members. And exclude the undesirables.

Once all the checkpoints were passed, began the descent of the stairs, slowly, and delayed by people coming up into the open air; and the biggest ones—over a metre sixty-five—had to lower their heads if they didn't want to smash their foreheads against the vault of the steep staircase. Which made some of them say that to go down into the Tabou it was necessary to pass under the Caudine forks. As one went down deeper, the smoke became more dense, the noise louder. "The racket was so intense that, in reaction, one could no longer see anything there."⁷

"The cellar of the Tabou, around two o'clock in the morning, is a den of hell," *Samedi-Soir* said perfidiously. Before adding: "A bread weighing one kilo that comes out of the oven, left on the table at noon, is at six o'clock the next morning reduced to a state of mouldy mush." That was perhaps true…Eight metres by fifteen. A vaulted, narrow and low passageway, some wooden tables and stools hard on rear ends, that dated from the previous ownership, some benches against the walls, a dollhouse cloakroom, a miniature bar behind which Paul, the barman, was active. While the two servers, Jacques and Georges, shoved by the dancers, holding with all their might trays loaded with rum and cokes, executed, over their customers' heads, a kind of high-wire act, and Mme

---

⁶ Juliette Gréco, *Jujube, op. cit.* The man whom she slapped was Louis Vallon, the director of the Mint.

⁷ Boris Vian, *Manuel de Saint-Germain-des-Prés, op. cit.*

Junger, wedged more or less behind her cash counter, aligned the bills. And beyond, at the back, against the iron grill, on a kind of platform in the shape of a straw hut, capped by a reed awning, the orchestra was unleashed: "five, six, eight or fifteen guys blew into metal tubes, beat on skins or finished mutilating a piano that had escaped from some second-hand dump."[8]

In the cigarette smoke, as thick as a London fog, in the acrid odour of blended bodily sweat, how many were they, squeezed into that dark basement? "A mass stuck together wriggled around in rhythm, each one trying to preserve a reduced vital space. Sometimes a couple went into a trance. To the sound of an unleashed clarinet, the young man projected his partner far from him, while holding on to her by the wrist. He then had to rapidly execute movements that stopped dead in their tracks, whirl around, dive down, while their feet were in high-speed motion."[9] The best dancers at the Tabou were Hot d'Déé and his wife, Suzanne; he had "a jade-like complexion, he was thin and supple, knee-high to a grasshopper," affirmed Vian, "a precious ebony statuette," Gréco preferred to say, who nicknamed him her "little thimble." This was a judicious image, since Suzanne was a seamstress.

During the pause, "the band went for a drink," as Vian said, the "poets" then took possession of the dance floor. Violently, "like devils coming out of a holy water font," in the midst of heckling, insults to provoke laughter and happy vociferations coming from the audience. At the beginning, when the Tabou was still a club for close friends, the poetic interlude, if one can describe it thus, would unfold in a good-natured if not respectful ambiance. It is said that on the evening of the inauguration Raymond Queneau, unable to endure it any longer, burst out laughing loudly on hearing a poet from the Beauce region, afflicted with a strong rural accent, mumble his way through his works on the little stage. And in return he found himself favoured with a severe reprimand: "Let me work, Sir, I am a poet!" With success, everything changed. Now the "poets" would howl out their texts with all the lung power at their disposal, accompanied by a mixture of boos and bravos. Which is a way like any other of encouraging them. If Gabriel Arnaud spoke, there was a general outcry: "Strip naked Gabriel, go make a crap Gabriel!" They would target him with foolish remarks, throw him coins, "and he

---

[8] *Ibid.*

[9] Marc Doelnitz, *La Fête à Saint-Germain-des-Prés, op. cit.*

would only begin his act under these conditions, getting himself more and more worked up and ending in a vociferating delirium bordering on hysteria."[10] He recited—he belched out, rather—"The Cheval de cirque" (The Circus Horse), "C'est Dimanche" (It is Sunday)"...Thus, like gladiators, they were several to have used Le Tabou as their forum for poetry. Radiguet, just sixteen years old then, the authentic nephew of the author of *Le Diable au corps* (*The Devil in the Flesh*), but whose real patronym was Alibert; Alain Quercy, also sixteen, the son of the minister Christian Pineau...A sample:

> A rope
> A gentleman at the end
> Concorde
> Are you getting off?
> The metro takes him away
> He doesn't get off
> And the next station?
> There won't be one.

Twenty years old, one metre sixty-eight, fifty or so kilos of energy and of black fever, a tousled head that seemed sculptured with a knife from a block of anthracite—dark hair, a smouldering gaze. It was "the archangel Gabriel," as he was called—Gabriel Pomerand, he whom the Tabou welcomed to the cries of "Koum Kel Kerr!", "Biniminiva!" or any other onomatopoeia borrowed from the "Lettriste" vocabulary.[11] He did not recite his poems, he screamed them, "and one wondered every instant where his voice came from and if he would have any left for the following word," said Boris Vian. Besides, the term "word" is saying far too much, if we may say so, since in general words have a meaning, whereas the ones Pomerand uttered didn't have any. "Syllable" would be more appropriate.

Gabriel Pomerand belonged to the "Lettriste" movement, of which he was one of the first members, a movement founded in 1945 by Isidore Isou—Isidore Isou Goldstein was his real name—who had just arrived from his native Romania. The two men met the same year, in a can-

---

[10] Boris Vian, *Manuel de Saint-Germain-des-Prés*, op. cit.

[11] The French term "Lettrisme" referred to the avant-garde literary school in the first half of the 20th century that advocated the use of onomatopoeias in poems devoid of meaning. [Translator's note]

teen frequented by penniless Jews; they had the same admiration for Lautréamont. A long discussion led to another, then another... And they needed nothing more to embark together, with a kind of furious enthusiasm, on what they called "Lettriste madness." In the tradition of dadaism and futurism, Lettrism saw itself as a radical challenging, strongly marked by eroticism, of culture and society, and proposed, among other things, to create a "proto-language," a kind of language of origins that played on the letters of the alphabet and graphic signs. As an example, here is a so-called "phonetic" poem titled "Tabou":

> *Yam Bambo yam Bambo*
> *Roum pika il cango so longo*
> *Roum pika il narabielnara*
> *Baïla Yambo roumbi al kié*
> *Mata roumba cousso ramba*
> *Yam Bambo yam Bambo.*

Lettrism would even attempt, further on, to associate itself with revolutionary movements, by advocating a "paradisiacal and creative" society. Not without first having a run-in with the justice system: "Isidore Isou, the 'leader of the lettrist school,' was indicted by M. Baurès, the investigating magistrate, for affront to public decency through his book. The work targeted by the indictment was titled *Isou et la Mécanique des femmes* (*Isou and the Mechanics of Women*)."[12] And the journalist, indignant, concluded his article: "Just like Flaubert, like Baudelaire! Isou doesn't deserve this."

Indeed, Isou didn't deserve this, because the Lettrist challenging, much more even than the preceding ones, Dadaist or Futurist, was first and foremost an enormous fraud. Even if, through certain of its aspects, it seemed to feed off the atmosphere of the times. Most particularly the atmosphere of Saint-Germain-des-Prés. Which did not prevent the Lettrists from exhibiting themselves elsewhere, as soon as an opportunity presented itself. At the Théâtre de Chaillot, on the evening of the première of *Nucléa*,[13] the play by Henri Pichette that the very young TNP scheduled, they pelted the public, during the intermission, with tracts composed in the form of telegrams: "Lettrists to Jean Vilar. Stop. Théâtre

---

[12] *Libération*, March 26 1949.

[13] May 3 1952.

National Populaire. Stop. Mediocre. Don't think you're a Copeau! It's only sawdust on Pipichette..."

But Bugajer, Ghislain Desnoyers de Marbaix, Michel Mourre, Albert Jules Legros, Matricon, Nonosse, Pac Pacco... the Lettrist poets of the Tabou did not leave a big imprint in the literary history of Saint-Germain-des-Prés. Only Gabriel Pomerand, through his talent for provocation, his audacity and determination, was able to give lettrism a genuine notoriety. To Boris Vian's question—who was preparing his *Manuel de Saint-Germain-des-Prés*—about the trades he had exercised in the past, he replied calmly: "gigolo." And when the same Vian asked him what his present occupation was, he did not hesitate any more than for the first question: "husband." It was true that he was married to Roxane Chiniara, a rich Egyptian heiress, related to King Farouk...[14]

This brazenness mixed with insolence and self-assurance, this nerve, came out more sharply during his lectures. The brochure announcing the one he presented on December 19 1948, on the stage of the Vieux-Colombier, reveals the tone: "You are invited to a great event that will take place at the Théâtre du Vieux-Colombier, during which Gabriel Pomerand will talk about the weather, and the choir of François Dufresnes will recite Lettrist poems."[15] There followed a kind of profession of faith, and the Lettrist ideas one caught as they passed by bore a certain resemblance to the ones that floated around, here and there, on the terraces of the neighbourhood bistros: "Men have only music to lull them into forgetting their knowledge and turn them away from their humanity. This is not so funny, but rather a proof of indigence. Some young people who are a bit foolish have taken on the task of advancing beyond the

---

[14] The day after his marriage, celebrated with great pomp in Cairo, in March 1950, *Samedi-Soir* ran as a headline: "To marry in Cairo a ravishing Thousand and One Nights heiress, the archangel of Saint-Germain-des-Prés was freshly shaven..." Barely back in Paris, Pomerand would be incarcerated in the prison of la Santé, by order of the Investigating Magistrate Baurès. Where he would undergo a psychiatric examination that concluded his state of mental health was good.

[15] It was on this same stage that Antonin Artaud, on January 31 1947, presented—or, rather, tried to present—a lecture titled "The Real Life Story of Artaud-Momo." Artaud, who had just emerged from three years of psychiatric internment at Rodez, was practically incapable of saying anything. In front of a distressed audience, where notably Jouhandeau and Audiberti were present. And Gide, who noted in his *Journal*: "Oh! No, no one in the audience wanted to laugh; and even Artaud took away from us the desire to laugh for a long time. He had forced us to share his tragic game of revolt against everything that, accepted by us, remained for him, purer than we were, inadmissible."

civilized jungle, into the very depths of the liana, where the presence of a living being has not yet left even a hint of his shitty footprints. What characterizes us is that we don't love life and that our own fills us with pity. Despising everything, including ourselves, we have promised ourselves to misbehave uselessly and publicly, disgusted in advance with obeying, even here, the conventions of this era of suicides. If, by chance, some poems or some new phrases remained after this fire, perhaps these derisory objects will satisfy us, because they alone will wait, beyond our death, for the final cataclysm."[16]

Pomerand often went in for this kind of outrageous behaviour. *Combat* describes an example of this in its edition of July 4 1949: "Gabriel Pomerand, the alter ego of Isidore Isou, the pope of Lettrism, gave the other evening, in the Salle de Géographie,[17] a lecture titled 'From the Pornographic to the Impoundment Mania.' It was as though we had returned, through the violence and coarseness of his text, to the heyday of Surrealism. The whole Saint-Germain neighbourhood was there. Yet no one rose when Pomerand, matching his action to his words, just like Ernst or Dalì in 1925, invited the audience to partake in a kind of universal marriage and, pointing to himself, proposed: "If someone wishes to taste this exotic fruit, I am here." Our only fear was that the Police Commissioner, whose presence had been reported, would pick up the fruit. But he, too, was good natured..." The Salle de Géographie would hear many others, with, no doubt, even stronger flavours: "The Advantages of Prostitution", "Objective Considerations on Pederasty"... Sapped by tuberculosis, Gabriel Pomerand would put an end to his life in 1972.

As Maurice Fombeure, committed to the tranquility of the neighbourhood, deplored, the so-called "literary" movements were in vogue in Saint-Germain-des-Prés. And It didn't happen yesterday: "Despite the periodic surge of literary fashions: Surrealism, Dadaism, Epiphanism, Existentialism, Lettrism, the neighbourhood keeps its character and its continuity."[18] Moreover Fombeure could have added to his list: Independantism, Semaphorism, Cacouac... The Lettrists wanted to revolutionize language; the Epiphanists, in whose midst Hervé Bazin was campaigning, were

---

[16] The author thanks Hélène Duc for having passed on this text to him.

[17] La Salle de Géographie, or Geography Hall, was situated near the Café de Flore, at 184 boulevard Saint-Germain

[18] Maurice Fombeure, quoted in Marcelle Routier, *Saint-Germain-des-Prés, op. cit.*

fighting against the ambient pessimism; the Semaphorists, lead by Yvan Audouard, claimed to be in possession of the modern way of expressing oneself clearly; the Cacouacs, disciples of a new philosophy, advocated the unconditional return to nature...A result of fashion, of course; movements pass, literature remains. They knew it, so they all wanted to be heard. As quickly as possible. And to be heard preferably at the Tabou, which was a formidable resonance chamber. By force, if necessary. So that on certain evenings the dance floor was transformed into a boxing ring and people were joyfully exchanging blows. To the extreme delight of journalists of the tabloid press who were always on the look-out: "Existentialists and Lettrists were abandoning themselves peacefully to the joys of the boogie-woogie, when the Independantists burst into the cellar and pitched into their literary adversaries. The Independentists, whose founder Ryce Awger [sic], virulent author of *La Robe du Centaure* (*The Centaur's Robe*), reproached the Existentialists for wearing striped socks and aping American novelists in their works. After their invasion of the Tabou, the Independantists, made up of a high-powered group of writers, withdrew in an orderly fashion to the Café du Cadran, their headquarters. The dean of the Independantists was 25 years old."[19]

Striped socks...It was true that they were part of the outfit of the perfect little male Existentialist. Like checked shirts, rubberized canvas shoes, like sneakers; and for the girls, tight-fitting black sweaters, pants or wrap-around skirts, also black. "A uniform," recalls Marc Doelnitz, "that made us recognizable from a distance. It was at the Saint-Ouen flea market, among the Jewish second-hand clothes dealers, that we would find the gifts shipped by the New York Jewish community for their coreligionists who had been stripped of everything, and put up for sale immediately. Mountains of checked shirts, pants with tight legs that were often too short, ankle socks with loud-coloured horizontal stripes and basketball boots, whose moderate cost had delighted us."[20]

If this was a fashion, then it was a fashion resulting from shortages. There was no provocation involved in this way of dressing that the press called "the Existentialists' clothing style"—and of which it would have spoken no differently if they had worn feathers, shells and knucklebones...Styles, in any event, that high fashion would hasten to imitate. As *Samedi-Soir*

---

[19] *Samedi-Soir*, March 6 1948. *La Robe du Centaure* is a novel by Ryce-Anger (and not Awger, as the newspaper states), published by the Éditions du Lutrin in 1947.

[20] *La Fête à Saint-Germain-des-Prés, op. cit.*

described the scene greedily:[21] "Catherine, a salesgirl at Carven, would dance in the evening the wildest boogie-woogie in Saint-Germain-des-Prés. Carrère[22] hired her. Now she is launched. Her boss, Mlle Carven, has made for her three 'Existentialist' outfits, with slit skirts that allow the most dynamic leaps. They are worn with basket-ball boots and a braided hairdo."

No provocation here. In any event much less than in the clothes worn by the Zazous, who flaunted insolently (and perhaps courageously), several years earlier, under the nose and gaze of the occupiers and the henchmen of Vichy, their hair arranged in waves over their foreheads, their shirt collars under their chins, their long jackets flapping around their knees, their padded shoulders…

"Let's admit it right away, none of the clubs that followed were able to recreate this incredible atmosphere, and the Tabou itself, alas! did not keep it for very long; besides it was impossible," affirmed Boris Vian. We can easily believe him. Especially because, in reality, the grand period of the Tabou would be short.

The club would perish as a consequence of its very success. As though it had been asphyxiated. Every evening, the line-ups extended in front of the entrance at number 33. They got longer and longer. Noisier and noisier. Shouts, laughter, slamming of car doors… To say nothing of this permanent suspicion of debauchery that hung over the place. Complaints from the neighbours about the noise at night piled up on the desk of the Police Commissioner of the 6th district. There were even petitions: "We inform you, we fathers, mothers and law-abiding workers, that we have decided, Mr. Commissioner, in view of your failure, and with great regret, to assure the policing ourselves and to hold you responsible for the consequences, whatever they may be, that will not fail to result from this. Rue Dauphine, that distinguished itself by its courage during the liberation of Paris, will distinguish itself by liberating itself from the Tabou."

From then on, pails of water would rain down in cataracts on the unfortunate entry-seekers at the Tabou. A deluge. It was reported that, one evening, a group of Scandinavian diplomats received the contents of a basin of blue dye; rumour had it that even hygienic buckets were emptied on people's heads… They were not in a joking mood on the rue

---

[21] January 22 1949.

[22] Maurice Carrère, the owner of the cabaret Chez Carrère, on 45 rue Pierre-Charron, Paris VIIIe.

Dauphine. Neither the dwellers nor the owners of the Tabou. Gripped by a kind of mercantile frenzy, the Guionnets were becoming more and more greedy; Loulou and Marcelle—of whom Boris Vian would say: "As owners of the Tabou, they are about the only ones of whom it can be said that they had nothing to do with its success as a cellar night club"—jacked up the prices. And declared brazenly, to anyone who would listen, that they were the real inventors of the Tabou.

That was too much. Frédéric Chauvelot threw in the towel. And, without hesitating, emigrated to the rue Saint-Benoît, this time in the heart of the "village," taking away in his valises Boris Vian, Juliette Gréco, Anne-Marie Cazalis, Marc Doelnitz—the winning quartet. With as a bonus Mme Junger, the cashier. They opened, at number 13, the Club Saint-Germain. Its boom would coincide with the decline of the Tabou. *Sic transit Gloria mundi.*

11

Under the influence of Boris Vian, The Club Saint-Germain became a temple of jazz, where all the musicians would stop over while visiting Paris, from Charlie Parker to Coleman Hawkins

Unleashed jazz at the Tabou. Jazz at the Club des Lorientais, where people would listen to it almost religiously (Anne-Marie Cazalis spoke readily of "Lorientais austerities") in the basement of the Hôtel des Carmes. Where Claude Luter, considered as having injected an authentic new life into the "New Orleans style," placed the emphasis on collective improvisation. It was organized around themes belonging to the repertoire of black musicians, while Mme Pérodo, the boss of the hotel, an amiable redhead from Brittany, passed around drinks. Jazz at the Méphisto; soon at the Club Saint-Germain; at the Club of the Vieux-Colombier, when Paul Annet-Badel would discover that he, too, had a cellar under his theatre; at the Rose Rouge, on rue de Rennes... The press pretended to be scandalized: "The cellar night clubs are multiplying in Saint-Germain-des-Prés at a rhythm that is stupefying the residents accustomed to living above ground and not below. At present, between the rue du Dragon and the rue de Seine, tons of coal are being displaced to free the space necessary for setting up dance floors in a good ten or so of these cellars."[1] So jazz was everywhere in Saint-Germain-des-Prés, having come back at the same time as peace. It was not the American GIs, however, who brought it in their bags. Chocolate, chewing gum, tins of corned-beef, yes—but not jazz.

---

[1] *Combat, December 23 1948.*

Was it a discovery? No. Rather a rediscovery, after four years of being forbidden. Indeed, well before the Second World War, Black American musicians sojourned in Paris. Sometimes for long periods, sometimes on the occasion of a tour. It started with Sidney Bechet, whose first trip to Europe went back to 1919, when he was the solo clarinettist of the Southern Syncopated Orchestra that Will Marion Cook directed. In 1920, he appeared for the first time in Paris, for two months, at the Théâtre de l'Apollo. He would return to the capital several years later, for the Revue Nègre, of which Josephine Baker was the star at the Théâtre des Champs-Élysées. Before settling permanently in Montmartre, in 1928. But Bechet was a real "tough guy," as one would say at the time, a "desperado." Already, in London, several years earlier, he had serious run-ins with the law. In Paris, he would be condemned to eleven months in prison and officially denied access there afterwards. There was a brawl between rival musicians, on rue Fontaine, that ended badly, shots were fired, some were wounded... Louis Aragon's intercession with the authorities wouldn't change anything. Once he served his sentence, Bechet would not be seen again in France until 1949. But he managed to get noticed, in London, by the Swiss conductor Ernest Ansermet, who did not hesitate to talk about genius when referring to him: "He follows his own path. And this is perhaps the road on which the whole world will swing tomorrow."

In these years between the two wars, North America, where a strict racism reigned, was not a paradise for Black musicians. Tours, especially, were trying. Black people were barred from restaurants, Black people were barred from hotels, Black people were barred from trains... They travelled then by bus; often it was the driver, a White man, who took care of buying sandwiches and drinks, while the musicians would wait in the vehicle.[2] One could understand, in these conditions, why a certain number of them preferred to expatriate themselves, in order to exercise their art freely. In France, notably, where such prohibitions did not exist. Thus in 1933 Bill Coleman moved to Paris, where he played in different ensembles before joining, two years later, the Quintet of the Hot Club of France run by Django Reinhardt and Stéphane Grappelli; with whom he recorded several discs, thereby participating in the popularity of the "swing style." The same year, Duke Ellington gave a concert at the Salle Pleyel. Louis Armstrong, in 1934, resided in the capital for six months,

---

[2] Certain historians think that the near-impossibility for musicians of colour to break into the world of classical music led many of them to opt for jazz.

on the rue de la Tour-d'Auvergne, while the trumpeter Freddy Taylor, for his part, appeared regularly at the cabaret La Villa d'Este, on the right bank. Dizzy Gillespie, who was still just a young unknown musician, played in Teddy Hill's orchestra, at the time of the Paris International Exhibition in 1937...

Naturally, French popular music of the 1930s was first and foremost the accordion and the rhythm in triple time. Nevertheless, singers and composers like Jean Sablon (often accompanied by Django Reinhardt), Mireille or Charles Trenet would bring a different sound to the song, a colour tinted, if one might say, with Americanism. Before poets or novelists, in turn, got involved in writing about jazz, thereby contributing to its propagation. To its renaissance, as a full-fledged art.

The Belgian poet, Robert Goffin, was one of those people. As soon as the Great War was over, he discovered this music that would shake up his whole life. And his works. He published in the Belgian literary review *Le Disque vert* (*The Green Disc*), one of the most important at the time, founded by the writer Frans Hellens, the first text devoted to jazz. And, as of 1922, a collection of poems whose title sufficiently indicated its contents: *Jazz-Band*. Then there was *Aux frontiers du jazz* (*At the Frontiers of Jazz*), a work published in 1932, with a preface by Pierre Mac Orlan. Afterwards there appeared a history of jazz, a biography of Louis Armstrong... Robert Goffin was one of the first to sense that this music conveyed an emotion, a sensibility radically different from those of other musics.[3] "Because this is really the definition of jazz: above all, an emotion," emphasized André Clergeat, a jazz historian.[4]

Another man, in the aftermath of the Second World War, would play a capital role, this time in the explosion of the "New Orleans style." Henri Bernard, the owner of a record store in Paris, on the rue de l'Odéon, was also a great collector of jazz recordings. These were fabulous archives that he put generously at the disposal of young musicians, thus letting them discover Jelly Roll Morton or King Oliver, musicians of the 1920s who would from then on become mythical. Claude Luter readily acknowledged his debt: "We met a collector, Henri Bernard, who possessed an

---

[3] It was Robert Goffin who would present to the French public, in May 1948, on the stage of the Théâtre Marigny, la Semaine du jazz (The Week of Jazz).

[4] André Clergeat is the author, among other works, of the excellent *Dictionnaire du jazz*, in collaboration with Philippe Carles and Jean-Louis Comolli, Robert Laffont, "Bouquins", 1994. One can read, by the same author, in collaboration with Jacques Aboucaya, *Le Jazz*, Fuzea, 2005. This chapter owes a great deal to his erudition.

extraordinary collection. We would go to him two times a week, we listened to his discs and we committed them to memory."[5]

Thus it was at his home that these young people would discover this music, so different from all the ones they had known. Here, the origins of jazz were offered to them. Luter and his friends were filled with enthusiasm. The times lent themselves to this. The Club des Lorientais opened in June 1946; Boris Vian, from time to time, came to perform there. " I frequented the Club des Lorientais," relates André Clergeat. "I was preparing at the time a "licence" in English at the Sorbonne. I went there as a neighbour. It would begin at 17 hours and would end at 19 hours. It was a student audience. And this orchestra, that had just discovered this improvisational, polyphonic music, was now making us discover it in turn! We, who had not gone beyond Yvonne Blanc's piano bar! As for Claude Luter, he played authentic Black music, inspired by Blacks."[6] An audience made up of students, it's true, and lycéens[7] ("They were between fourteen and seventeen years old and hadn't yet lost sight of their matriculation exams").[8] A more decorous audience than the one at the Tabou. Because the Club des Lorientais was a kind of temple, and one came to celebrate mass there. The ambiance: "All of Luter's Paris fans had arranged to meet in this temple of classical jazz in order to take communion according to the 'New Orleans' rite. Claude Luter, in person, officiated with his knee and his trumpet with his customary ease. The Paris smart set and the tourists didn't go to the rue des Carmes. Students and school kids make up the major part of his faithful fans. A crowd, as motley as could be, filled up the three cellars linked in a row, which was the domain of the Luter groupies. Obviously, there were many checked shirts and heads of long hair. All of them were talking jazz..."[9] Raymond Queneau expressed this in other terms: " Youth in a pure state could be found there, penniless young people but very sure of themselves and of the value, intangible at the time, of that to which they were committing themselves and for which they were sacrificing quite a few things.... In fact interest in the theatre and the cinema constitute with a passion for jazz the three principal activities of this youth."[10]

---

[5] Interview published in *Saint-Germain-des-Prés, 1945-1950*, op. cit.
[6] Interview with the author, December 2007.
[7] The terme "lycéens" means high school students. [Translator's note]
[8] *Samedi-Soir*, May 3 1947.
[9] Jean Tanous, *Combat*, September 17 1948.
[10] Préface à Jean Queval, *Rendez-vous de juillet*, Le Point du jour, 1949.

Saint Germain des Prés

Jazz was now in the public arena. As of January 1946, Don Redman's orchestra appeared on a Paris stage. It was the first Black American group to return to France since the declaration of war, in 1939, that caused the cancellation of concerts scheduled by Jimmie Lunceford's ensemble. This music forbidden during the Occupation, this music that people listened to almost secretly at surprise parties, would henceforth be listened to in broad daylight. Or rather in the penumbra of cellars.

In Saint-Germain-des-Prés, the intellectuals, following in Vian's footsteps, went mad over jazz: "Boris knew everybody: the Prévert brothers, Sartre, Simone de Beauvoir, Queneau, and all those who were part of the intelligentsia of Saint-Germain-des-Prés, and with his wife, Michelle, he did a lot of publicity for us. He would tell them: 'One must be curious. Go listen to Claude.' And they would come."[11] Because Boris was literally "mesmerized by American jazz."[12]

When she came home from the United States, in May 1947, after a lecture tour of four months in American universities, it was at the Club des Lorientais that Simone de Beauvoir threw a party to fête her return: "I invited twenty or so friends to celebrate my return from America," she wrote to Nelson Algren. "I found a nice little cellar where we can dance, we will have good jazz records and a little orchestra. I have bought a large quantity of bottles: whisky, cognac, gin, vodka, and I have dressed as elegantly as I could, wearing the Mexican outfit purchased in New York and the glass necklace that you liked."[13] And henceforth, thanks to these letters she sent almost every day to Chicago, it is possible to understand the infatuation of the Parisian public—a certain Parisian public, the one made up of intellectuals and artists—for jazz. "The jazz concert has perhaps been the best thing I have seen and heard in years. The Salle Pleyel, as vast as Carnegie Hall, was teeming with a screaming audience, mostly young people, mad with enthusiasm. They were killing each other to enter by force whereas all the seats had been reserved eternities ago...

---

[11] Interview with Claude Luter, published in *Saint-Germain-des-Prés, 1945-1950, op. cit.*

[12] Dominique Desanti, interview with the author, February 2006.

[13] *Lettres à Nelson Algren, op. cit.* (Letter of June 12 1947). Simone de Beauvoir's lectures were about the writer's responsibility, as Existentialist a theme as any. Hence the surprise of the reporter of the *New Yorker* on discovering her: "Since in Paris she is considered Sartre's feminine double, we were prepared for a half-hour of lugubrious conversation. Well, surprise! Mlle de Beauvoir is the prettiest Existentialist we have ever seen; she is as intense, sweet, modest and delighted as a provincial girl from the Midwest with her two weeks in New York."

Besides Armstrong, a marvellous pianist by the name of Hines or something like that was playing, and the clarinet, the trombone, the drums, and the double bass were the best in the USA. A big fat Black woman, Middleton, sang admirably.[14] In the afternoon a pleasant get-together was organized at the home of old Gallimard who opened up his beautiful apartment to the Blacks of *Présence africaine* (African Presence) in order to receive Louis Armstrong. All of the black French intellectuals, all of the Parisian artists were crowding in." On March 22 1948: "I attended a magnificent concert by Mezz Mezrow in an immense hall overflowing with frenzied young people, applauding, screaming, throwing kisses, I was filled with enthusiasm. I adore the good old jazz."

She would be spoilt for choice. In the column he wrote for *Combat*, on February 25 1949, "It's Going to be Hot at the Salle Pleyel," Boris Vian announced the Jazz Festival 49, which would take place in the hall of the Faubourg Saint-Honoré from May 8 to 15: "We expect to see Charlie Parker, the brilliant alto saxophone, a creator with Dizzy Gillespie of the bop style, Miles Davis, a trumpeter still relatively unknown in France, but very sensational, Max Roach, one of the two best drummers at present in the United States (the other is our friend Kenny Clarke), Ray Brown, Ella Fitzgerald's favourite bassist. They also talk about Art Tatum, Sidney Bechet… In any case, things are going to get hot at the Salle Pleyel…" And, in fact, things did get hot! Moreover it was during the course of this same festival that Miles Davis heard Bechet play for the first time: "He thought that it was very similar to Johnny Hodges. This is not a silly remark, really, when you think of it…"[15] He also fell under the spell of Juliette Gréco. And vice versa: "I had never seen a man as handsome and I have never seen a handsomer one since," recalled Gréco.[16] "I was in the wings and he was playing. I could see him in profile: an Egyptian god." They were, both of them, barely more than twenty years old, they were in love, they knew no doubt that their love was condemned in the short run—distance, ordinary racism… Their idyll belongs today to the jazz legend. And to the official history of Saint-Germain-des-Prés.

In Saint-Germain-des-Prés, where, henceforth, the Club Saint-Germain would enjoy pride of place. The inauguration, on Friday June 11 1948,

---

[14] These were Earl "Fatha" Hines, 1903-1983, and Velma Middleton, 1917-1961.

[15] *Combat*, May 13 1949.

[16] Quoted in Bertrand Dicale, *Gréco, les vies d'une chanteuse, op. cit.*

became a social event—"the last big unifying event in Saint-Germain-des-Prés."[17] The rue Saint-Benoît remained blocked by cars for several hours, while the bottleneck was spreading little by little, like a tide, on the rue de l'Université, and the boulevard Saint-Germain... The police was overwhelmed. "Nearly three thousand people thought they had been invited. Two thousand seven hundred at least remained outside, for lack of room."[18] And invitation cards. Certain people did not hesitate to get them on the black market—going, it is said, as far as paying up to 5000 francs. At the entrance, François de La Rochefoucauld, better known in Saint-Germain-des-Prés under the pseudonym of François Carennes, was designated to scrutinize the precious passes, assisted by Tarzan (ninety kilos for one metre seventy-eight), a famous figure in the neighbourhood, "the biggest loudmouth among the loudmouths at the Tabou," according to Vian. *Samedi-Soir*—which knew everything!—asserted that the future Duke de Liancourt, just twenty-eight years old, "screened the clientele with a glacial authority" and turned back all the BOFs.[19] And, with a photo as proof, *Samedi-Soir* also declared that he was spinning out love's sweet dream with a young model from Schiaparelli, Annabel Schwob de Lur...[20]

Christian Casadesus had a vivid memory of this inaugural evening: "The rue Saint-Benoît was obstructed by the line of cars. The whole of Paris was there. A compact crowd, that pushed against the sidewalk to enter. When the door finally opened, Bois Vian on the trumpet tore into *Some of These Days*, the piece that Sartre had made famous in *La Nausée* (*Nausea*)."[21] Eight days later, *Samedi-Soir*, still at it, gave an account of the evening. In its fashion: "At ten paces from the Flore, the Club Saint-Germain-des-Prés, the new headquarters of mundane Existentialism, was inaugurated in a climate resembling the storming of the Bastille. Right at 11 in the evening, a New Look[22] crowd, estimated at several thousand people, tried to storm the new catacomb. Three hundred invitations had

---

[17] *Ibid.*

[18] Marc Doelnitz, *La Fête à Saint-Germain-des-Prés, op. cit.*

[19] During the years that followed the Second World War, this abbreviation (Beurre Oeufs Fromage/Butter Eggs Cheese) designated the shopkeepers who had become rich in the food supply business thanks to the black market during the Occupation.

[20] *Samedi-Soit*, January 29 1949. The newspaper was referring of course to the future Annabel Buffet.

[21] Interview with the author, November 2006.

[22] "New Look" designated the dress style launched by Christian Dior, precisely in 1948. It was at the time the latest in fashion: tight waist, long skirt...

been sent out. At midnight the traffic was interrupted on the Place Saint-Germain-des-Prés. At midnight thirty, in the cellar of the Club, renowned for it coolness, the thermometer hit 60 degrees Centigrade. An enormous Tarzan, entrusted with the screening at the door, was trampled on. In the cellar, Odette de Joyeux began to groan: 'I can't breath anymore. –Breath what?' Asked Boris Vian, himself livid. Odette Joyeux fainted right then and there. In any event, more than twenty customers were reported to have passed out that night. Maurice Chevalier and Nita Raya, who stayed for a quarter of an hour, each lost 800 grams. Sartre, awaited like the Messiah, made his entrance at one in the morning. At 1:03, overcome by nausea, he withdrew hurriedly, surrounded by seventy reporters. ... The new Tabou resembles an aquarium, a steam room, the vaulted ceiling of an overhead metro and a Surrealist chapel. Light is provided by candles and the walls are decorated with the old debris of a Louis XIV frigate."[23]

Samedi-Soir went too far! The "old debris" of a frigate were sculpted and painted pieces of wood of the finest quality, coming from an antique wooden horse merry-go-round—this one, indeed, built with the remains of a former and authentic frigate. From the time of Louis XVI, not of Louis XIV! A large and magnificent cardboard horse's head, the famous painting by Émile Binet, *Saint-Germain-des-Prés*, the portrait of a bearded woman—"who resembled Christian Bérard," according to Marc Doelnitz—completed the decorations in which, moreover, Christian Bérard himself had a hand. The cellar was very attractive: "Situated in the basement of the Deux Magots, admirably decorated in a wild yet agreeable style, the night club is home to the best jazz in Paris, an excellent little orchestra, and young adults dance there like gods. It is the young man with the trumpet who conducts."[24]

Before slamming the door at the Tabou, Frédéric Chauvelot made sure he had a fall back position. And not just of any kind: the most beautiful basement in the neighbourhood that he had been eyeing covetously for a long time. Three cellars connected to one another, situated under the large building that housed the Society for the Encouragement of National Industry dominating the square, opposite the church of Saint-Germain-des-Prés. It turned out that the wife of the President of that society, Louis Breguet, was a friend of Anne-Marie Cazalis. The latter

---

[23] *Samedi-Soir*, June 14, 1948.

[24] Simone de Beauvoir, *Lettres à Nelson Algren, op. cit.* (Letter of August 8 1948). The "young man with the trumpet" is of course Boris Vian.

was thus in charge of negotiating the deal. Which she concluded in the best conditions, since Louis Breguet happened to be completely charmed by the project: not only would the rent be modest, but the Society of Encouragement committed itself to take charge of a portion of the renovations. Paul Boubal would make up the difference, because Christian Casadesus succeeded in convincing him to participate in the financial mounting of the operation. Not without difficulty, because the owner of the Café de Flore was not the kind of man to rush into things with his eyes closed. And then one fine day: "From Boubal's place, whose apartment dominated the square, one could see very well the Flore's terrace and the junction of the rue Saint-Benoît. One evening when I was dining at his home, I asked him: 'Imagine a club there, on the rue Saint-Benoît, opposite the bar du Montana, and all the people who would arrive by car, the crowd that would stand in line...' Whereupon, he answered me: 'I want to be part of it.' He negotiated with Chauvelot, then we went to a lawyer, maître Izard, to close the deal."[25]

So work could start. A staircase in concrete, cobbled together, came down to the sidewalk on the rue Saint-Benoit, from which the club would be accessed, up by number 13—so that indeed, as Simone de Beauvoir said, one might believe that the cellar belonged to the Deux Magots. "The three rooms, encumbered with iron scrap, were just waiting for the rag and bone men to empty them, for the demolition crews to connect them through a system of arcs, for the electricians to pierce the walls and place their wires, for the people of the CPDE to lower a transformer four metres down."[26] All that was left to do was to install a bar, bathrooms, a cloakroom, and a service area... The Club Saint-Germain-des-Prés was born. Everyone would call it the Club Saint-Germain. It was shorter and more convenient.

Thirty years later, when writing her Mémoirs, Anne-Marie Cazalis would not be wrong when she affirmed that Frédéric Chauvelot, a shrewd businessman, was able, thanks to his contacts in the world of fashion and show business, to sustain and develop the Saint-Germain-des-Prés phenomenon. A phenomenon that would, in actual fact, with

---

[25] Christian Casadesus, interview with the author, November 2006.
[26] Boris Vian, *Manuel de Saint-Germain-des-Prés, op. cit.* The CPDE was the Compagnie parisienne de distribution d'électricité (The Parisian Company for the Distribution of Electricity). Électricité de France (France Electricity) was created in April 1946, but when Vian wrote these lines, he was still using the former nomenclature.

the Club Saint-Germain, move into high gear. Until it knew a kind of apotheosis. The atmosphere that reigned at the Tabou, the party for the party's sake, without any reservations, had nothing more in common with the one at the Club Saint-Germain. Under the influence of Boris Vian, it became within several weeks a true temple of jazz, where all the musicians passing through Paris would stop. And they were many, in those post-war years: Charlie Parker, Max Roach, Hot Lips Page, Buck Clayton, Kenny Clarke, Moody, Don Carlos Byas, Ernie Royal, Coleman Hawkins... The temple of jazz and the real rendezvous of fashionable people. Because at the Club, henceforth, they dressed well. No more checked shirts, no more wrap-around skirts or sneakers; on the occasion of Duke Ellington's appearance, on June 19 1948, the invitation card stated explicitly: "Evening attire."

That evening, organized by the cinema producer Jules Borkon, a sort of preview of the two concerts that the musician was to give at Pleyel, was such an event that the press became its resonating chamber[27]. First of all by "covering" the arrival of the Duke, received like a star at the Gare du Nord railway station, where Boris Vian was part of the welcoming committee: "And the Duke, preceded by an impressive pile of baggage, appeared at last on the step... Stampede of admirers, of autographs, an entourage following him until he exited the station (all the stars of Saint-Germain-des-Prés were present, the dark Gréco, the redhead Simone Signoret, and I would make sure not to forget my blond wife). Duke, smiling, is greeted in the main hall of the station by Claude Bolling's band. Newscasters, autograph seekers, crowds, crowds, crowds..."[28] A few hours later, on rue Saint-Benoît, "four policemen (hired, without white gloves, at 80 francs for the evening) casually pushed back the celebrities who were shoving one another without any courtesy and who, in their social absent-mindedness, had forgotten to reserve their seats. Mme Schiaparelli's dress projected a black spot among the multicoloured evening gowns."[29] Among the guests: Yves Allégret, Alexandre Astruc, Georges Auric, Sylvia Bataille and her husband, Jacques Lacan, the

---

[27] As for Vian, he did a review of these two concerts in *Combat*, on July 25: "He is a great guy. I loathe saying things like that, it seems idiotic. But in the case of Duke, it is so true. Heck, when you think of the importance the Americans have given to that twit Gershwin. They have something better at hand. And he, at least, is alive..."

[28] *Combat*, July 20 1948.

[29] Jean Maury, *Combat*, July 20 1948.

Bouglione brothers, Jean Genet, Yves Montand, Simone Signoret, Roger Vailland, Nicole Védrès, Richard Wright—in short, the smart set of Saint-Germain-des-Prés. At midnight, when Duke Ellington finally arrived, the excitement reached its paroxysm. The doors closed behind him and, as the journalist of *Combat* said, everyone could suffocate to his heart's content. "Clark Gable and Katherine Hepburn who were supposed to come, would perhaps remain outside, but so much the worse."[30]

The golden age of the Club Saint-Germain was beginning. Between "Jazz Nights" and "Theme Nights"—"Night of Innocence," "1925 Night"—Parisian personalities in the public eye were jostling one another to get in. Using a major alibi: charity. As *Combat* explained to its readers, in its edition of June 30 1948: "Henceforth, just like the Lady Bountiful women of the neighbourhood, the Existentialists would have their good works. Since charity required money and the Existentialists hardly had any, the curious visitors would pay. Once a month, in the cellar of the rue Saint-Benoît, a big gala would be organized in favour of a charitable association. The first 'Night,' the '1925 Night,' would be held on July 9, for the 'Children of Artists.' The ladies invited would have to wear dresses made twenty-three years earlier, the orchestra would forget swing in order to remember 'Tea for Two,' 'Zaza,' or 'Nono Nanette.'"

And, in fact, on Friday July 9, just at midnight, Boris Vian, blowing into his trumpet, opened the dancing to the rhythm of the Charleston, while Princess Rospoli, wearing a cloche hat pulled right down over her eyes, and a dress cut above her knees, put on high-heels in the purest style of the Roaring Twenties, soon imitated by "a whole high class society in bewildering outfits: Mmes de Toulouse-Lautrec and de La Rochefoucauld, Marie-Laure de Noailles, Mme Lazard."[31] It was the fashion designer Pierre Balmain who thought up the idea of this "1925 Night," when he had just designed the costumes for a revival of *Pas sur la bouche* (*Not on the Mouth*), the operetta by Maurice Yvain, created, precisely, in 1925. And these "bewildering outfits"—dresses with multicoloured spangles, fans made of ostrich feathers, paste headbands, aigrettes—over which the journalists were going into raptures, were the very ones worn by his models, who had come with him for the event. They were joined by Mathilde Casadesus, Nicole Védrès, the eccentric Renée Passeur, with her false eyelashes hanging out... In the audience

---

[30] *Ibid.*

[31] *Samedi-Soir*, July 17 1948.

one caught sight of Christian Bérard, Louis Ducreux; the ex-star of the ABC and the Folies-Bergères, the beautiful Spinelly, an authentic top performer of the 1920s and 30s, sang *Nuit de Chine* (China Night) at the top of her lungs, no doubt to remind herself of her youth, while André Luguet, who had just celebrated at the Théâtre Antoine the 100th performance of *Les Mains sales*, howled in her ear, to cover the noise of the music: "My poor Spi, now I can tell you this. You see, Rosine, my daughter... Well, I almost thought of you the day that I made her!"[32]

The "Beach Night," the "American Night" would soon follow... And that famous "Night of Innocence," on June 1 1949, during which would be chosen "the Village Maiden of Saint-Germain-des-Prés." The invitation, printed on immaculate lacy paper, set the tone for the evening and informs us, at the same time, about the price of the festivities: "Night of Innocence* Wednesday June 1 1949* At the Club Saint-Germain-des-Prés* 13, rue Saint-Benoît* In aid of Children Charities* Dress code in the spirit of innocence compulsory* Seating capacity limited at 150* Pick up tickets at the Club by showing this card (members 200 francs, guests 500 francs)." Two days later, under the pen of Sylvain Zegel, *Combat* ran the headline: "Among the good angels and the guilty consciences, Saint-Germain-des-Prés crowned its innocent maid." Then it gave a detailed account of the evening: "The members of the jury were severe. First of all because there were in the audience psychoanalysts and personages whose innocence could not be questioned. The walls were adorned with daisies, streamers and Chinese lanterns. Among the jurors could be found the angelic Boris Vian, the pure Anne-Marie Cazalis, the innocent Marc Doelnitz, the juvenile Merleau-Ponty, the ingénue Simone Signoret, the discreet France Roche or yet Pierre Brasseur. They asked of the postulants questions of a bawdy nature and made them undergo tests... Howls of joy greeted the election of the 'Rosière' (Innocent Maid) who had successfully handled all of the exams." Among the jury members we also note the presence of the painter Félix Labisse, and of François Chalais. The winner, barely twenty years old, was called Édith:[33] with miraculous red hair, all decked out in pink, like a baby, a ribbon tied in her hair, she had "more freckles than it

---

[32] *Ibid.* Colette said about Spinelly (Élise Fournier, 1887-1966): "An incomparably feminine body, a supple back, radiant breasts, a conquering ankle, a face, a mouth that seem to drink the air without letting her lips touch it" (*La Jumelle noire*, November 14 1937, "Spinelly à l'ABC", Flammarion, 1973).

[33] She was the actress Édith Perret, who was then a student in Charles Dullin's course.

was decent to have," declared Vian. A "certificate of satisfaction," signed by Frédéric Chauvelot, testified to the ingenuousness of "Édith-la-Rosière" (Édith the Innocent Maid). For his part, Marc Doelnitz disguised himself as a little boy: "I appeared as a little boy in shorts, with a beret pulled down to my eyes, a good conduct cross around my neck, and stockings. There was a multitude of good sisters, of priests, of sacrificial virgins in undergarments. Zacharias, a musician in the Claude Luter orchestra, had made himself up as an astonished Harpo Marx and angels were dancing. The success was equal to the enterprise's moral quality..."[34] As for Juliette Gréco, she wore the costume of the perfect little girl, Anne-Marie Cazalis sported the crown of a young girl making her first communion (and "her most deceitful air," said Gréco). Boris Vian, with his pants rolled up above his knees, played the reed-pipe—a faun or a shepherd?...

But the rivals of the Club Saint-Germain, worried about this success that was depriving them of a good part of their clientele, had already lit backfires. "Saint-Germain-des-Prés is no longer a land of peace," *Samedi-Soir* explained to its readers. Ever since the birth of the club on the rue Saint-Benoît and the resurrection of the Rose Rouge, the Tabou looks like a poor relation. Boris Vian, Anne-Marie Cazalis and Gréco have dropped it and have abandoned it to its fate as a neighbourhood bistro. It was necessary to save the Tabou. From that night on its organizers took action to save it..." How? By organizing a "Night!" An umpteenth Night, one called the "Fête in the Village," in the month of July 1949. With an orchestra used for country weddings, paper garlands—and, at midnight, a herd of goats that tumbled down a steep staircase...Or a "Night of Lust," as an answer, naturally, to the "Night of Innocence," during the course of which the young Diane Erdos, 17 years old, would be completely undressed by the jury, in front of Freddy Baume's camera, before winning the coveted title of "Miss Vice"...But the Vice Squad, that got wind of the affair, viewed the film for itself. One did not play around with morals, in those years of generalized prudishness. The Tabou would remain closed for two months, by a prefectorial decision. While between the cellar nightclubs the war went on more relentlessly.[35] Even if it was limited to a musical war, a jazz war: the Club du Vieux-Colombier was "New Orleans," the Club Saint-Germain was "bop"...

---

[34] *La Fête à Saint-Germain-des-Prés, op. cit.*

[35] *Le Parisien libéré* of June 11-12 1949 carried this headline: "The war of the cellar night clubs seethes in Saint-Germain-des-Prés."

Everyone was putting on his "Night": "Venitian Night," with Boris Vian dressed up as a Doge; "Night at the Port," where Lilli Palmer, Rex Harrison and Jean-Pierre Aumont danced to the rhythm of rascally refrains coming from sailors' bars; "Chicago Night," where the crew of the film *Rendez-vous de Juillet* (July Rendezvous), then in full production, got their kicks, as we would say today: Daniel Gélin, Jacques Becker, Nicole Courcel, Maurice Ronet; "Unusual Night", "Cannibal Night", "Western Night", "New Orleans Night"…

At the Tabou, at the Club Saint-Germain, at the Rose Rouge, at the Club du Vieux-Colombier—inaugurated at the end of 1948, after the "Lorientais" shut up shop—where Claude Luter played, a renegade from the rue des Carmes, and Sidney Bechet, on his return from America, it was a continuous party: "Evening after evening, the hours were madly light-hearted and carefree. From a slow with Dolorès del Rio, the exotic Hollywood star, I fell into the arms of a dancer from the Katherine Dunham ballet troupe. Everyone offered himself a celebration according to his means. During these days following the world conflict when nevertheless the only issues were the Cold War, the balance of terror and the Berlin blockade, we were really not conscious of dancing on a volcano. The world couldn't be crazy enough to start it all up again, and then the uncertainties of the dark years had taught us to take advantage immediately of what was offered to us."[36]

---

[36] Marc Doelnitz, *La Fête à Saint-Germain-des-Prés, op. cit.*

12

The publication of I Will Spit on Your Graves *and of* The Second Sex *caused a scandal. Through them, it was Saint-Germain-des-Prés that was being attacked, Existentialism, the Tabou, the corrupt youth of the cellar night clubs ...*

Le Prix du Tabou (The Tabou Prize) was awarded for the first time in the month of December 1947 to the novelist Sally Mara, for her novel *On est toujours trop bon avec les femmes* (*One is Always too Good to Women*), published by the very young Éditions du Scorpion, housed on the rue Lobineau, that is to say in the very heart of the Saint-Germain-des-Prés village. A strange prize! And that did not in the least hide its agenda. Boris Vian, associated with the Éditions du Scorpion, took it upon himself to explain to us how it worked: "Le Prix du Tabou, a prize awarded in advance, like the others, presents this distinctive characteristic of being the only one to admit this without the slightest embarrassment. It is the only honest prize of the year, awarded by the authors of Le Scorpion to the authors of Le Scorpion, and feted by the director of Le Scorpion."[1] A director whose avowed goal was to boost his sales.

The latter, Jean d'Halluin, was an enterprising man. He was on a roll and knew how to attract promising young authors, like Yvan Audouard or Jacques Robert; his "in your face" covers, red and black, designed by the painter Jean Cluseau-Lanauve, coincided with the taste of the day and drew the eye to bookstore windows. "Jean d'Halluin was one of the first to understand the major role that the Café de Flore played in the mythology of Saint-Germain-des-Prés. Sure that he was doing

---

[1] *Manuel de Saint-Germain-des-Prés, op. cit.*

the right thing, he wanted to get Paul Boubal to write his Memoirs, but Boubal never wanted to do it..."² On the other hand, Raymond Queneau agreed very willingly to collaborate with the Éditions du Scorpion, on condition he could use an assumed name in order not to displease his editor and patron, Gaston Gallimard. This name, the three accomplices, d'Halluin, Vian, Queneau, would make up: Sally Mara, whom the editor introduced thus to its readers: "A young Irishwoman of great talent who experienced for her French professor, Michel Presle, an unrequited passion, and died miserably in rather unclear conditions." As for the title—*On est toujours trop bon avec les femmes*—one can easily guess Vian's style here. Raymond Queneau, ex-Surrealist, mad about mathematics, future founder, with the mathematician François Le Lionnais, of l'Oulipo (OUvroir de LIttérature POtentielle/The Working Room for Potential Literature), was delighted to play this good trick on the Parisian literary milieu.³

A trick? Yes, but not the first one. One year earlier, Jean d'Halluin published at Scorpion, with a big publicity barrage, the novel of a Black American author, Vernon Sullivan, *J'irai cracher sur vos tombes*. The so-called Black American writer was none other than Boris Vian. And the book, a skilful mixture of eroticism, pornography, violence and racism, all of it floating in the humid atmosphere of the South, provoked, as soon as it appeared, a first-class scandal that would end on the benches of the 17th Magistrates Court.

The American novel was at the time extremely fashionable. In fact, everything coming from the States—books, but also films, jazz...—and of which the French had been deprived for more than four years, was, at present, the object of a veritable infatuation. *Autant en emporte le vent* (*Gone with the Wind*), although translated and published as of 1939, was still listed among the bestsellers. Gallimard, for its part, launched the "Série Noire" (Black Series) through Marcel Duhamel's initiative, a collection whose name, invented by Jacques Prévert, indicated clearly that the purpose was to acclimatize in France the authors of black novels and Anglo-Saxon detective stories: Peter Cheney, Horace McCoy, James

---

² Christian Casadesus, interview with the author, November 2006.

³ Raymond Queneau had already been, in 1933, the first winner of the Prize of the Deux Magots for his novel *Le Chiendent*. Other books receiving awards from the jury members of the Prix du Tabou: *Marie-Octobre* by Jacques Robert, in 1948, *De deux choses l'une*, by Maurice Raphaël the following year. Both, of course, published by the Éditions du Scorpion, as the prize regulation dictated.

Hadley Chase, etc. In addition, the French public, just recently delivered from a moral order imposed by Vichy, craved more licence. Soon, the brand new Éditions Jean Froissart would enjoy an enormous success with the work by Cécil Saint-Laurent, *alias* Jacques Laurent, *Caroline chérie* (*Darling Caroline*) a popular novel that would crystallize the naughty desires of a society thirsting for emancipation.

This was what Jean d'Halluin had understood well. And this was what he explained to Boris and Michelle Vian, one evening when he met them in a queue at the movies. And because he knew, as did everyone in Saint-Germain-des-Prés, that Boris, without having ever set foot there, had an excellent knowledge of the United States, he asked the latter to uncover there the providential author. It went without saying that he would translate and adapt the work into French. Vian did not take long to give his answer. Rather than a laboured translation, he proposed to write directly a false Black American novel. "A first: the imitation of the crude style, of the violence, of the humour of this literature of which the French seemed to be so fond for the past two years. A good prank. The infatuation was such, that editors extremely eager to promote new American authors could easily impose, in the confusion, a writer who didn't exist."[4] Jean d'Halluin didn't hesitate either. Vian knew Anglo-Saxon literature well enough to pull off this pastiche. It was yes.

J'irai cracher sur vos tombes would be written in two weeks, from August 5 to 20 1946. A record. In Vendée and in Paris. The story is about a "white Negro," Lee Anderson, ravaged by hatred following the lynching of his young brother, who becomes through vengeance a serial rapist and murderer of white girls. Was Vian even a bit worried about the outcome? The fact remained that he solicited the advice of Marcel Duhamel, another great specialist of American literature: "One day Boris handed me a manuscript and asked me to tell him if, in my opinion, it was an original or a translation of an American text. The systematic violence, a certain attitude towards Black people seemed fabricated to me and put me off a bit. But for me, Vernon Sullivan, the author, was really an American. Boris seemed quite happy. He really tricked me…"[5]

Produced in an equally record time, the book was in the bookstores in the month of November, under the name Vernon Sullivan, Boris Vian appearing only as the translator. Few were in the know and those few

---

[4] Philippe Boggio, *Boris Vian, op. cit.*

[5] Marcel Duhamel, *Raconte pas ta vie, op. cit.*

promised to keep it a secret. An absolute secret, but not really watertight, as we will soon see. D'Halluin did his work well. *Franc-Tirerur,* in its November 25 issue, published "advanced sheets" of the book, carefully chosen, while Boris went up to the front line and presented the work before a learned assembly of journalists brought together at the Club du Faubourg: "A literary work must provoke a shock, engender as violent a malaise as possible." He took up this idea again and developed it in a text that was one-half a "please insert," one-half an advertising claim, that he sent to the press: "The first novel of this young author whom no American editor dared publish denounces in pages of an unheard-of violence, and in a style which is equal to that of great predecessors like Caldwell, Faulkner and Cain, the unjust suspicion levelled against the Blacks in certain regions of the United States."[6] And he added: "A harsh depiction, marked by a cruel and total eroticism, that will undoubtedly scandalize as much as the most daring pages of Miller. A novel such as has never been written."

Who was the first to leak the secret? Very quickly, as of January 1947, that is to say barely two months after its publication, the rumour spread: Vernon Sullivan did not exist, the author and translator were the same person. And what had to happen indeed happened: on February 7, the Public Prosecutor's Office opened a preliminary investigation against the author and editor of *J'irai cracher sur vos tombes,* based on a complaint by the Cartel for Social and Moral Action. Its director, Daniel Parker, an architect by profession, pointing to the Daladier law of July 1939, still in use, concerning the protection of the French family. A singular man, this Parker. On the one hand, he was a kind of uptight prude, an austere puritan who was not afraid, in the past, to attack the books of Henry Miller and who campaigned actively to close the brothels; on the other, he was a convinced pacifist, a defender of deserters and conscientious objectors…

Coup de theatre: on April 29, a travelling salesman, Edmond Rougé, an ex-Nazi collaborator, strangled his mistress in a hotel room on the rue du Départ, in Montparnasse; on the bed was discovered a copy of *J'irai cracher sur vos tombes,* opened on the very page where was described the murder by strangulation of one of the heroines of the book… An outcry in the press: we told you so, this contemptible book is an incitement to crime, a perverter of our beautiful youth, etc. "We move from obscenity to horror. The newspapers flash the headline: 'The Novel that Kills' and

---

[6] Quoted in Philippe Boggio, *Boris Vian, op. cit.*

the scandal takes on overblown proportions."[7] All this annoyed Vian. Even if he could not refrain—it was in his nature—from feeling jubilation over the spectacle of the journalists' stupidity, the "rubbish churners" as he called them, who published his photo next to the one of the murderer, who piled on the commentaries, quoting without scruples passages from the book: "The excerpt that inspired the assassin", "Having read these words, Edmond strangled Marie-Anne", "an Existentialist crime"...All the while the clever editor, for his part, speeded up the reprints of the work. A news item had come to the rescue of the book's sales: moderate beforehand, they at last took off.

Naturally, through *J'irai cracher sur vos tombes*, it was Saint-Germain-des-Prés that was being targeted, Jean-Paul Sartre, Existentialism, the Tabou, the corrupt youth of the cellar night clubs... The press attacked Vian in order to make him confess the hoax; so that he would spill the dope, once and for all. But he held his ground. One evening, at the Tabou, an American female journalist persisted: she declared in a loud voice that he, Boris Vian, was the author of *J'irai cracher sur vos tombes*. She absolutely wanted him to acknowledge it in public. Dominique Desanti witnessed the scene: "Every time the music stopped, he came back to sit at the table where the journalist was waiting for him. And she started up again...'What makes you think such a thing?' he asked her, sardonically. And she answered: 'Your language, your way of speaking.' He pretended to be astounded: 'But I don't always talk about spit!—Well, she said, who wrote it, this book, if it isn't you?—It is signed, the author is Vernon Sullivan!' It went on like that the whole evening. It amused him. Moreover, Boris' conversation always unfolded in a kind of second degree, so that his interlocutors never knew exactly what to think of it. Was it simply a case of 'dubbing' the conversation, as though it were a game, or did he really believe what he was saying?..."[8]

In this affair, one must admit that Boris Vian was not pussyfooting around. And he even overdid it, exploiting his success to the very limit. Too much, perhaps, at the risk of justifying his detractors. Thus it was that a year later, on April 23 1948, he presented at the Théâtre Verlaine,[9] in Paris, *J'irai cracher sur vos tombes*, a stage version of his novel, put

---

[7] Geneviève Beauvarlet, *Boris Vian*, Hachette, 1982.

[8] Interview with the author, February 2008.

[9] The Theatre Verlaine, now no longer in existence, was located at 66 rue Rochechouart, in the 9th district. Later it took the name of Théâtre des Arts.

together and rehearsed in barely several weeks. "It was last December, one year after the publication of the book, that I was asked to work on its story for the theatre," Vian explained complacently. "I first made an adaptation of it in three acts and three décors. Then, on the advice of Pasquali, the director, it was reduced to only one décor: the back shop of Lee Anderson."[10] A very watered down version, as one can imagine, of the eponymous novel. It was indeed impossible to bring to the stage the rape, murder and sadism episodes that account for the substance of the book! And more than one enticed spectator would go home disappointed... As Noël Arnaud reminds us in his work *Les Vies parallèles de Boris Vian* (*The Parallel Lives of Boris Vian*):[11] "In the first rank of the voyeurs one remarks all those who for the past eighteen months have been vociferating against depraved novelists, against erotic literature, against corruptors of our beautiful youth, against the 'pornographer' Boris Vian." Vian himself, moreover, took the precaution of advising his future audiences: "I am anxious to warn people who expect to find scenes of rape or obscene words in this play that they will be wasting their time."[12] On the other hand, the whole part evoking the social and racial problems which the Black Americans confronted had been considerably enriched; but it was not this aspect of the play that drew the public. Not a large one in any event, no doubt discouraged by a reserved or sarcastic critical reception—such as the article by René Barjavel, who feigned to treat the performance in an offhand manner: "A very small thing around which they have tried to make a lot of noise and which we would not talk about if it had not made possible the putting on stage of four of the prettiest girls in Paris."[13] And on July 10, on the eve of the summer holidays, for lack of spectators, the Théâtre Verlaine closed its doors.

But Daniel Parker wouldn't give in and Boris Vian had not yet paid his debt to the justice system, even though a providential amnesty law, promulgated on August 16 1947, that exempted from legal proceedings works published before that date, gave him shelter temporarily. The

---

[10] *Combat*, April 21 1948.

[11] Christian Bourgois, 1984.

[12] *Combat*, april 21 1948.

[13] *Carrefour*, April 28 1948. Surrounding Daniel Ivernel, who played the role of Lee Anderson, the "four prettiest girls in Paris" were Anne Campion, Véra Norman, Jacqueline Pierreux and Danielle Godet.

more or less controversial performances of *J'irai cracher sur vos tombes* no doubt contributed to reminding the prudish architect about the "Edmond Rougé Affair" and the grievances that went with it. In addition, the editor, taking advantage of the scandal and its commercial fall out, put himself in the wrong by reprinting the book several times. And so Boris Vian was again summoned before the judge. As he explained it, the very next day, to the journalist of *Combat*, Jean-François Devay, who had come to interview him at his home. Was it self-interest? Weariness? Suddenly, during the course of the conversation, he acknowledged, as he had already done so the day before to the judge, that he was indeed the author of *J'irai cracher sur vos tombes*. Not without indulging, at the end of the interview, in one of those pirouettes which were customary with him: "I was summoned yesterday before M. Baurès, the Examining Magistrate,[14] who condemned me for affront to public decency." The journalist then asked him: "So you are being pursued for an amnestied offence?" Vian exclaimed immediately: "Oh no! Scorpion has reprinted the book quite a lot since then, 100,000 copies, I think."[15] But the reprinting was done in another printing firm and the new printer was not prosecuted. There followed a dialogue that Jean-François Devay reproduced up to the last coma:

"—It appears that you finally admitted, before M. Baurès, that you were the author of *J'irai cracher* ...

—Yes, but I lied.

—Could Vernon Sullivan exist?

—Obviously. The proof is that my books are written in a completely different style.

—Why did you accuse yourself?

—To save him. If he were prosecuted in France, he would have a bad time across the Atlantic.

—Will you introduce me to Vernon Sullivan?

—With pleasure. He will be in Paris at Christmas. Don't repeat this."[16]

It mattered little that Boris Vian, true to habit, was joking, pretending to retract, henceforth there was no doubt about it, and *Samedi-Soir,* several

---

[14] This was the same judge Baurès, certainly very much in demand in Saint-Germain-des-Prés, who would have Gabriel Pomerand jailed in 1950 (see note 14, page 147).

[15] Philippe Boggio, in *Boris Vian (op. cit)*, put forward the figure of 500,000 copies sold since the book's publication.

[16] *Combat*, November 24 1948.

days later, was not afraid to tell the truth bluntly: "Boris put himself to work seriously, aligned his twelve pages per day and finally produced *J'irai cracher sur vos tombes*. To spice up the best seller with a note of mystery, the Black man Vernon Sullivan was created. At first Scorpion printed 10,000 copies. This figure grew tenfold afterwards."[17] At the same time the newspaper informed its readers that the "author" risked two years in prison and a fine of 300,000 francs.

The affair came to an end in May 1950, before the 17th Magistrates' Court. Boris Vian and Jean d'Halluin were condemned jointly for "affront to public decency." With a derisory fine, in comparison to the sums the two men had pocketed. And the fact that the novel was henceforth prohibited did not cause them great harm: By that date, all the juice had already been squeezed out of *J'irai cracher sur vos tombes*... Let us be reassured: as of 1953, an amnesty law would allow its publication again."[18]

As far as scandals go, the one caused by the publication of *Le Deuxième Sexe* in 1949 wasn't bad either.[19] Even if this one was not orchestrated! In *La Force des choses*, Simone de Beauvoir related the genesis of this book, the project of which took shape in October 1946. Determined to undertake an essay on her own experience, she became aware of the fact that a first question had to be asked before she could even begin: "What had it meant for me to be a woman?" Just as she was ready to overlook it, considering that her femininity had scarcely hindered her in any way in her life and ventures, Sartre advised her nonetheless to reconsider her position: "All the same, you were not raised in the same way as a boy: you should look at that more closely." "I did look," Beauvoir continued, "and I had a revelation: this world was a masculine world, my childhood had been sustained by myths forged by men and I had not reacted at all in the same way as though I had been a boy. This interested me so much that I abandoned the project of a personal confession in order to concentrate on the feminine condition in its generality."[20]

---

[17] *Samedi-Soir*, December 4 1948.

[18] In 1959, Michel Gast would film for the cinema a rather unfaithful adaptation of the novel, with Christian Marquand and Antonella Lualdi in the principal roles. We know that while attending the projection of the film Boris Vian succumbed to a heart attack.

[19] The first volume, *Les Faits et les Mythes*, appeared in June, the second, *L'Expérience vécue*, in November.

[20] Simone de Beauvoir, *La Force des choses*, op. cit.

Three years of work. Dozens of books consulted at the National Library. "I was indebted to my university training for my efficient working methods: I knew how to classify and peruse books quickly, to eliminate those which were only plagiarisms or fantasies; I drew up an almost exhaustive inventory of everything that had been printed in French and in English on the issue; it inspired an enormous body of literature but, as in many other cases, only a small number of these studies count."[21] Never had the feminine question, considered as a whole, given rise to such a labour. Nor such an approach: total, objective and free from any generally accepted ideas. It was a veritable enterprise of demystification. Or, better still, of demythification. The conclusion of the first chapter, titled "Biological Facts", gives the reader insight into the tone of the book: "She [the woman] is of all the female mammals the one who is the most profoundly alienated, and the one who most violently refuses this alienation; in no other is the enslavement of the organism for the reproductive function more imperious or accepted with more difficulty: puberty and menopause crises, monthly curse, long and often difficult pregnancies, painful and sometimes dangerous births, sicknesses, accidents are characteristics of the human female: one would say that her destiny is all the heavier because she rebels against it more by asserting herself as an individual."[22]

The first volume was rather well received by the public: 20,000 copies sold in several days. And the accustomed digs from *Samedi-Soir*, like that article titled "Simone de Beauvoir describes the torments of Lady Chatterley,"[23] went by almost unnoticed. Beavoir affirmed, in *La Force des choses*, that it was the launch of the second volume, in the autumn, that unleashed the scandal. Certainly. But it appeared to have been set in motion as of the month of May, with the pre-publication, in *Les Temps Modernes*, of a chapter called "The Woman's Sexual Initiation." François Mauriac's sadly famous remark to Jean Cau is widely known: "I've learned everything about your boss's vagina." He did not content himself with this remark, however, making as he did a kind of appeal to young people in *Le Figaro* of May 30 1949: "What are we bringing, today, to the young people of this world who read our magazines and our books and who capture the message of Saint-Germain-des-Prés?... We have reached the limits of the contemptible from the literary point of view... But the contemptible

---

[21] *Ibid.*

[22] Simone de Beauvoir, *Le Deuxième Sexe*, vol. I, *Les Faits et les Mythes*, Gallimard, 1949.

[23] *Samedi-Soir*, May 28 1949.

is never beautiful. Do Sade and his emulators fall within the province of psychiatry or literature? Does the subject discussed by Mme Simone de Beauvoir: 'Woman's Sexual Initiation,' belong in the table of contents of a serious philosophical and literary review? Are we not the victims of an equivocation, of a confusion exploited by the directors of the modern consciousness who conform to a preconceived plan?" And he ends by calling on "all twenty-year-old Christians" to express themselves, to give their opinion on the issue. Replies, for or against, to this opinion poll, published in *Le Figaro* from June 25 to August 6, would not be lacking.[24]

Mauriac was not the only one to react in this way. Even among the intimates of the author, some of them balked. Albert Camus, for his part, as though deeply wounded in his virile Mediterranean pride, reproached Simone de Beauvoir for having ridiculed the French male. During the course of the summer, *Paris-Match* got involved and offered its readers substantial excerpts from the book, under the title "Simone de Beauvoir, the first woman philosopher, has just written 800 revolutionary pages on a pedestal table of the Flore." The article accompanying these passages was rather favourable to her: "Everyone, in the sky of dreams in Saint-Germain-des-Prés, reserves the place of honour for this beautiful woman with the austere and serene face."[25] The problem was not there. In actual fact, whether they were benevolently or malevolently disposed, when they spoke about *Le Deuxième Sexe*, journalists never forgot to cite Saint-Germain-des-Prés, this crucible of all the turpitudes imaginable, suspected of corrupting morals. And, of course, of greatly corrupting the youth.

The Vatican blacklisted the book. The Communists were unanimous in rejecting the work, affirming—an irrefutable argument—that it would make the female workers of Billancourt laugh a lot.[26] Coming from the Right, the same discourse: "I was a 'poor little girl,' neurotic, repressed, frustrated, disinherited, virago-like, insufficiently screwed, envious, an embittered woman crammed with inferiority complexes with respect to men, and with respect to women resentment was eating me up."[27]

---

[24] They can be consulted *in extenso*, compiled by Ingrid Galster, in her remarkable work *Le Deuxième Sexe de Simone de Beauvoir*, Presses de l'Université Paris-Sorbonne, 2004.

[25] *Paris-Match*, August 6 1949.

[26] Marie-Louise Barron, *Les Lettres françaises*, June 23 1949 : "I can imagine the big laughing success Mme de Beauvoir would have in a Billancourt workshop, for example, by presenting her liberating program of defrustration."

[27] Simone de Beauvoir, *La Force des choses, op. cit.*

"Embittered"? "Insufficiently screwed"? At the same time that she was working on the composition of *Le Deuxième Sexe*, Simone de Beauvoir experienced a burning passion for Nelson Algren. She was a woman who loved and was loved. The tone of the letters that she wrote every day to this lover, so sexually desired (as well as that of the rare letters from Algren that we know), do not allow us to doubt for one moment the sensual blossoming that she enjoyed in this love: "I will not allow you any respite at night, I will make sure that you really love me."[28]

---

[28] Simone de Beauvoir, *Lettres à Nelson Algren, op. cit.* (dated April 14 1948).

13

At the Club de la Rose Rouge, a new style was born, the cabaret theatre, that would mark a milestone and from which the café théâtres would be able to claim to take their inspiration twenty years later

In an interview he gave to *La Gazette de Lausanne* (The Lausanne Gazette), in October 1958, Boris Vian returned to the post-war period and attempted to explain, with the necessary distance, the reasons that turned this Parisian neighbourhood into one of the most famous places in the world: "In 1945, the young people lived in attics measuring three square metres. They would look for spots where they could meet." These were, as we have seen, the Bar Vert, the Tabou, "where anyone could improvise on the trumpet, dance without paying anything, quote anything that went through his head... There occurred an astonishing artistic and intellectual concentration around the old steeple of Saint-Germain-des-Prés: The Lorientais, where Claude Luter made his début... Further away the Fontaine des Quatre-Saisons; the Rose Rouge, with the Grenier-Hussenot company and Yves Robert who invented new forms of cabaret theatre and where the Frères Jacques performed..."

The Frères Jacques, but also, soon, Juliette Gréco, Léo Ferré, Cora Vaucaire, Mouloudji, Catherine Sauvage, the mime Marceau... In the whole country, a formidable cry for air pushed aside the old pre-war artistic glories, in favour of the newcomers—all those who during the years of the Occupation had been preparing themselves in the shadows and let their talent ripen secretly, before exploding in broad daylight. All the while Jean Sablon, Lucienne Boyer or Damia, stars of the 1930s, saw their star grow pale. Inexorably. Another generation was taking over. It would substitute jazz for the accordion, the song based on a text for the song for the voice, vitriol for rose water, the absurd for the rational.

In the opening pages of his work *Le Cabaret "rive gauche"* (*"The Left Bank" Cabaret*), Gilles Schlesser placed this excerpt from *Combat*, dated December 1944: "The day after the Parisian insurrection, the Parisian shows seemed to have aged and to have sunk into an already far-distant past."[1] It was true. Because in this immediate post-war France, where new ideas were spreading faster and deeper than one would have first thought, marked by political ambiguity and the uncertainties of the moment, the public would demand to find on the stage, embodied by new performers, the echo of these political, aesthetic and artistic changes. And it was in Saint-Germain-des-Prés, more often than not on little makeshift stages, that audiences would find them.

Changes? Yes. But changes that came from far, the inheritors of that "Café de Flore spirit" of which Simone de Beauvoir spoke in *La Force de l'âge* and which the Prévert of the Groupe Octobre or Agnès Capri illustrated. And it came from even further: the troupe of Les Copiaus, and that of the Comédiens routiers. As Martin Pénet, a historian of the chanson, explains it: "During the 1930s, the so-called avant-garde chanson, engaged or poetic, had at its disposal a very restricted audience. Nevertheless, it was during these same years that the new avant-garde, the one which would see the light between 1947 and 1950, over by Saint-Germain-des-Prés, was taking root. Three currents, that we can clearly identify, appeared in fact from those very years. A theatrical current, first of all, with the travelling troupe of Les Copiaus, created by Jacques Copeau, that included in its ranks Gilles and Julien. Then there was Léon Chancerel's, whose Les Comédiens routiers performed Choral singing and seemed to prefigure groups like les Frères Jacques or les Quatre Barbus (The Four Bearded Guys). Finally the Groupe Octobre."[2]

"Copiaus?" Copiaus, like Copeau. He who had directed the Théâtre du Vieux-Colombier since 1913, left the place abruptly in 1924.[3] And withdrew

---

[1] Gilles Schlesser, *Le Cabaret "rive gauche.» De la Rose rouge au Bateau ivre (1946-1974)*, L'Archipel, 2006.

[2] Interview with the author, November 2006. This chapter owes a great deal to the erudition of Martin Pénet.

[3] See *supra*, Chapter 1.

to Burgundy. Disappointed by the failures, the financial problems, the loss of interest shown by all kinds of people, he hoped to find in the provinces "an audience that was less frivolous, less distracted, less driven by pleasures, less enervated by the constant variations in fashion, less unsettled in its taste and less fluctuating in its judgement than the Parisian public."[4] Some disciples followed him in his retreat: Michel Saint-Denis, his nephew, Marie-Hélène Copeau, his daughter, and Jean Dasté, his future son-in-law, Étienne Decroux, Aman Maistre, Jean Villard, Léon Chancerel[5]...Actors, mimes, singers. The travelling troop of the "Copiaus"—this was how the Burgundy peasants would call them with their accent—was born from this gathering of friendships and talents. Without large financial means, the Copiaus reinvented in their way a French style *commedia dell'arte*. They would go from village to village, performing in the open air, on raised platforms slapped together, Molière farces, collective creations, with masks, improvisations, dance, mime, acrobatics, music...

Two men, Jean Villard and Aman Maistre, coming from the troupe, would join forces, under the name of "Gilles and Julien," transposing in their duo the spirit and technique of the Copiaus. "Their attitude on stage overturns all the conventions. Dressed in black pants and a black sweater (at a time when the tuxedo was de rigueur), they adjusted the lighting carefully. Gilles was seated before the piano, while Julien leaned on it nonchalantly with his elbows."[6] They had a repertoire that made no concessions, violently engaged, antimilitaristic, anarchistic, denouncing capitalism. Like the chanson *Dollar*, written in 1932. In short, they revolutionized the nature of the song as it was conceived at the time. Thus they opened up the road for the post-war interpreters: Juliette Gréco's black dress—her black working clothes, as she called it—stripped of all oraments, it accentuated the face and the hands of the singer; Mouloudji, wearing a black sweater, black pants, would not be afraid to interpret *Le Déserteur* (The Deserter), on the stage of the Théâtre de l'Oeuvre, the very day that Diên Biên Phu fell...

In actual fact, all through the 1930s, the chanson—at least, a certain chanson of quality—by working its way underground, or by taking side roads, imperceptible at the time, was preparing the wide avenues through which it would make its way after the Liberation. Mireille and

---

[4] Jacques Copeau, "Les Copiaus", *Revue de Bourgogne*, 1925.
[5] Léon Chancerel would leave the Copiaus in 1929 to create the Comédiens routiers, while Michel Saint-Denis would found the Compagnie des Quinze.
[6] Gilles Schlesser, *Le Cabaret "rive gauche"*, op. cit.

Jean Nohain, Charles Trenet, Marie Dubas, the Groupe Octobre, the Comédiens routiers, the Quatuor vocal des Compagnons de Route (The Vocal Quartet of the Road Buddies), that became later on the Quatre Barbus (The Four Bearded Guys) … : It was from this living pond that the young post-war artists would draw their inspiration.

But already Marianne Oswald, Agnès Capri or Lys Gauty brought a new style to the chanson.[7] Neither soppy nor whining. Rather a kind of realism, social or poetic.

Marianne Oswald had fled the Berlin of the Third Reich. With her husky, rough voice, her dramatic ugliness, her fire-red hair that seemed to burn her face, her expressionist gestures, she became as of 1932 a habitué of the cabaret Le Boeuf sur le Toit (The Ox on the Roof); Jean Cocteau wrote *Anna la Bonne* (*Good Anna*) for her; she added to her repertoire the French adaptations of the songs in *L'Opéra de quatr'sous* (*The Four Penny Opera*) and recorded, in 1935, *Embrasse-moi* (*Kiss Me*), by Jacques Prévert and Wal Berg—fifteen years before Juliette Gréco.

Lys Gauty, who declared to the press in 1951: "I believe I can say that I have defended what is best in the subtle and beautiful chanson, I have been one of the first to sing chansons of literary quality like the ones in *L'Opéra de quat'sous*,"[8] can be placed at the crossroads of the popular chanson and the avant-garde chanson. In her repertoire stand side by side, besides the famous and magnificent *Chaland qui passe* (The Passing Barge), the songs of *L'Opéra de quat'sous*, the charming story of the Two Snails, by Prévert and Kosma, and some compositions by Jean Tranchant—the Tranchant of the black period—like *La Ballade du cordonnier* (The shoemaker's Ballad).

Agnès Capri, a former student of Charles Dullin, began her career in 1936, in that nursery of real talents that was the Boeuf sur le Toit. Then it was the ABC that consecrated her. Before she opened her own cabaret in 1938, on the rue Molière, behind the Palais-Royal. A padded little hall, decorated by Sonia Mossé, a miniature stage, hidden behind a red curtain, a projector. "Agnès Capri, with an innocent air reflected in her angular face, sang the chansons of Prévert; she recited his poems, verses

---

[7] Marianne Oswald (Alice Bloch), 1901-1985; Agnès Capri (Sophie-Rose Friedmann), 1915-1976; Lys Gauty (Alice Gauthier), 1908-1994

[8] Florelle, the interpreter of the French version of the film by G.W. Pabst *L'Opéra de quat'sous*, also recorded these same songs, very fashionable among the intellectuals. Juliette Gréco will take them up during the 1950s, soon to be followed by Cora Vaucaire.

by Apollinaire; I enjoyed the acid freshness of her voice: I never grew weary of hearing her in *La Pêche à la baleine* (Whale hunting), nor of seeing the blossoming between her lips of the poisonous autumn crocus."[9] The Parisian intelligentsia hurried towards Agnès Capri's place. Germaine Montero would make her début there with a recital of Spanish songs.

In 1941, Capri engaged a young unknown, Cora Vaucaire, she who would be called, about ten years later, "The White Lady of Saint-Germain-des-Prés," because of her immaculate dress: "The place was not large. I remember some very beautiful automats, there were two at each side of the wall. So she [Agnès Capri] had mounted a show and had invited Raymond Bussières, Serge Reggiani, Jean Carmet, a stage actress by the name of Jenny Burnay. Mouloudji was also there, he, too, was very young. And there was Jacqueline Bouvier, who became Mme Marcel Pagnol."[10] And, of course, the lady of the house herself: "She was a marvellous woman, very intelligent and with incredible possibilities. When she did not have them, she invented them... Besides I never suspected that she had such a pretty voice, high pitched but delightful.... Agnès Capri had taste, wit, she is the one who invented everything in this trade, and notably the café theatre. In actual fact, hers was the first café theatre."[11]

But, on the horizon, the clouds were accumulating. The hunt for Jews was open. The first big round ups occurred in Paris as of the spring of 1941. First foreign Jews, then French ones, arrested right in the street or in their homes. At the end of the year, Agnès Capri closed her cabaret, went over to the free zone, then embarked for Algiers. Curtain.

The White Lady of Saint-Germain-des-Prés... White, because of the dress she wore when singing. Perhaps, but above all to distinguish her from the other, "The Black Lady"—Juliette Gréco.[12] She went on stage for the first time on June 22 1949, at the Boeuf sur le Toit. Incredible: "the nymph of Saint-Germain-des-Prés," as the newspapers called her, began her career on the right bank! And almost by accident.

---

[9] Simone de Beauvoir, *La Force de l'âge, op. cit.*

[10] Cora Vaucaire, in *Cora Vaucaire l'intemporelle*, interviews with Martin Pénet, Éditions de Fallois, 2006.

[11] *Ibid.*

[12] "At that time we were all broke. The young people in Saint-Germain-des-Prés wore black because it didn't get dirty, and I wore white because it could be washed..." Cora Vaucaire revealed to Martin Pénet (*ibid.*).

The Tabou then the Club Saint-Germain turned Gréco, within a few seasons, into a really Parisian figure, as they say. Even though she had not done anything yet, other than playing walk-on parts, contenting herself, as journalists desperate for stories emphasized, with being the muse of Existentialism. "She was a star, but she was a star of nothing," observed Guillaume Hanoteau. She was photographed; not a week went by without the press talking about her, with *Samedi-Soir* in the lead, evoking her long hair, her pale complexion. "They are starting to copy her way of making her eyes up. They are also copying her non-hairstyle, her use of black and her pants are all the rage."[13] And yet, since the short-lived adventure of *Victor ou les Enfants au pouvoir*, the theatre was ignoring her, the cinema forgot her, she hardly shot anything except silhouette appearances—a nun, a prison warden—in 1947, in *Les Frères Bouquinquant* (The Bouquinquant Brothers), by Louis Daquin, and Jean Cocteau had not yet started work on his film *Orphée* (*Orpheus*), in which she would play the role of Aglaonice, the queen of the Bacchants.[14] It didn't matter: "She watched. Indifferently."[15] Anne-Marie Cazalis, her friend and accomplice confirmed this: "Gréco was waiting, sprawled out on the present moment as though on a park bench. Patiently, she gazed at the sky."[16] She was waiting? For what? Her destiny, no doubt. There it was! It arrived.

Spring 1949. Louis Moysès, the founder in 1925 of the Boeuf sur le Toit, that famous landmark that moved from the rue Boissy-d'Anglas to the rue de Penthièvre, before settling in on the rue du Colisée, had just died. His sister and only heir, Mme Henriot, caught off guard, found herself at the head of an establishment that she was incapable of administrating, since she knew nothing about show business. It then occurred to her to have recourse to Marc Doelnitz, master of Parisian nocturnal entertainment, friend of duchesses and stars, whose reputation went beyond the limits of the 6th district and who had recently distinguished himself by participating in the organizing of large social festivities: at the home of Arturo Lopez, the king of tin; at the chateau of Corbeville, the domain of the fashion designer Jacques Fath...

---

[13] Juliette Gréco, *Jujube, op. cit.*

[14] We have seen that Juliett Gréco also participated in two films by Alexandre Astruc that would never be commercialized: *Aller-retour* and *Ulysse ou les Mauvaises Rencontres*.

[15] Juliette Gréco, *Jujube, op. cit.*

[16] *Les Mémoires d'une Anne, op. cit.*

One afternoon—it is Gréco herself who related the episode—while Doelnitz was visiting the Boeuf, empty at that hour, putting together plans and programs likely to awaken the old sleeping cabaret, an idea germinated suddenly in his brain. An idea that Anne-Marie Cazalis, who was accompanying him, had just whispered in his ear: "And if Gréco sang?" However softly she whispered, Juliette Gréco heard her. Sing? Why sing? An actress is what she wanted to be, not a chanteuse. And because she remained silent, as was her custom, she thought she had gotten rid of that preposterous idea. She was mistaken. Because that very evening, while they were walking down the rue Blanche after dining at the restaurant La Cloche d'or, along with Sartre, all of a sudden Anne-Marie, turning towards the philosopher, announced in a loud voice: "Gréco would like to sing!" To which Sartre replied quite naturally: "If she wants to sing, let her!" But this time, Gréco protested so strongly that he could not refrain from asking her to explain this refusal. An explanation she was well obliged to give: "I don't know how to sing, and besides I don't like the songs that are heard on the radio—Which ones do you like?—The ones by Agnès Capri, Yves Montand...—Be at my place tomorrow morning at 9 o'clock," concluded Sartre.

9 o'clock, the next morning, at 42 rue Bonaparte. Sartre was already seated behind his desk. He pushed a pile of books towards the young woman: Claudel, Tristan Corbière, Jules Laforgue, Raymond Queneau; between the pages, he slid some bookmarks. Finally, she would keep only two texts: a poem by Jules Laforgue, "Notre petite compagne" (Our Little Companion), another by Queneau, "C'est bien connu" (It's well known)."[17] Two texts, but she would take three home, because Sartre, as though to bring her luck, had just offered Gréco an inestimable gift: *La Rue des Blancs-Manteaux* (The Street of the White Coats), the song that Inès hums in *Huis clos*, and whose text is found *in extenso* in the brochure of the play:[18]

---

[17] "Notre petite compagne" would become *L'Éternel feminin* and "C'est bien connu" would be called *If you think* when Gréco would sing them. Yvette Guilbert, however, had already sung "Notre petite compagne", on a musical theme by Émile Waldteufel; she recorded it in New York on October 23 1918 (reference: Columbia Amérique A 2740). The author thanks François Bellair-Dubas, who shared this information with him.

[18] Later on Sartre would give Gréco two other texts; "La Perle de Passy" and "Ne faites pas suer le marin." She would never sing them, because both were lost or stolen.

GARCIN
Yes. And we... we will be saved. Remain silent. Look inward, never raise your head. Agreed?

INÈS
Agreed.

ESTELLE, *after hesitating*
Agreed.

GARCIN
Well then, goodbye.

He goes to his sofa and places his head in his hands. Silence. Inès begins to sing for herself:

On the rue des Blancs-Manteaux
They have erected a platform
And put bran in a pail
And it was a scaffold
On the rue des Blancs-Manteaux...

And he sent it to Joseph Kosma, who would compose the music for the three texts.

In retrospect, this adventure seemed crazy, like one of these marketing stunts, as one would say today, for which Cazalis had a genius. She launched Saint-Germain-des-Prés, she could easily launch Gréco. Nevertheless, if one did not know the outcome of the affair, one would not have bet a cent on it. Even though Hélène Duc affirms today that on hearing the young girl sing *Mon amant de Saint-Jean* (My Lover from Saint-Jean), on the very evening of her arrival at the Servandoni boarding house, in 1943, she understood right away the kind of singing career that could open up for the latter.[19]

Kosma worked fast. And well. Dropped off at his place at 10 in the morning, the three poems were already transcribed into music when Gréco, still flanked by Anne-Marie Cazalis, returned in the afternoon. It was the month of June; it was hot in the attic where Joseph Kosma lived, under the

---

[19] Interview with the author, May 2006.

rooftops, on the rue de l'Université; bees were entering through the open window, attracted by the little glass of fortified sugary wine that Mme Kosma served the two young women. "Kosma went to the piano. She didn't open her mouth for fear that a sound would come out. Anne-Marie and Kosma began singing in unison to encourage her and in a rasping voice that sounded as though it were being strangled she attempted the impossible:"[20]

> *If you think, if you think*
> *Little girl, little girl, if you think*
> *That it that it that it will always go on*
> *The season of, the season of*
> *Season of love, then you've goofed up,*
> *Little girl, little girl, then you've goofed up ....*

Time was running out. Because the Boeuf sur le Toit—unfortunately rebaptised L'Oeil de Boeuf (The Bull's Eye) by Doelnitz—would be reopening in several days. The pianist Jean Wiener took up his place again at the keyboard, the one he occupied in the past, with Clément Doucet, at the time of the first Boeuf, when Cocteau and Darius Milhaud were present. He would direct Gréco. She did not know a thing about her new activity; he made her work unremittingly, endeavouring to teach her in a few sessions what one normally learns in several years.

The press was prowling around, enticed by the personalities of the young woman and of those who surrounded her: Saint-Germain-des-Prés was always good box office material, even when it was transplanted on the right bank. In its issue of June 18 1949, *Samedi-Soir* announced the reopening of the Boeuf, under headlines that they wanted to be sensational: "Cocteau wants to get Sartre to sing at the Boeuf sur le Toit." Fortunately, the article itself made up somewhat for the title. After recalling the circumstances that surrounded the creation of the establishment, after the First World War, and the names of the celebrities that frequented it assiduously, from Chanel to Cocteau and including Gaston Gallimard, Raymond Radiguet or Picasso, the editor—anonymous, as usual—wondered: "Will the Oeil enjoy the same extraordinary popularity that the Boeuf did? Marc Doelnitz, who has faith, and also social relations, believes in the victory of his Oeil: 'On the evening of the première,' he said, 'we will have the smart set of Paris and the smart set

---

[20] Juliette Gréco, *Jujube, op. cit.*

of Hollywood. Marlene Dietrich will be there and Charles Boyer will be at Sartre's table. Louis Jourdan and the whole old guard of the Boeuf.'" But nature taking over, the article, as always, ended in tomfoolery: "The surprise of the evening will be Sartre's début as a singer. After thinking about it, Sartre refused to sing his refrains himself. It is the nymph Gréco who will be asked to lend her voice. We will hear her in a realistic chanson: 'La rue des Manteaux blancs'*[sic]*."

The première was set for June 22. Marc Doelnitz put together a copious program. A series of sketches, where first the master of the house himself would appear, disguised as a comical Hamlet, facing another Hamlet, just as comical, to be played by Bernard Zacharias, a fugitive from the Claude Luter Orchestra, and a black Ophelia, the dancer Tommie Moore, an escapee from the Katherine Dunham Ballet; then a parody of the silent films, *Le Souper tragique* (The Tragic Supper)...The public remained patient, applauded, laughed politely at Doelnitz's jokes, who pretended to be strangling himself on stage by swallowing down a plate of spaghetti. In reality, everyone was waiting for Gréco, because everyone came for Gréco. She appeared at last, a bit after midnight—with her lunar complexion, her long black hair, her black sweater, black pants, bare feet in golden sandals. And who began valiantly, tied up in knots by stage fright, the first of her three songs: *La Rue des Blancs-Manteaux*. Next came *L'Éternel féminin* and, finally, *Si tu t'imagines*. Praise from the critics: "The smart set of Paris, for once, must have left their judgment in the cloakroom. They were understanding and indulgent. They kindly applauded the little fool who didn't know how to sing and who trembled, with tears in her eyes."[21] Raymond Queneau, arriving too late at the Oeil de Boeuf, at the moment when the young woman ended *Si tu t'imagines*, noted in his Diary, that very evening: "A pretty voice, but no practical experience." An opinion she shared willingly: "Her photo that had been spread out in the newspapers of the whole world several months before did not at all deserve in her eyes to occupy that place. Now she would have to justify this. That night, on returning home, Jujube went directly to the mirror in the bathroom. She looked at herself straight in the eyes, critically. And that is how Jujube took the oath in front of Gréco to justify herself as much as would be humanly possible and to do everything necessary to try to reach that goal."[22]

---

[21] *Ibid.*

[22] *Ibid.*

She would keep her word. As of autumn. And on the left bank this time, returning to the very heart of Saint-Germain-des-Prés. At the Rose Rouge, on the rue de Rennes, where Nico Papatakis, the young director, had just engaged her: "Flattered, she accepted. Nico gave Gréco a salary of five francs per performance and warm encouragement."[23]

The Rose Rouge was a kind of consecration for this generation of young artists, sure of finding there an informed public. And large. Every evening, towards midnight, the little basement on the rue de Rennes was stormed, so to speak, by the crowd of spectators. There were many actors among them, who came to breath in the air of the times: "As soon as they took off their makeup, all the actors in Paris left their dressing rooms and gathered in the heavy smoke of the Rose Rouge, where the cellar rats had already heated up the hall with be-bop music."[24] Something new was in the process of being invented here, something that had elements of comedy, cabaret, and music hall... Which the press, from *Samedi-Soir* to *Combat* summed up in a fashionable formula: "the *up to date* cabaret." And yet, the Rose Rouge was not created in one day. And indeed, after its founders separated, there were, for several years, two Rose Rouges...

1946, on rue de la Harpe, right in the Latin Quarter, a Senegalese dancer, an ex-star of the Folies-Bergère, Féral Benga, opened a little African cabaret restaurant. He called it "La Rose Rouge." Benga, born in 1906, whose first name was really François—for which he substituted Féral, no doubt more exotic, on arriving in Paris, around 1925—had his hour of glory before the war. A partner of Joséphine Baker in the luxurious revues of the Folies, he also triumphed on the big European stages, notably at the Wintergarten in Berlin. In 1930, he participated in *Le Sang d'un poète* (*The Blood of a Poet*), by Jean Cocteau, posed for sculptors, opened a cabaret on the rue Tilsitt. Which the war would force him to close.

The Rose Rouge was hardly frequented except during the weekends, when, after the meal service, the restaurant transformed itself into an African ballroom. A funny place, where the boss played all the roles: "This big Senegalese, Féral Benga, is simultaneously the boss, the cook and the star of the cabaret La Rose Rouge. After preparing the couscous, the Sudanese mafé and the gary of Dahomey with hot sauce, he sets aside the cook's hat and puts on the nicely cut jacket to do the honours and show people around the house. Then he goes out. We see him coming back

---

[23] *Ibid.*

[24] Cécile Philippe and Patrice Tourenne, *Les Frères Jacques*, Balland, 1981.

almost naked. He leaps, gesticulates, rolls his terrible eyes, while the tam-tam, pim-pah, sha-sha and tin-tin reverberate. It is the bakou dance[25]."

Concerned about making a dormant business profitable, Féral Benga began searching for an associate to whom he could entrust the running of the establishment. That was how he met Nico Papatakis. Papatakis had led a romantic life. The life of a real adventurer. Born in Addis-Abeba in 1918, of an Abyssinian mother and a Greek father, he found himself forced into exile in 1935, when Mussolini's army invaded Ethiopia. He would be a manservant in Greece, under the dictatorship of General Metaxas, a painter's model, before arriving in France in 1939.[26] Where he became, like many others, a regular patron of the Café de Flore. Did his desire to be in the theatre come from there? During the war he took Solange Sicard's course on comedy. Where he crossed Juliette Gréco's path: "She already had the impressive voice of a tragic actress, a very well placed voice, a stunning presence."[27] Saint-Germain-des-Prés was a big family.

Nico Papatakis did not come alone to the Rose Rouge, a group of pals followed him: Michel de Ré, Mireille Trépel, Yves Deniaud, Jean Rougeul... The hall was repainted yellow, the kitchen served as a dressing room for the artists, a little stage was set up. Michel de Ré put on short plays by Prévert: *En famille* (Within the Family), *Tentative de description d'un diner de têtes* (*An Attempt to Describe a Dinner of Heads*)—shows that bore a certain resemblance to those of the defunct Groupe Octobre. People could hear Yves Robert sing Brecht and Bruant, Jacques Douai, Francis Lemarque, Stéphane Goldmann... Gérard Philipe and Maria Casarès, often accompanied by Roger Blin and Georges Vitaly—all four were rehearsing nearby, at the Théâtre des Noctambules, on the rue Champollion, the play by Henri Pichette, *Les Épiphanies* (*The Epiphanies*)—passed by almost every evening. One could also see frequently Simone Signoret, Alain Cuny, Louis Aragon and Elsa Triolet... Even if the hall was tiny, even if one could not see well from any spot, even if the seats were uncomfortable, the formula was pleasing; it was new, funny, caustic. The Rose Rouge on the rue de la Harpe, the ancestor of the left-bank cabarets, never emptied.

---

[25] *Samedi-Soir*, January 15 1947.

[26] Nico Papatakis, *Tous les désespoirs sont permis*, Fayard, 2003. During the 1960s, a convert to the cinema, Papatakis would produce notably the film *Les Abysses*, inspired by the affair of the Papin sisters.

[27] Nico Papatakis, quoted by Bertrand Dicale, *Gréco, les vies d'une chanteuse, op. cit.*

Alas, there were more guests than paying customers among the frequenters. And the accounts suffered as a result. Enough for the partners to separate at the beginning of the year 1948. All the more because a sponsor, brought in by Maria Casarès, proposed his services to Nico Papatakis... While Benga, on the rue de la Harpe, returned to his roots—Africa, its dances and its myths—Papatakis and his friends packed up and settled in a bit further away, in Saint-Germain-des-Prés, at 76 rue de Rennes, in the basement of the former Brasserie Lumina, that had been closed since the war.

This second Rose Rouge would have a lot of trouble becoming viable: "They had transported from the boulevard Saint-Michel to the rue de Rennes their material and artists, but during the move had lost their audience."[28] Paul Tourenne—one of the four Frères Jacques—who went there in the month of June in the hope of landing an engagement, entered an almost deserted hall: "Seated at the piano, Léo Ferré, still unknown, sang for a few scattered spectators, before the act of the mime Marceau who was in the process of inventing, in an atmosphere of almost total indifference, his personage Bip."[29]

It was precisely from the Frères Jacques that salvation would come for the Rose Rouge no. 2. Summoned for an audition, they were engaged right on the spot. And made their début on June 15. "The date has remained engraved in my memory," said Paul Tourenne. Success would not be long in coming: "These four young singers totally renew the genre. They please their audience without being vulgar, transform average songs like *Le Général Castagnetas* into masterpieces and masterpieces like *Les Nombrils* (The Navels) into apotheoses. With them, one can laugh without feeling shame. They operate at the Rose Rouge of which they are the spinal column."[30] And a damned good spinal column, since they would remain there for five years! And once they left the cabaret would sink slowly into failure and oblivion.

Four young singers, indeed. Not one of them was called Jacques. At the beginning was André. André Bellec, an administrator in the Ministry of Work and Culture, an association committed to promoting a truly popular culture. He had wanted for a long time to create a vocal group, a quartet, of which each member would be simultaneously a singer, dancer,

---

[28] Guillaume Hanoteau, *L'Äge d'or de Saint-Germain-des-Prés*, op. cit.

[29] Paul Tourenne, interview with the author, March 2001.

[30] Boris Vian, *Manuel de Saint-Germain-des-Prés*, op. cit.

mime and actor. The creative ferment that accompanied the Liberation impelled André Bellec to carry out his idea. All the more because he received the artistic support of Léon Chancerel, the founder, as we mentioned, of the Comédiens routiers, who found the idea captivating. There remained the task of discovering three other singers. His brother Georges would be the first. He would find the two others—François Soubeyran and Paul Tourenne—on the spot, in the very offices of the Ministry of Work and Culture. André, Georges, François and Paul. Four destinies had just decided to become one.

Fate would take care of giving them a name. While the team found itself together in a radio studio, each one asked the question out loud: "Brothers? English names are fashionable. Frères? Yes, but what brothers? ..." In the control booth, a scolding voice arose suddenly to demand silence: "Will you finally stop playing the fools ('faire les Jacques')!"[31] It was July 14 1945. A date that could not be forgotten. Thus baptized, all the Frères Jacques had to do was invent a style for themselves. Another happy coincidence would provide it. Jean-Pierre Grenier and Olivier Hussenot had just established their theatrical company, one of the first to see the light after the Liberation. It had a very precise goal: the refusal of seriousness, the penchant for parody. That was also the Jacques' objective. They were immediately engaged by the Grenier-Hussenot troupe. They soon appeared at the Théâtre Agnès-Capri, in *Orion le Tueur* (*Orion the Killer*), by Maurice Fombeure, and in *Parade pour rire et pour pleurer* (*Parade for Laughter and Tears*), a series of sketches, or rather circus numbers, mounted around texts by Verlaine and Jules Laforgue. For this *Parade*, that put on stage travelling performers coming out of a trailer, Jean-Denis Malclès, the creator of the costumes and décors, chose to dress the whole troupe in tight-fitting leotards—a sort of homage to the Picasso of the blue period. The Frères Jacques would keep their black tights. To which they would add a coloured doublet, white gloves, a hat and a moustache... "The Complete Athletes of Song," as Yvan Audiard would nickname them, had found their style.

Agnès Capri, that indefatigable talent scout, was pushing them towards the cabaret, convinced as she was that inside a theatrical company, no matter how innovative and brilliant, they ran the risk of having their most precious characteristics blunted: this unleashed sense of the

---

[31] "Faire les Jacques" in French means "to play or act the fool." Hence the name "Les Frères Jacques," chosen by the singing quartet. [Translator's note]

ridiculous, for example, which was already their trademark, this talent for caricature, for poetry, these chansons that were broken down and set up like cartoons, with close-ups, "bubbles" and underlined mimicry. So off they went on their adventure, from the right bank to the left bank: the Boeuf sur le Toit, Chez Colette Mars, la Vie Parisienne, Chez Carrère... And, finally, the Rose Rouge. Where they found their true audience: "They would come in from the back of the hall, in black tights, sweaters of green, yellow, red and grey silk, carrying their props, calling out joyously to the spectators, and would get up on the stage by means of two small steps. Then it was sheer joy. The Frère Jacques' audience, one of the most faithful in the world, knew by heart their first successes: *L'Entrecôte* (The Steak), *Le Général Castagnetas*, *La Queue du chat* (The Cat's Tail) and applauded their new chansons wildly, *Barbara, La Marie-Joseph, Inventaire* (Inventory)... And their audience asked for more and went overboard with non stop applause."[32] The Frères Jacques were soon joined by the Grenier-Hussenot team, then by Yves Robert who, the following year, would take over the artistic directorship of the cabaret. Thus began with all of them the great era of the Rose Rouge.

Every evening, towards ten o'clock, a crowd thronged on the sidewalk of the rue de Rennes. People used their elbows to enter: "It is necessary to get hold of a porter seated behind a register, throw him a thousand francs or shout one's name to him in order to acquire the favour of descending the staircase," related Guillaume Hanoteau, a witness of the days, and, especially, the nights of Saint-Germain-des-Prés. "Descending the staircase" was a tricky manoeuvre, so steep and encumbered it was: all those who could not find a seat in the hall seated themselves unceremoniously on the steps. Many called, few chosen, because "the space was so narrow and the public so dense that everyone was practically seated on his neighbour's lap and drank from one glass or another, for lack of being able to find one's way around," wrote a columnist of *La Tribune de Genève* (*The Geneva Tribune*) who had come to assess the phenomenon personally. "It was crowded. I can't remember having found a place to sit. Way at the back, standing, yes. Or on the steps. Nico let his pals enter. But it was jam-packed!"[33] On the ceiling, the ventilators were purring, without really appeasing the heat; on the beige walls, brown silhouettes, as though

---

[32] Geneviève Latour, *Le Cabaret-Théâtre, 1945-1965*, Bibliothèque historique de la Ville de Paris, 1996.

[33] Nicolas Bataille, interview with the author, March 2008.

drawn with a stencil, vaguely depicted a rocky décor: animals, characters... "Everything is special there," said, going overboard, Yves Gibeau, the special reporter, it should be mentioned, from *Combat*, "Everything: the place, the attractively furnished cellar, the atmosphere, the decorations, the regular customers—genuine and phoney Existentialists—and above all the show that, at 12:30 a.m., follows the rhythms of a reduced but lively orchestra. The dancers—it must be said that given the cramped area of the dance floor and their number, have a lot of trouble executing perfectly their highly fanciful steps—then go back to their tables."[34] Because at the Rose Rouge, until midnight, people danced. Like elsewhere: be-bop, boogie-woogie, slow... On a dance floor of four by four metres. With a real orchestra, an orchestra led by Michel Devillers—the Great Orchestra of the Rose Rouge—which by some miracle fit into that space as big as a pocket handkerchief. Roger Guérin on the trumpet, Maurice Meunier on the clarinet, Alix Bret on the double bass, Géo Daly on the vibraphone, Bernard Planchenault on the drums. At the piano, according to the evenings: Christian Chevalier or Henri Patterson.[35]

At midnight and a half, "the lights are turned off... Mystery. An invisible announcer presents the program."[36] The curtain opened. There she was then, she whom everybody called Gréco—it would take time for them to give her back her first name. Gréco: a beautiful name, sombre and tragic, that suited this young woman whom no one ever taught how to smile or move on stage. There she was, in her black uniform—sweater and pants—her hands clasped behind her back. With her three songs, to which had come to be added, offered by Joseph Kosma, *La Fourmi* (*The Ant*) by Robert Desnos and the already legendary *Feuilles mortes* (*Dead Leaves*), written by Jacques Prévert: "So Gréco had five songs in her repertoire and judged it to be enough."[37] Gréco surprised, Gréco shocked. But already the most knowledgeable guessed that with her the chanson had undoubtedly one of its newest post-war talents. This presence, this way of grabbing the public, almost physically, this note of velvet, suddenly, in her voice... "Gréco is certainly an unusual girl. In her black 'outfit,' with her long, shoulder-length hair framing her face, sad, heavy but not without beauty, she captivates,

---

[34] *Combat*, September 19-20, 1948.

[35] Henri Patterson would become later on Juliette Gréco's official accompanist for a good twenty years.

[36] *Combat*, September 19-20 1948.

[37] Juliette Gréco, *Jujube, op. cit.*

disturbs, even amuses. Perhaps she has not yet found the right way of singing the chansons of Sartre or Queneau? We listen to her nonetheless with much interest, especially in *Les Feuilles mortes*, one of the most beautiful songs around. And even this stage fright, that she does not conceal well, she who seemed not be afraid of anything, adds to her personality."[38]

Let the press put its mind at rest; the black "outfit" belonged to the past. We know the story, dozens of magazine articles, almost as many books, have told it. Seeing that his resident performer's success would be lasting, Nico Papatakis suddenly became aware of the fact that her wardrobe left something to be desired. Precisely, the Pierre Balmain fashion house was getting ready to sell off its creations, in its showrooms on rue François I. He brought his star there; and there you had both of them in the hands of salesladies, in a luxurious fitting room, Papatakis facing the young woman who made—she was the one who said it—"some comical attempts to fit into the models' shopsoiled dresses." In vain, because not one really appealed to her: this "pretty madame" style, that the high fashion designer cultivated in those years, was really not hers. So they brought her a recent model: a kind of black sheath, very simple, prolonged by a sumptuous train of gold satin speckled with velvet. The dress pleased Papatakis who purchased it at once. Gréco remained silent. Even though her thought process was still going on. A little later, in her hotel room, she undertook to detach the train with the help of a pair of embroidering scissors, "the scissors of vengeance," she said. Painstakingly, stitch by stitch. "Once the work was done, all that was left was the main black slip. She put it on that very evening, without advance warning. Nico nearly fell backwards."[39] There was a mocking reaction from *Samedi-Soir*, as usual, as of the following week:[40] "The event of her singing stint at the Rose Rouge, is her appearance in a black dress. This is the first time she is wearing a black dress since the war. 'It's happened,' said a furious Existentialist, 'they have demobilised her!'"

Was she beautiful, this Gréco of the Rose Rouge, in her long black dress, with this "heavy face, not without beauty" that the columnist of *Combat* remarked? On this matter, there was no doubt: she did not consider herself beautiful. Was it for that reason she decided to change her face? Starting with the nose. The whole business would perhaps have

---

[38] Yves Gibeau, *Combat*, December 21 1949.

[39] Juliette Gréco, *Jujube, op. cit.*

[40] December 24 1949

remained strictly private if Gréco, one day, had not confessed to Simone de Beauvoir that she envied the line of the latter's nose. Which the lady hastened to tell Nelson Algren, that very evening, in her daily letter: "They are going to cut her nose; looking at mine, one day, she declared: 'I will have a nose like that one,' and the surgeon is going to construct for her the nose that God bestowed on me..."[41] As a result, the news spread around the whole neighbourhood, and even beyond—Gréco's nose: if it had been shorter, the whole face of Saint-Germain-des-Prés would have been changed... And the newspapers hastened to pass on the Saint-Germain-des-Prés gossip: "That nose will have made lots of printer's ink flow, it will have touched off polemics!... The first nose was a catastrophe, the second too. The third was saved by the magical and British hand of Sir Archibald Mac Indoe, a famous surgeon." It was Gréco herself who affirmed this. Many years later, it was François Mauriac's turn to declare: "Her personage is composed with a science that leaves nothing to chance. She is a statue of ivory and jade. Many chanteuses are interchangeable. Gréco is the unique masterpiece of Gréco."[42]

At the Rose Rouge, the intermission has just ended. "The curtain opens on the second part. Suddenly we forget the heat, the lack of air. We are no longer in this basement of whitewashed walls. We climb up to the Dome of the Invalides. We pursue Fantômas through the girders of the Eiffel Tower, we travel on Philéas Fogg's steamer or on the Maharajah's elephant. The master of these magic spells is an Yves Robert who gave up a singing career for stage directing. Does he command an army of stagehands? It is his actors, and they are only seven or eleven with the Frères Jacques, who transport the décors and make the scene changes in front of the audience. Yves, it is true, has at his disposal an accomplice more effective than all the machinery of the Châtelet, poetry. A poetry that allows him to suggest a palace thanks to a shadow, and a drama thanks to a noise..."[43]

With the arrival of Yves Robert and his actors—Rosy Varte, Jacques Dufilho, Jena-Marie Amato, Jacques Hilling, Edmond Tamiz, Guy Pierauld...--in the basement of the rue de Rennes, it was like a current of fresh air, laden with fantasy and imagination, that swept over the little stage. Little, yes: barely four metres wide, two deep, as much in height, without passages or stage equipment. The Grenier-Hussenots warned

---

[41] Simone de Beauvoir, *Lettres à Nelson Algren, op. cit.*

[42] *Le Figaro littéraire*, January 27 1952.

[43] Guillaume Hanoteau, *L'Âge d'or de Saint-Germain-des-Prés, op. cit.*

the spectators: "We wish to ridicule the official theatre, through a new repertoire that we must build."[44] On that score, the public would not be disappointed. Until 1953, the date when Yves Robert would leave the Rose Rouge definitively, there would be a succession of short plays, sketches and numbers which, indeed, would revolutionize the cabaret. A new style was born—the cabaret theatre—the heir of the Groupe Octobre and of Agnès Capri, and by which, twenty years later, the café theatres could claim to be inspired. And to which the critics, immediately, offered their fervent support: "Each new cabaret show on the rue de Rennes always contains enough novelty, surprises, humour and poetry for us to want to see it again."[45]

The authors went to work without delay. André Roussin inaugurated the formula with *L'Étranger au theatre* (*The Stranger at the Theatre*): dialogues in school kid slang interpreted by clowns—"an excessively droll, disconcertingly comical farce."[46] Albert Vidalie followed suit: *Terror of Oklahoma* is a kind of parody of the western, with cowboys and Indians, a pretty saloon girl, a stagecoach attack and even Abraham Lincoln in person. "It has everything, gunshots, a fantastic horse ride, a scalping, arrows, gasoline and lofty sentiments. Yves Robert makes his début as a stage director in this theatrical film, unfolding at high speed in a space of three square metres."[47] Then Jacques Prévert presented *L'Opéra des girafes* (*The Opera of the Giraffes*) and *Branle-bas de combat* (*Preparations for Action*). And proved that he had not lost his touch since the 1930s and the heyday of the Groupe Octobre. Yves Gibeau, in *Combat*, on December 21 1949, marvelled: "Yves Robert's staging is a delight. It is enough for Jacques Dufilho, the admiral of the warship, to come on deck, richly attired, with binoculars in his hands, for the audience to split its sides with laughter."

Yves Robert called to arms the authors of Saint-Germain-des-Prés: Guillaume Hanoteau gave him a succulent *Fantômas* (an old project of Robert Desnos that the poet, having died in a concentration camp, did not have the time to complete), where certain actors can play up to seventeen roles—there was not a minute to lose in the wings, reduced to the bare minimum, during the costume changes. Boris Vian and Pierre Kast brought *Cinémassacre*: the same amorous encounter scene as conceived by Cecil B. De Mille, Vittorio de Sica, Alfred Hitchcock, Marcel Carné,

---

[44] Quoted by Cécile Philippe and Patrice Tourenne, *Les Frères Jacques, op. cit.*"
[45] Jean-François Devay, *Combat,* December 17-18, 1949.
[46] *Combat, September 19-20 1948.*
[47] *Combat*, November 29 1948.

etc. As for Yves Robert, he watched over the adaptation of Jules Verne's masterpiece, *Le Tour du monde en 80 jours* (*Around the World in 80 Days*). The audience howled with laughter.

The big event, however, the apotheosis of the Rose Rouge style, was the creation, on October 21 1950, of Raymond Queneau's *Excercices de style* (*Exercises in Style*). A creation that nearly did not see the light of day. When Yves Robert asked him for permission to stage his text, Queneau shrugged his shoulders: how could one get spectators interested in these purely intellectual rantings?[48] Published in 1947, the *Exercices de style* constitute another step in the exploration of language that Queneau had been carrying out for a long time, and which would culminate in the establishment of the Oulipo movement, in 1960. The *Exercices de style* was a challenge, a literary game in which Queneau diabolically multiplied the constraints and the traps: telling the same story in ninety-nine different ways by illustrating each time a different stylistic genre—a story, simple notes, alexandrines, a sonnet, anagrams...How can one describe the story told in this manner? Banal? Not even that: inexistent. In the S bus, a man complains in a loud voice that his neighbour is pushing him. That is all.

Story
One day towards noon near Monceau Park, on the back platform of an almost full S line bus, I noticed a character with a very long neck, who wore a soft felt hat trimmed with a woven braid instead of a ribbon. This individual suddenly shouted at his neighbour, claiming that the latter was stepping on his feet on purpose each time passengers were getting on or getting off. In any event he quickly dropped the issue to rush to get a seat that had become vacant.

Notes
In the S, at rush hour. A guy about twenty-six years old, wearing a soft hat with a band replacing the ribbon, with a neck too long as though someone had shot at him. People get off. The guy in question is angry with his neighbour. He reproaches the latter for jostling him every time someone passes by. In a whining tone that tries to appear nasty. As he sees a vacant spot, he rushes towards it.

---

[48] The chanteuse Marie Dubas, however, had already shown an interest in these *Exercices de style* as soon as they appeared, even planning, with Queneau's agreement, to stage them. But the project never materialized.

Saint Germain des Prés

Alexandrines
One day in the bus bearing the letter S
I saw a whippersnapper of some kind or other
Who was moaning even though on his turban
There was a braid in place of a ribbon.
He was moaning, this young man with his insipid appearance,
With his overstretched neck, his foul-smelling breath,
Because a citizen who seemed to be an adult
Barged into him, he said, if any passenger
Hoisted himself panting and pursued by the hour
Hoping to have lunch in his chaste dwelling
There was no scandal at all and the poor guy
Ran towards a spot and sat down foolishly.

And so forth...

The project would not have gone any further, but Yves Robert insisted. Despite Raymond Queneau's opinion, despite the opinion of the Frères Jacques, "full-fledged partners" in the Rose Rouge, approached about performing in these *Exercice* and who seemed very reticent about it... The stage director's powers of persuasion finally succeeded in gaining everybody's support. On stage, the *Exercices,* boiled down to fifty-seven, made for a dazzling show. For the ear as well as for the eye. Pierre Philippe, the accompanist of the Jacques, wrote a musical score, while Serge Creuz designed the décors and costumes. Funny, absurd, zany. The audience clamoured for more. Starting with Jean-Paul Sartre himself: "There was a night club, the Rose Rouge, where we used to go quite often, because the Frères Jacques would sing there. We had discovered them some time earlier, and we would go to the Rose Rouge to see them again."[49] There would be six hundred performances in total; the Frères Jacques would record the *Exercices de style* in 1954; a photo of the quartet surrounding Raymond Queneau on the platform of the 84 bus—the former S—immortalized the recording.

The success of the Rose Rouge would encourage many forms of competition. If not of counterfeit versions. The Fontaine des Quatre-Saisons (The Fountain of the Four Seasons), on the rue de Grenelle, an imitation, in a more comfortable and bigger version of the cabaret on the

---

[49] Jean-Paul Sartre, quoted in *Simone de Beauvoir*, a film by Josée Dayan, 1979.

rue de Rennes, opened its doors, in the back of a courtyard, in June 1951. Under the leadership of the Prévert brothers. Pierre acted as the artistic director, Jacques, having become in a way the official poet of Saint-Germain-des-Prés ever since his collection of poems *Paroles* (Words) appeared in 1946, supplied the house with sketches and one act plays. For the opening program: *Le Dîner de têtes* that dated back nonetheless to 1931... This did not escape the attention of *Combat*, which put out the headline: "Jacques Prévert-51 met Jacques Prévert-31 at a dinner of heads." Soon the Grenier-Hussenot Company would make its headquarters on the rue de Grenelle, then one could hear three singer wearing striped leotards—les Garçons de la Rue (The Street Boys)... In short, enough to remind many people of the wonderful evenings at the Rose Rouge.

Other establishments did not wait for Papatakis' success to launch themselves. As of 1949, the Saint-Yves, for example, set itself up without embarrassment in the lobby of the hotel bearing the same name, on the rue de l'Université. "They sang with their backs leaning against the reception desk. The guests didn't seem to mind the racket on the ground floor and would come in, even while the performances were going on, to pick up their keys, make a phone call.... "We performed our acts in 1900 costumes."[50] Right in the middle of a kind of flea market, a Belle Époque bric-a-brac where were piled up, higgledy-piggledy, posters by Chéret, turn of the century Japanese fans, lanterns, photos by Nadar or Reutlinger... Because the master of the house, Romi—antique dealer, collector, printer—made the repertoire of the caf'conc come alive again, rejuvenated by new performers. In these circumstances, three pretty girls were swishing their skirts around, impersonating by turns pretentiously elegant ladies, street singers or street prostitutes: Simone Chobillon, Lily Bontemps, Claudine Chéret. The servers—with their white aprons, black jackets, napkins folded over their arms, in the purest tradition—participated in the show. On certain evenings, you could even hear Louis-Armand Fèvre there, squeezed into his Grande Armée uniform—"the last of the Bonapartists," as he was called—blare out patriotic choruses at the audience. "It was funny, very parodic..." recalled Nicolas Bataille.

The neighbourhood hotels really welcomed music. And the chanson. After the Hôtel des Carmes, where the Lorientais found shelter as of 1946,

---

[50] Jacques Fabbri, *Être saltimbanque*, Robert Laffont, 1978; quoted by Gilles Schlesser, *Le Cabaret "rive gauche"*, op. cit.

after the Hôtel Saint-Yves and its 1900 craziness, it was the turn of the Hôtel Saint-Thomas-d'Aquin, on 3 rue du Pré-aux-Clercs. Francis Claude opened there, in 1948, the Quod Libet. It was a little cellar—sixty people could fit in there comfortably—whose walls he lined with newspaper. On the eve of its inauguration, they noticed that there was no stage! Nothing to worry about: an old champagne crate would serve as a platform. Léo Ferré, who lived above, made his real début at the Quod Libet. Just like Catherine Sauvage—red hair, in a frieze dress and sandals.

The following year, Agnès Capri reopened her cabaret on the rue Molière. Cora Vaucaire made her stage debut at the Échelle de Jacob—where she would become, as we stated, "the White Lady of Saint-Germain-des-Prés"—a new night club, opened on the very terrain where the former restaurant Chéramy had stood. Two singers, Marc and André, the partners of Léo Noël and Brigitte Sabouraud, established themselves on the Quai des Grands-Augustins. A funny spot, in the style of the bistros frequented by bargemen, with fishnets and buoys hung up on the walls. All that was lacking were seagulls' cries. It was called L'Écluse (The Lock). Soon, a tall, dark young lady would sit down behind the upright piano: Barbara. But she already represented the post-Saint-Germain-des-Prés period that was beginning...

14

On the little stage of the Théâtre des Noctambules,
The Bald Soprano faced the public. "Fortunately,
we will never again hear of M. Ionesco,"
exclaimed a critic

Does the rue Champollion belong to Saint-Germain-des-Prés? Certainly not. But ever since the Lorientais colonized the rue des Carmes, the whole of the Sainte-Geneviève slope, like some belt-drive effect, found itself linked to that neighbourhood. The first Rose Rouge, on rue de la Harpe; the Gipsy's, a cabaret on rue Cujas... A kind of Saint-Germain-des-Prés pocket right in the heart of the Latin Quarter. In any event this is what Boris Vian pretended to believe in 1958, when he drew up retrospectively, at the request of *La Gazette de Lausanne*, his cultural inventory of the neighbourhood: "Georges Vitaly launched Audiberti and Schéhadé at La Huchette; at the Noctambules Gérard Philippe and Maria Casarès conjured up mad love to Henri Pichette's rhythms." Vian did not forget anyone. He also named Eugène Ionesco, Samuel Beckett; he spoke of Jean Vilar, Henri Cartier-Bresson's photos, Dior and Jacques Fath... Ten or twelve years after its explosion, the spirit of Saint-Germain-des-Prés became quite simply the spirit of Paris...

When Gérard Philipe returned to Paris, in the autumn of 1947, from Italy where he had just finished the shooting of Christian-Jaque's film, *La Chartreuse de Parme* (*The Charterhouse of Parm*a), it was to be reunited with his partner, Maria Casarès, on the stage of the Théâtre Édouard-VII. They would perform *Les Épiphanies*, the first play of a young, almost unknown poet, Henri Pichette. Six long months of shooting a film, in

Rome, Milan, on the shores of Lake Como—it was the first Franco-Italian super-production since the war—allowed the two young actors to develop a kind of artistic companionship—and even a bit more—that would never flag.

Spiritual heir of Rimbaud and Antonin Artaud, with whom, moreover, he came into contact, Pichette belonged to that generation—he was twenty years old in 1944—whose youth had been wrecked by the war.[1] Youth work crews, Resistance, French Forces of the Interior, combats in a regiment of the Algerian infantry... And now the Cold War, dragging along with it the threat of another apocalypse. Thus it was war and, in a more general manner, all forms of oppression that the play denounced. Just like the collection of poetry that Henri Pichette published that same year 1947, at the Éditions Fontaine, under the provocative title *Apoèmes*.

Gérard Philipe made his acquaintance during the performances of *Caligula*. Introduced by Georges Vitaly, the young poet read him some of his still unpublished texts: "He listened attentively, mentally engrossed, as though he had converted my rhetorical flowers into his own substance."[2] A friendship was born as a result of this meeting, intensified by a mutual admiration. As a result, when he undertook the writing of his dramatic poem *Les Épiphanies*, he handed over the first sketches to Gérard Philipe. Twelve pages to be exact, where unfolded, inscribed in red ink, a large, sober, and rounded handwriting that contrasted with the lyricism and luminous disorder of his style. Philipe was immediately conquered. He believed he could recognize in it the tone, the exaltation, the violence, in a word, the new language that his generation was awaiting: "Poetry is a broadside launched against habit," said Pichette. And while he was getting ready to return to Italy and *La Chartreuse de Parme*, the actor made Pichette promise to send him the rest of the text. The latter would do that scrupulously, page by page, until the very last one. In Rome, Maria Casarès read *Les Épiphanies*, and she, too, became enthusiastic. As Renée Faure, their partner who played the role of Clélia Conti in the film, noted: "At that time I was joining the Comédie-Française, I tried to get them to come there with me, but both of them were getting ready then to perform *Les Épiphanies* which they had just discovered, and that alone interested them."[3]

---

[1] Henri Pichette, 1924-2000, born Harry Pichette of a Quebec father naturalized as an American and a French mother.

[2] Henri Pichette, *Tombeau de Gérard Philipe*, Gallimard, 1961.

[3] *Les Lettres françaises*, December 3 1959.

Saint Germain des Prés

Back to Paris, then. A Paris in the throes of multiple strikes: Peugeot, Berliet, Michelin, the metalworking industry, the mines, the metro system, the buses, the railways... At the end of November 1947, in a France almost paralysed, it was estimated that two million workers were on strike. But given the name of Gérard Philipe, the rising star of French cinema—*Le Diable au corps* (*The Devil in the Flesh*) had triumphed on the Parisian screen since September 12—all doors opened wide. Notably those of the Théâtre Édouard-VII, the director of which, Pierre Béteille, accepted the play on trust alone, without even reading it... Gérard Philipe and Maria Casarès in the same cast, that is to say, two stars whom audiences adored, basking completely in the glow of their film successes, what more could one ask for? He already imagined full houses. Things could not have been going better. Until October 30, when M. Béteille, comfortably seated in an orchestra seat, attended the sixteenth rehearsal. Catastrophe. If the ceiling of his theatre had suddenly collapsed over him, he could not have been more alarmed: "He declared that he was shocked by certain words, by certain attitudes, by certain thing as well that he did not understand."[4] Puzzled by this text in which "insults and cries of hope flow together in such strange ways," aghast, he looked for a loophole. He ended up backing out.[5] So he explained to the cast—fifteen actors, besides Gérard Philipe, Maria Casarès and Roger Blin—that he had made a mistake in the dates, that Sacha Guitry was supposed to present his new play shortly at the Édouard-VII and that, consequently, the stage would only be free from six to eight o'clock. "We packed our things and left in a fit of laughter," related Georges Vitaly, the stage director, "and took refuge that very day in the Théâtre des Noctambules."[6]

After difficult beginnings, the Noctambules hall, which championed a quality repertoire, became a centre for theatrical renewal. One hundred seats, "a theatre no larger than a cradle," said Henri Pichette. But it was on this little stage that would be developed the whole dramatic output in the second half of the 20th century. Often in front of small audiences. Soon, here, Eugène Ionesco would reveal himself with *La Cantatrice chauve* (*The Bald Soprano*), Arthur Adamov with *La Grande et la Petite Manoeuvre* (*The Large and Small Manoeuvre*), Boris Vian would

---

[4] *Lettres françaises*, November 13 1947.

[5] Jacques Lemarchand, *Almanach du théâtre et du cinéma 1949*.

[6] In *Gérard Philipe, Souvenirs et témoignages* collected by Anne Philipe and Claude Roy, Gallimard, 1960.

put on *Équarrissage pour tous* (*Everybody for the Glue Factory*). And Dürrenmatt, Ugo Betti…

In fact, it was Gérard Philipe, welcomed with open arms by the directors, Pierre Leuris and Jean Claude, who made the decision to rent the Théâtre des Noctambules at his own expense. And his initiative did not fail to round up the journalists, who had never thronged in front of the hall on the rue Champollion in such large numbers. This was because after the incident at the Édouard-VII they were now smelling a ruckus—a flop, for example! Courageously, Maria Casarès was the first to attack: "Pichette's play may appear scandalous to certain people. But it deserves to be performed and we will perform it."[7]

In his *Tombeau de Gérard Philipe* (*Memorial in honour of Gérard Philipe*), Henri Pichette remembered the work sessions and how the actor often asked him to read his text himself, out loud: "Reading rehearsals where, so to speak, he wanted me to give him the *A*. If something seemed wrong, he would start laughing with a kind of laughter that implied discretion or a need to escape. Here and there, he would ask to repeat, he would propose a nuance, he would go deeper, he would take notes." Wise and grave. But, once the rehearsal was over, he was the first to suggest going over for a drink to the Rose Rouge, on the rue de la Harpe.

December 3: while a piano played the musical interludes composed by Maurice Roche, Gérard Philipe moved forward on stage, in front of the backdrop painted by Roberto Matta. The spectators were not wrong in thinking that he would jump out into the hall, so great did his tension appear to be: "I see under his head of hair in an attractive disarray his eyes wide open in acquiescence…. Would he have endorsed the *Épiphanies*, if he had not had a lyrical and risk-taking temperament? Gérard represented the poet. He performed without makeup, carried an all-purpose sweater. He was breathtaking: in his head was a fountain of memory, he was as tense as a roebuck trembling as though in tune with the leaves, and his hands moved more extravagantly than ten birds."[8] A navy blue sweater indeed, an open white collar, dark trousers, tousled hair, like so many young men of his age—it was precisely to the young men of his age that he would address the revolt and anguish with which their generation could identify. He spoke, as though burning at a white heat: "Since the world's first heartbeat, I have been spinning around…" This energy, this sort of

---

[7] Quoted in *Combat*, December 5 1947.

[8] Henri Pichette, *Tombeau de Gérard Philipe, op. cit.*

poetic electricity laced with lightning flashes, Henri Pichete himself was able to transmit to his actors: "Don't cool down anything; be in it; you are on stage; you are the world; life is also what you are evoking; live it. The street, the river, the migrating bird, the comet, the connecting thread of the century pass through the stage. It is a moment in the life of the world."[9]

"Épiphanie," from the Greek *epiphaneia*: appearance. Here, the appearances "are the poet's visions through the revelations of Genesis, of Love, of War, of Madness."[10] That end in the Fulfilment, where the poet is seen triumphing over the Devil and regaining possession of the world. Because the poet emerges victorious from all these epiphanies which are so many trials—victorious "because he alone is rich enough to 'organize' the great 'metamorphosis' and 'espouse' the universe."[11]

Les Épiphanies would leave André Breton dumbstruck with admiration. Maurice Genevoix as well, whom one was not expecting there: "What filled us with wonder in this young man of twenty-three, and what continues to astonish, is this way of pushing words in front of him: torches that light up the shadows, battering rams that break down walls." Julien Gracq, a quarter of a century later, still remembered performances at the Théâtre des Noctambules: "*Les Épiphanies* have not lost anything of their freedom and their over-all freshness. Again I find here a language both inexhaustible and ingenuous, that seems closer than any other to its panic sources,—a clear water and yet completely effervescent, that bursts out and frees itself and crackles in thousands of bubbles—a poetry in a state of expansion."

On the evening of the première, all of Saint-Germain-des-Prés was present: "All the pals had come to see what Philipe was doing, whom we had known from the time he lived on the rue du Dragon."[12] Leading them were the regulars of the Tabou—at the height of its popularity rating in that winter of 1947. Among them, one remarked the young high fashion designer Pierre Balmain wearing a checked shirt.

It was an immediate success. Despite some grousing: "Some spectators grumbled, didn't like me; all, however, admired Gérard."[13]

---

[9] Quoted by Gérard Lieber, in *Dictionnaire des pieces de théâtre françaises du xxe siècle, op. cit.*

[10] Geneviève Latour, *Théâtre, reflet de la IVe République*, Bibliothèque historique de la Ville de Paris, 1995.

[11] *Ibid.*

[12] Nicolas Bataille, interview with the author, March 2008.

[13] Henri Pichette, *Tombeau de Gérard Philipe, op. cit.*

It was a success, especially, with the young public, which the text of *Épiphanies*, nevertheless, hardly treated gently: "And so will I go forth, pursuing myself from earths to moons and even further through fluids, completely free, scornful of all the ordeals, an ideal matter, a parent branch, the pierced opening of an absent brain, until the final heartbeat of the world."

Despite the obscure passages and the poetic grandiloquence, the Casarès-Philipe couple was so beautiful, so fervent—she, with her hair loose, her lips lacquered with rouge, all dressed in black, pulsating—that, as Adrienne Monnier noted at the time in her column in the *Mercure de France*, "the lovers' jargon was seated on one of the lofty chairs of poetry." And Jacques Lemarchand, the wise, clairvoyant critic, drawing up the balance sheet at the end of the season, stated: "It was one of the most discussed plays of this year, because it was irritating, strong, sometimes puerile, often aggressive, extraordinarily beautiful in many of its parts, and suddenly gratuitously provocative."[14]

The spring of 1950, the Théâtre des Noctambules. That one again! A little troupe of very young actors, directed by Nicolas Bataille, that had just won the prix d'Avant-Garde (The Avant-Garde Prize) at the Concours des jeunes compagnies (The Competition for Young Companies), came to audition for the directors. With a short play, or rather an "anti-play," as the author himself called it, an unknown of Romanian origin, Eugène Ionesco. The title of which resembled a hoax: *La Cantatrice chauve* (*The Bald Soprano*). "It's marvelous," exclaimed Pierre Leuris, "Unfortunately it takes up only one hour! What do you want me to do with one hour? Listen, I'm willing to put you on the program, but at 18 hours, because I have a show at 21 hours. I'll supply you with the stage manager, the electricity, everything, I won't ask you for anything."[15] But the theatre was not rich. The actors even less so. They would perform without scenery, surrounded by curtains. A few indispensable pieces of furniture, however—a sofa, an armchair, a hassock...—would be lent by antique dealers of the Village Suisse. As for the costumes, they were the ones worn by the actors in the film *Occupe-toi d'Amélie* (*Take Care of Amélie*), graciously loaned by the director Claude Autant-Lara.

---

[14] In *Almanach du theatre et du cinema 1949*.

[15] Quoted by Gonzague Phélip, in *Le Fabuleux Roman du Théâtre de la Huchette*, Gallimard, 2007. The play put on at 21 hours was *Équarrissage pour tous* by Boris Vian.

Everything began several months earlier, in the back room of a bistro in Saint-Sulpice. A group of close friends, all young actors, was doubling up with laughter while reading a play, *L'Anglais sans peine* (*English Made Easy*). Ionesco later on explained the first title: wanting to learn English, he obtained a method called Assimil. And he discovered, in that succession of often crazy sentences, in any event deprived of any immediate meaning, chosen simply for their grammatical difficulties—for example: "My grandmother's dress is larger than my cousin's scissors"—a kind of vertigo, a disruption of language that opened up for him a kind of parodic world, more real, perhaps, than the real world. And on which he would build his whole theatrical production to come.

"We were twenty years old and this was exactly the theatre we were waiting for. It didn't resemble anything that already existed. Ionesco let off a firecracker in the theatre of the 1950s! Characters from a Jules Verne text who spoke and behaved on stage like Ibsen characters. 'Play it like *Hedda Gabler*,' I told the actress who took on the role of Mme Smith," Nicolas Bataille declares today, and, indeed, the dramatic interplay of the actors, the ceremonious staging, pasted on this farcical text, would prove to be irresistible.[16] A young Romanian lady from among his friends, who was a translator, entrusted him with the text: M. and Mme Smith, a couple who no doubt have not had anything more to say to one another for a very long time, receive at their home another couple, whose two members, M. and Mme Martin, don't recognize one another. Here was a text that everyone thought was unplayable. And, moreover, which the Grasset publishing house had just rejected.

"We'll perform it!" decided the enthusiastic young adults. Who started rehearsals right away—without a theatre, without a producer, without money. The rehearsals would last five months, depending on everyone's schedule, generally at Ionesco's home itself. They looked for another title: *L'Heure anglaise* (*The English Hour*), *Big Ben Folies*...Nothing was suitable. Until the day when the actor who played the role of the chief of the fire brigade committed an irresistible slip: instead of talking about "une institutrice blonde" (a blond teacher) as the text dictated, he said "une cantatrice chauve" (a bald soprano). The title was found. The play was created on May 10 1950. And, no doubt, this troupe of beginners did not imagine for one instant that it had just opened up, on that poor little stage, a major period in the history of world theatre: the one that would be called the "Theatre of the Absurd."

---

[16] Interview with the author, 2001.

At the Noctambules, most of the spectators and many critics would remain impermeable to Ionesco's manner: "*La Cantatrice chauve:* among other things, attempts to get the theatrical mechanism to function without a purpose. An exercise in creating an abstract or non-figurative text. Pushing the farcical to its extreme limit."[17] But Raymond Queneau did not miss the appointment. He came three times a week, rounded up the journalists, called his friends to arms: "You should go to the Théâtre des Noctambules one of these days. A play that will please you, I think," he suggested to Marcel Duhamel.[18] While the actors, in the afternoon, took on the job of sandwich-men on the boulevard Saint-Germain. All this was in vain. *La Cantatrice chauve* would not survive until the arrival of summer. Patience, it would have its revenge![19]

The Théâtre des Noctambules was one of those little halls similar to the many that still existed at the time, especially in the 5th and 6th districts: the Théâtre du quartier Latin, adjoining the Noctambules—that Michel de Ré directed—the Théâtre de la Huchette, at number 23 on the street bearing the same name, the Théâtre de Babylone, on 38 boulevard Raspail... It was in this last one that was created, on January 3 1953, *En attendant Godot* (*Waiting for Godot*), by Samuel Beckett, in the staging by Roger Blin.[20] No one wanted that one either... And Blin started to despair: "I was very excited by this play and I was eager to mount it very quickly."[21] But all the theatre directors, one after another, slammed the door in his face. Except Jean-Marie Serreau, who directed the Babylone at the time. The theatre was on the verge of bankruptcy. Serreau nevertheless put on the play. His audacity would be rewarded: scarcely ten days after the performances started, the news was already spreading in Paris that something was happening on the boulevard Raspail... And the hall was filled to capacity every evening. The success would last more than a year. But the Théâtre de

---

[17] Eugène Ionesco, *Notes et Contre-notes*, Gallimard, 1966. "Fortunately we will never again hear of M. Ionesco!" predicted a journalist. The play nonetheless had its defenders, the critics Jacques Lemarchand, Guy Durmur, Renée Saurel, Jean Pouillon, Gustave Joly. And also Albert Camus, André Breton, Benjamin Péret.

[18] Marcel Duhamel, *Raconte pas ta vie, op. cit.*

[19] Revived with *La Leçon*, in February 1957, at the Théâtre de la Huchette, *La Cantatrice chauve* has been playing on the same stage without interruption for more than fifty years. A unique phenomenon in the world history of the theatre.

[20] The Theatre de la Huchette—90 seats—is today the only survivor of all these little halls.

[21] Quoted by Geneviève Latour in *Théâtre, reflet de la IVe République, op. cit.*

Babylone would still not survive. And it would close its doors in the month of November 1954.

Few—very few—resources, few spectators, the lack of comfort in the hall and in the dressing rooms, this was commonplace in those little theatres in Saint-Germain-des-Prés and the surrounding areas. But it was not enough to discourage authors, actors, set designers, or stage directors. When Georges Vitaly took charge of the Théâtre de la Huchette in 1947, everything had to be done. And he went to work with his partner, Marcel Pinard: "Taking turns they swept the hall, did some touch-up painting, repaired a foldaway seat or helped carry a set. We installed the first electric organ in any theatre, with two resistors and six projectors. We succeeded in producing miracles, in inventing. Places as poor as ours are like monasteries where the audiences accept illusion, and dreams much more readily. We show them a match and they believe it is a greasy pole."[22]

---

[22] Georges Vitaly, interview with André Gintzinburger, *Acteurs*, no. 5.

15

"This indefinable something that made up the charm of the village and that was quite simply poetry. That which wells up from human contacts"

1952, 1953, 1954...Time passed. In Saint-Germain-des-Prés as well. And faster than elsewhere, perhaps. After the Théâtre de Babylone, it was the Noctambules' turn to close. Transformed into a cinema. At the Rose Rouge, Nico Papatakis stepped down. His cabaret would not survive for long after the change in management. "The golden age of Saint-Germain-des-Prés is ending," deplored Marc Doelnitz;[1] "Saint-Germain-des-Prés is dead," Anne-Marie Cazalis answered him like an echo[2]...Dead and buried.

Gréco was now singing as a star at the Olympia, on the Boulevards, and the movies were already courting her; she traded her miserable little room at the Louisiane for a townhouse. Ever since she obtained the Prix Goncourt for her novel *Les Mandarins* (*The Mandarins*), Simone de Beauvoir emigrated to Montparnasse, on the rue Schoelcher. "Besides, everybody was abandoning the high-class ship, transformed into a big tourist boat. Annabel, after managing a cabaret in Megève and participating in elegance contests, would marry Bernard Buffet. Thanks to abstract painting, Corbassière would discover the comfort of a Rolls Royce. Frédéric Chauvelot would go off to cultivate his vines and François de la Rochefoucauld would become the Duke de Liancourt."[3] As Guy Béart's song said so aptly, "There is no after in Saint-Germain-

---

[1] *La Fête à Saint-Germain-des-Prés, op. cit.*
[2] *Les Mémoires d'une Anne, op. cit.*
[3] Marc Doelnitz, *La Fête à Saint-Germain-des-Prés, op. cit.*

des-Prés. Neither the day after tomorrow nor the afternoon. There is only today."

Tourists, tourists... It was true, the poorest, dumpiest café, between the Seine and the rue du Four, opened up to a public coming from five continents its hastily cleaned basement that it baptized right away as a "cellar nightclub:" a dozen or so stools and lop-sided tables, a few candles inserted in bottles, bad music—and everybody believed it! On some evenings, four, five tourist buses, parked head to foot, would congest the square. English, Americans, Swedes... eager, no doubt, to breath in the intoxicating perfume of debauchery, to share some imaginary excesses with the natives of Saint-Germain-des-Prés—the ones that the press took pleasure in suggesting. "Where is the Tabou? Where is the Rose Rouge? Where is the Club Saint-Germain?..." But all the natives of Saint-Germain-des-Prés have left. All of them. Even Jean-Paul Sartre: "We continued, of course, to go to the Flore, but it was beginning to lose its lustre because it was really becoming a store selling surprise packages. People would come to look at us and we were beginning to have our fill of it. They would ask, on entering: 'Where is Sartre's place? Where does he write?' So we ended up deserting the Flore."[4] A few more years and Sartre would not even dare walk in front of the church, for fear of autograph chasers. And beggars of all kinds: "Even to go to my publisher Gallimard, I use the rue Jacob to avoid being recognized."[5]

Saint-Germain-des-Prés died. On what day, at what time? Who dealt it the fatal blow? And what if the guilty ones were none other than those who invented it? Saint-Germain-des-Prés died because they no longer believed in it, because they had ceased being young. That is the banal fate of all generations: growing old. Where did they go, those who were there from the very beginning? This "excitable, dynamic youth, bursting with ideas, ready for anything, ready for nothing, miraculously realising their project, living like nowhere else, sustaining themselves with cocktails that, however expensive they were, were still less so than the cheapest of meals, a dishevelled youth that didn't stop throwing one challenge after another in the face of an era that was amorphous in appearance, tainted, boring and bored. It was as though this Existentialist nursery, with its Tabou entourage, its foot-stamping, the strident soaring of its

---

[4] Jean-Paul Sartre in *Simone de Beauvoir*, a film by Josée Dayan, op. cit.
[5] Words reported by Othilie Bailly in Marcelle Routier, *Saint-Germain-des-Prés, op. cit.*

saxophones, sought to shake all of the old accumulated dust."[6] The dust settled. One fine day, "the excitable youth," the "dishevelled youth," woke up in the skin of a teacher, a judge, a civil servant, a banker, a lady postal clerk... Or even in the skin of a famous actor.

The times changed. The immediate post-war period ended as well. The Cold War which, finally, in Paris, would only be a laughing matter, at worst a pretext for getting oneself scared, would soon give way to real wars—the disaster of Diên Biên Phu, Algeria... In Moscow, at the 20th Congress of the Soviet Union Communist Party, in February 1956, Khrushchev declared loud and clear that a conflict was not inevitable; the victory of the working class did not necessarily take the form of armed struggle. In the West, the surprise was great, especially so when the contents of a report that the First Secretary of the Party delivered before dumbfounded delegates started leaking out. There was indeed plenty to cause surprise in the brutality of the indictment: the denunciation of Stalin's crimes was unequivocal. Everything was revealed, with figures to prove it: the deportations, the rigged trials, the executions. This did not fail to bring up questions immediately. As Simone de Beauvoir emphasized, when evoking these moments in *La Force des choses*: "It was not enough to knock Stalin off his pedestal, they should have analyzed the system that had made his tyranny and his 'bloody crimes' possible. The people who were now denouncing 'the personality cult' had worked with Stalin: why had they not said anything? Up to what point did their complicity go or not go? And to what extent can they be trusted?"

There were as many silences as there were questions. Especially in Paris, where the Communist Party maintained a cautious blackout: the readers of *L'Humanité* would only be entitled to a few vague comments from the report "attributed" to Khrushchev. The hour for de-Stalinization had not yet struck. In fact, Jacques Duclos, the First Secretary of the Communist Party had barely returned from Moscow when he had the name of Stalin acclaimed at a meeting in Paris held at the Salle Wagram. And when *Le Monde*, on June 6, began publishing the famous report, voices were raised, within the Party, questioning its authenticity. Consequently, the 14th Congress, that was held at Le Havre during the course of the summer, chose purely and simply to overlook the subject. But if Paris pretended to be deaf, the report, in the East, had the effect of a bomb. Three months later, Soviet tanks entered Budapest to

---

[6] Colin-Simard, "Saint-Germain-des-Prés, terre de poussière et de feu", art. cité.

quell the insurrection. And the "travelling companions" began to doubt. They would not stop doubting. Thus began the hemorrhaging of the Communist party. Which, devalued, began its slow, irremediable descent into hell...

How could it survive, this group of young people, this community—a community bred by circumstances but a community nonetheless[7], born in the deepest poverty, ten years or so earlier, on the banks of the boulevard Saint-Germain? Several thousands of young adults, united by the same past and the same ardour—the heavy legacy of the Occupation and the fondness for partying—sharing the same hopes, the same enthusiasms, in a common desire to live intensely and together their rediscovered freedom. As Juliette Gréco declared: "under a pile of lies and speculations, there was a reality. The anxiety. The anxiety of those who were searching for one another with the crazy yearning for an encounter, for friendship and for sharing."[8]

How could the spirit of Saint-Germain-des-Prés survive in this new world that was emerging in the middle of the 1950s? Because to the helplessness, the anxiety of the young "Existentialists" of 1945 corresponded, ten years later, another anxiety. The material comfort anxiety of a society that was getting rich—4.8% annual growth on the average over the period from 1950 to 1970—of a prosperous, well nourished youth, free in its thoughts and actions. The youth of the "thirty glorious years," to quote the expression of the economist Jean Fourastié. It had nothing to do with the penniless Bohemians at the Tabou and the Bar Vert, who had just spent four years, with empty stomachs, under Nazi rule. Returning to Saint-Germain-des-Prés during the 1970s, Marc Doelnitz noted: "The new denizens of Saint-Germain-des-Prés are not happy, all weighted down by the car, the remote control, the video recorder, the credit card, the second home.... We used to be lighter. We had nothing. Except for a few doors open to us through friendship. We reckoned we owed nothing to society. On the other hand we did not expect any gift from it."[9]

Simone de Beauvoir had sensed this disintegration of an era, of a way of life. As early as 1950, when she had just finished *Le Deuxième Sexe*, she started on a novel whose objective was to relate the disappointments, the

---

[7] The expression "communauté de circonstance" (a community of circumstance) comes from Vincent Gille, in *Saint-Germain-des-Prés* 1945-1950, op. cit.

[8] *Jujube*, op. cit.

[9] *La Fête à Saint-Germain-des-Prés*, op. cit.

disillusions of the left-wing intelligentsia during the years that followed the war. The formidable élan vital, the blazing fire of camaraderie that followed the conflict petered out quickly, given the squabbling of the different clans and the settling of political scores. This so recent past, still so warm, woven with friendships that had now unravelled, with lost illusions, palpitating with so many emotions, this past that was in the process of disappearing, would come through in the writing of *Les Mandarins*, which was an attempt to revive and, perhaps, à posteriori, to better understand it: "Only a novel could in my opinion draw out the multiple and whirling meanings of this changed world in which I had awakened in August 1944: a changing world that had never ceased moving."[10] Thus it was around the theme of thwarted friendship and wrecked hopes—those of a whole generation of intellectuals—that the book would revolve: "To talk about me, I had to talk about *us*, according to the meaning this word had implied in 1944."[11]

"We," emphasized Simone de Beauvoir. Because in this formidable movement of ideas, this artistic, political, literary, philosophical, and theatrical burgeoning that exploded in Saint-Germain-des-Prés, around 1944-1945, with the return of freedom, there was room for everything and everybody: "the Prévert Gang" and the "Sartre Family," Bernard Buffet's first picture and Antonin Artaud's last drawings, Jean-Paul Riopelle's paintings and those of Jean Fautrier—Fautrier who dreamed of an ideal picture, where everything he had learned would be useless, a badly composed picture, badly drawn, with ugly colours, but a picture which existed!...—"The Black Lady" and "the White Lady"—Juliette Gréco and Cora Vaucaire—the Café de Flore and the Bar Vert, the Existentialists, the Communists, the Lettrists, the singers, the actors, the film directors, Jean Cocteau and Gabriel Pomerand, the Tabou and Le Divan bookstore, jazz bop and New Orleans jazz, Sidney Bechet and Boris Vian, Jean-Paul Sartre and Jacques Laurent, Maurice Ronet the painter and Maurice Ronet the actor, Simone de Beauvoir and Marguerite Duras, Marc Doelnitz's duchesses, wearing new-look suits and stiletto heels, and Pépita, the dead broke model of dead broke painters, Miss Vice and La Rosière of Saint-Germain-des-Prés, the kids from rich families and the kids from poor ones. ... Fraternity. A façade-like fraternity, but a fraternity nonetheless.

---

[10] Simone de Beauvoir, *La Force des choses, op. cit.*

[11] *Ibid.* It will be noted that *Us (op. cit)* was the title chosen by Claude Roy for the second volume of his autobiography which covers these same post-war years.

This was the fraternity that Daniel Gélin remembered: "I didn't go to the 'neighbourhood;' it was the neighbourhood that drew me in. I would go there without any specific rendezvous, without any purpose, simply to breath in an atmosphere: an atmosphere full of tenderness, friendship and singing spirit. We would be seated around one table or another in a restaurant or a café, gathered together by the lightest of coincidences: young guys coming from milieus and having opinions that were sometimes completely opposed, but that had no importance whatsoever: all barriers were abolished. A guy from the left would converse with an unconditional Gaullist, a Catholic with an anticlerical... Every moment spent there had a savour of tenderness and renewal. We were happy with one another and no one cheated."[12]

A state of grace? Without any doubt. But which, in the end, lasted only a short time. Five years? Six years? Ten? On that subject, opinions differ. Everyone has his own Saint-Germain. The newspapers, those that report anything at all, the invading businesses, the tourists who are always one fashion behind,—and time, the onslaught of time—got the better of it. They destroyed "this indefinable something that made up the charm of the village and that quite simply was poetry. Because it was really all about a kind of poetry. The kind that wells up from human contacts."[13] Poetry, like a spark.

No, the state of grace could not last any longer. Nor could the loves, the friendships, or the ideas. That was it, Saint-Germain-des-Prés' eternity...

> *To live one day at a time*
> *The slightest of loves*
> *Took on in those little streets*
> *An eternal dimension*
> *But at night was night*
> *It was soon over*
> *This was the eternity*
> *Of Saint-Germain-des-Prés*[14]

---

[12] *Deux ou trios vies qui sont les miennes, op. cit.*

[13] *Ibid.*

[14] *Il n'y a plus d'après* (There is no after), a song by Guy Béart, Éditions Espace, 1960.

Chronology

542
Childebert I, son of Clovis, besieges Saragossa. As part of his booty, on his return: the tunic of Saint Vincent, martyred two centuries earlier.

558
Consecration, in Paris, of the Abbey constructed on the advice of the Bishop Germain, future Saint Germain, to receive the tunic of Saint Vincent. Devastated by the Normans, the building is reconstructed around the year one thousand. It contains the burial places of Childebert, Saint Germain, Descartes, Boileau, Mabillon

1792
The monks are driven out; the abbey is reconverted into a prison. More than three hundred people will be summarily executed during the September massacres. All that is left today of the abbey, ravaged by a fire in 1794, is the church, one of the most ancient in Paris, and the palace of the abbey.

1873
A hosier's shop, with the sign of "Les Deux Magots", opens on Saint-Germain-des-Prés Square.

1893
Colette, at twenty years old, moves into 28 rue Jacob, the year of her marriage to Willy.

1909
First issue of the *Nouvelle Revue Française.*

1910
Nathalie Clifford Barney moves to rue Jacob.

1913
Jacques Copeau, assisted by Louis Jouvet and Charles Dullin, founds the Théâtre du Vieux-Colombier.

1915
Adrienne Monnier opens the bookstore La Maison des Amis des Livres, on 7 rue de l'Odéon.

1919
Opposite, at number 12, the bookstore Shakespeare and Company is set up, created by the American Sylvia Beach.

1924
Gaston Baty, at 143 boulevard Saint-Germain, installs his theatrical company in the ephemeral Baraque de la Chimère.

1930
At the Deux Magots, some dissident Surrealists, among whom are Georges Ribemont-Dessaignes, Jacques Baron and Jacques Prévert, draw up their satirical tract against André Breton: *Un cadavre*.

1932
Jacques Prévert lives at 39 rue Dauphine. He participates actively in the creation of the Groupe Octobre.

1936
Jean-Louis Barrault rents a vast space, located under the roof timbers, at 7 rue des Grands-Augustins. He founds there the Compagnie du Grenier des Augustins that will mount *Le Tableau des Merveilles*, adapted from Cervantès by Jacques Prévert. The Groupe Octobre meets there frequently.

1937
April 26. Bombardment of the little Spanish town of Guernica.
In the Spring. Picasso, who has taken over Jean-Louis Barrault's attic and turned it into his studio, paints *Guernica* there.

1937 or 1938
Simone de Beauvoir comes to the Café de Flore for the first time.

1939
Paul Boubal buys the Café de Flore.

1940
Closed during the June debacle, the Flore reopens as of the month of July.

1941
Spring. Jean-Paul Sartre creates the ephemeral resistance movement Socialisme et Liberté.
July. Performance of the *Suppliantes*, by Aeschylus, in a staging by Jean-Louis Barrault, at the Roland-Garros Stadium. This spectacle will give Sartre the idea of writing *Les Mouches*.
Winter. Jean-Paul Sartre and Simone de Beauvoir frequent the Flore assiduously, where they write.

1942
Albert Camus publishes *L'Étranger* and *Le Mythe de Sisyphe*.

1943
June 2. The creation of *Les Mouches* by Jean-Paul Sartre at the Théâtre de la Cité (Sarah-Bernhardt), in a staging by Charles Dullin.
June. Simone de Beauvoir, soon followed by Sartre, moves into the Hôtel La Louisiane, on 60 rue de Seine.
Summer. Publication of *L'Être et le Néant*, by Jean-Paul Sartre. Publication of *L'Invitée* by Simone de Beauvoir.
Autumn. Juliette Gréco arrives in Saint-Germain-des-Prés and moves into the Servandoni boarding house.
November. The creation at the Comédie-Française, by Jean-Louis Barrault, of *Le Soulier de satin*, by Paul Claudel. For the whole duration of the Occupation, the Café de Flore is the refuge for Parisian intellectuals and artists: "At the Flore we were at home" (Sartre).

1944
March 19. Reading at Michel Leiris' home, Quai des Grands-Augustins, of the play by Picasso: *Le Désir attrapé par la queue*.

June 2. The setting up of the Gouvernement provisoire de la République française (GPRF).
June 6. Landing of the Allied Troops in Normandy.
June 10. Dress rehearsal of *Huis clos*, by Jean-Paul Sartre, at the Théâtre du Vieux Colombier.
August 19-25. Liberation of Paris.
August 28-September 4. Publication in *Combat* of Sartre's account of the Liberation of Paris: "Un promeneur dans Paris insurgé."

1945
August 6. Explosion of the bomb at Hiroshima.
August 9. Explosion of the bomb at Nagasaki.
September. Publication of Simone de Beauvoir's novel, *Le Sang des autres.*
September 26. First performance of *Caligula* by Albert Camus.
October. Publication of the first two volumes of *Les Chemins de la liberté* (*L'Âge de raison* and *Le Sursis*), a novel by Jean-Paul Sartre.
October 15. First issue of the review *Les Temps Modernes.*
October21. Legislative Elections: 160 seats for the Communist Party, 152 for the MRP, 142 for the SFIO.
October 29. Lecture by Jean-Paul Sartre, "L'existentialisme est un humanisme."
October 30. Première of the play by Simone de Beauvoir, *Les Bouches inutiles*, at the Théâtre des Carrefours.
November 13. General de Gaulle is elected unanimously as Head of the Government by the Constituent Assembly and forms a government with the MRP, Socialists, and Communists.
December 28. In *Les Lettres françaises*, a violent article by Roger Garaudy against Jean-Paul Sartre : "Un faux prophète : Jean-Paul Sartre ."
Launch of the Mouvement lettriste by Isidore Isou.

1946
January 20. Charles de Gaulle resigns from the Presidency of the Provisional Government.
January. Don Redman's Jazz Orchestra performs in Paris. This is the first Black American group to return to France since the declaration of war, in 1939.
June. Opening, on rue des Carmes, in the basement of the Hôtel des Carmes, of the Club des Lorientais, where Claude Luter performs.

November. Publication, at the Éditions du Scorpion, of *J'irai cracher sur vos tombes*, by Vernon Sullivan, translation by Boris Vian.
Publication of *L'Existentialisme*, by Henri Lefebvre, and of *La Sainte Famille existentialiste*, by Henri Mougin, two Communist tracts against Existentialism.
Opening of the first Rose Rouge cabaret on rue de la Harpe.

1947

February 7. Opening of a preliminary investigation by the Public Prosecutor's Office against the author and translator of *J'irai cracher sur vos tombes.*
April 11. Opening of the Tabou, a cellar nightclub located on 33 rue Dauphine, where Boris Vian plays the trumpet and the hosts of which are Juliette Gréco, Anne-Marie Cazalis and Marc Doelnitz.
May 3. An article, in *Samedi-Soir*, gets Parisians to discover Saint-Germain-des-Prés.
September. In the USSR, a report by Andreï Jdanov at the Constitutive Conference of the Kominform confirming the existence of two "camps": the imperialist and anti-democratic camp vs. the anti-imperialist and democratic camp.
December 3. Creation of *Les Épiphanies*, by Henri Pichette, at the Théâtre des Noctambules, in a staging by Georges Vitaly, with Gérard Philipe.
Publication of *L'Existentialisme n'est pas un humanisme,* a work by Jean Kanapa, a blistering attack against Sartre and his philosophy.

1947-1948

Beginning of the Cold War.

1948

Spring. Nico Papatakis opens the second Rose Rouge cabaret, on 76 rue de Rennes.
June 11. Opening of the Club Saint-Germain, on 13 rue Saint-Benoît.
June 15. Debut of the Frères Jacques at the Rose Rouge.
Summer. World Congress of Intellectuals for Peace, in Wroclaw, during which Fadeïev violently attacks Jean-Paul Sartre.
November. Shooting, at the theatre du Vieux-Colombier, of *Ulysse ou les Mauvaises Rencontres*, a film by Alexandre Astruc. Boris Vian is summoned by the judge Baurès concerning *J'irai cracher sur vos tombes.*

Winter. Opening of the Club du Vieux-Colombier, where Claude Luter and Sidney Bechet perform.

In *Situations II*, Sartre notes: "The politics of Stalinist Communism is incompatible with the honest practicing of the literary profession."

1949

January. Kravchenko Trial, in Paris.
June. Publication of the first volume of *Le Deuxième Sexe*, by Simone de Beauvoir: *Les Faits et les Mythes*.
June 1. Election, at the Club Saint-Germain, of "la Rosière de Saint-Germain-des-Prés ."
June 22. Debut of Juliette Gréco at the cabaret Le Bœuf sur le Toit.
November. Publication of the second volume of *Le Deuxième Sexe : L'Expérience vécue.*
Autumn. Juliette Gréco sings at the Rose Rouge.
December 6. Première in Paris of Jacques Becker's film, *Rendez-vous de Juillet*, that features the youth of Saint-Germain-des-Prés.

1950

March 19. The Stockholm Appeal.
May. Boris Vian and Jean d'Halluin, Director of the Éditions du Scorpion, are jointly condemned for "affront to public decency." *J'irai cracher sur vos tombes* is henceforth forbidden. Creation at the Théâtre des Noctambules of *La Cantatrice chauve* by Eugène Ionesco, in the staging by Nicolas Bataille.
October. Yves Robert mounts, at the Rose Rouge, *Les Exercices de style* by Raymond Queneau.
December. The Cold War occupies people's minds. Simone de Beauvoir to Nelson Algren: "Most of the non-Communist intellectuals believe that they will be forced to make declarations and perform acts contrary to their convictions if the Russians arrive here…. Everyone agrees that Sartre will be swiftly liquidated, and I will be in great danger."

1954

October. Publication of *Les Mandarins,* by Simone de Beauvoir, who will obtain the Prix Goncourt.

Index

A

Abetz, Otto 63
Aboulker, Stéphane 36
Achard, Marcel 65
Adamov, Arthur 2, 43, 47, 48, 52, 205
Agnès Capri 182
Alazé, (M.) 68
Algren, Nelson 95, 109, 120, 157, 196
Allégret, Yves 46, 95, 162
Amato, Jena-Marie 196
Amiel, Denys 17
Anchorena, Hortensia 73, 76
Anchorena, Marcello 73, 76
Annet-Badel, Paul 80, 81, 153
Ansermet, Ernest 154
Antelme, Robert 125
Apollinaire, Guillaume 18, 74, 183
Aragon, Louis 18, 31, 190
Armstrong, Louis 154, 155, 158
Arnaud, Gabriel 144
Arnaud, Noël 172
Arnault, Michel 9
Artaud, Antonin 81, 133, 217
Astruc, Alexandre 94, 130, 131, 134, 162
Aubier, Jean 74
Auboyneau, Robert 143
Auclair, Michel 87
Audiard, Yvan 192
Audiberti, Jacques 2, 43, 47, 52, 203
Audouard, Yvan 149, 167
Aumont, Jean-Pierre 166
Aurenche, Jean 29, 34, 36
Auric, Georges 162
Aury, Dominique 47
Autant-Lara, Claude 82, 208
Aymé, Marcel 80

B

Bair, Deirdre 70
Baker, Josephine 154, 189
Balachova, Tania 81, 93
Balmain, Pierre 163, 207
Bamberger, François 132
Baquet, Maurice 24
Barbezat, Marc 79
Barbezat, Olga 79.
   See Kechelievich, Olga
Baron, Jacques 20
Barrault, Jean-Louis 23, 24, 25, 30, 31, 32, 33, 55, 59, 60, 62, 65, 73
Bassan, Jean 63

Bataille, Georges *20, 73, 162*
Bataille, Nicolas *44, 45, 46, 65, 94, 193, 200, 208*
Bataille, Sylvia *73*
Baty, Gaston *17*
Baume, Freddy *165*
Baurès (judge) *173*
Bazin, Hervé *148*
Beach, Sylvia *19*
Béart, Guy *213*
Beaumont, Jacques de *130*
Beauvoir, Simone de *vii, ix, xiv, 1, 2, 34, 35, 39, 40, 41, 42, 43, 45, 50, 52, 56, 57, 58, 61, 67, 68, 69, 70, 72, 74, 77, 78, 79, 86, 88, 95, 109, 110, 111, 112, 113, 114, 120, 124, 126, 130, 138, 157, 174, 175, 176, 177, 196, 213, 215, 216*
Bechet, Sidney *154, 158, 166, 217*
Becker, Jacques *166*
Beckett, Samuel *31, 203*
Becque, Henry *13*
Bedel, Maurice *120*
Beigbeder, Marc *102*
Bellec, André *191*
Benda, Julien *120*
Benga, Féral *189, 191*
Bérard, Christian *94, 141, 142, 160, 164*
Berger, Jean *114*
Berg, Wal *182*
Bernard, Henri *155*
Bernard, Jean-Jacques *17*
Berstein, Serge *96*
Bertin, Pierre *51*
Besnard, Lucien *17*
Besset, Arlette *26, 27*

Béteille, Pierre *205*
Betti, Ugo *206*
Bibesco, Elizabeth *13*
Bilemdjian, Sophie *100, 101*
Binet, Émile *47, 160*
Bing, Suzanne *13*
Blanc, Yvonne *156*
Blin, Roger *24, 31, 36, 48, 190, 205, 210*
Blondin, Antoine *2*
Blum, Léon *21, 120*
Boll, André *81*
Bolling, Claude *162*
Bontemps, Lily *200*
Bost, Jacques-Laurent *35, 52, 57, 70, 74, 77, 130*
Boubal, Henriette *47*
Boubal, Paul *44, 46, 51, 52, 53, 57, 168*
Boucher, Pierre *36*
Bouglione (brothers) *163*
Bouhélier, Saint-Georges de *17*
Bouquet, Romain *13*
Bourget, Paul *9, 37*
Bourget, Pierre *89*
Bourla, Jean-Pierre *43, 67*
Boussigue, (M.) *47*
Bouthoul, Gaston *36*
Bouvier, Jacqueline *183*
Boyer, Charles *188*
Boyer, Lucienne *180*
Braque, Georges *19, 73*
Brasillach, Robert *85*
Brasseur, Pierre *81, 164*
Bray, Yvonne de *94*
Breguet, Louis *160*
Bret, Alix *194*
Breton, André *18, 20, 207*

Brodsky, Michel *130*
Brooks, Romaine *20*
Brown, Ray *158*
Bruant, Artistide *2, 190*
Brunon, Georges *98*
Bryen, Camille *47, 131*
Buffet Annabel. See Schwob de Lur, Annabel
Buffet, Bernard *68, 213, 217*
Bugajer, Bu *147*
Burnay, Jenny *183*
Burnier, Michel-Antoine *123, 125*
Bussières, Raymond *24, 26, 27, 29, 183*
Byas, Don Carlos *162*

C

Café de Flore *57, 62*
Calmy, Jacques *102*
Campan, Zanie *74*
Camus, Albert *ix, 71, 72, 74, 75, 77, 78, 79, 81, 88, 97, 106, 107, 109, 110, 124, 128, 176*
Capelier, Margot *24, 30*
Caracalla, Jean-Paul *7, 19*
Carennes, François. See La Rochefoucauld, François de
Carette, Julien *13*
Carmet, Jean *183*
Carné, Marcel *25, 31, 46, 197*
Carrère, Maurice *150*
Cartier-Bresson, Henri *203*
Caryathis. See Jouhandeau, Élise
Casadesus, Christian *51, 130, 159, 161*
Casadesus, Mathilde *163*

Casarès, Maria *73, 78, 190, 191, 203, 205, 206, 208*
Cassan, Marguerite *41*
Cassou, Jean *122*
Castelot, André *85*
Cau, Jean *94, 138, 175*
Caussimon, Jean-Roger *114*
Cazalis, Anne-Marie *xiii, xv, 68, 71, 94, 99, 130, 134, 137, 141, 151, 160, 161, 164, 185, 186, 213*
Cazes, Marcellin *22*
Cendrars, Blaises *18*
Césaire, Aimé *120*
Chabannes, Jacques *25*
Chalais, François *94, 164*
Chancerel, Léon *180, 181, 192*
Chanel, CoCo *187*
Chaplin, Charlie *viii, 80*
Chapuis, Pierre *82*
Chase, James Hadley *168*
Chauffard, R.J. *79, 80, 81*
Chauvelot, Frédéric *136, 137, 141, 151, 160, 161, 162, 213*
Chavance, Louis *36*
Cheney, Peter *168*
Chéramy, Augustin *129, 130*
Chéret, Claudine *200*
Chevais, François *66*
Chevalier, Christian *194*
Chevalier, Maurice *63, 142, 160*
Chobillon, Simone *200*
Christian-Jaque *203*
Clarke, Kenny *158, 162*
Claude, Francis *65, 201*
Claude, Jean *206*
Claudel, Paul *9, 18, 19, 59, 61, 64*
Clayton, Buck *162*
Clergeat, André *155, 156*

Clifford Barney, Natalie *19, 20*
Clovis *4*
Club du Tabou *129, 134, 135, 136, 137, 141, 142, 143, 145, 147, 149, 150, 151, 160*
Cluseau-Lanauve, Jean *167*
Cocteau, Jean *3, 32, 49, 55, 67, 69, 70, 71, 73, 80, 94, 182, 184, 187, 189, 217*
Coleman, Bill *154*
Colette, Sidonie-Gabrielle *8, 20, 36, 64, 69, 164*
Compagnie des Quinze *81, 181*
Concert Mayol *61*
Cook, Will Marion *154*
Cooper, Gary *129*
Copeau, Jacques *8, 9, 10, 11, 13, 14, 15, 16, 80, 180*
Copeau, Marie-Hélène *13, 181*
Corbassière, Yves *95, 137, 213*
Cossery, Albert *68*
Courcel, Nicole *166*
Coutaud, Lucien *56*
Cravenne, Marcel *36*
Creuz, Serge *199*
Crolla, Henri *41*
Cuny, Alain *190*
Curie, Marie *120*
Curie, Pierre *120*
Cuzin, François *57*

D

Dalì, Salvador *148*
Daly, Géo *194*
Damia *180*
Daquin, Louis *184*
Dasté, Jean *181*
Dasté, Marie-Hélène. See Copeau, Marie-Hélène
Davis, Miles *158*
Delavaquerie, François *6*
De Mille, Cecil B. *197*
Deniaud, Yves *190*
Desanti, Dominique *57, 126, 138*
de Sica, Vittorio *197*
Desnos, Robert *20, 21, 23, 32, 48, 91, 194*
Desnoyers de Marbaix, Ghislain *147*
Desseau, Pierre *131*
Devay, Jean-François *173*
Devillers, Michel *194*
Devouassoux, Simone *57*
Dicale, Bertrand *66*
Dietrich, Marlene *129, 188*
Dior, Christian *134, 159, 203*
Doelnitz, Marc *94, 134, 135, 141, 142, 149, 151, 160, 164, 184, 185, 187, 213, 216, 217*
Doisneau, Robert *95*
Domarchi, Jean *136*
Dominique, Olga. See Kosakiewicz, Olga
Dorgelès, Roland *2*
Douai, Jacques *190*
Doucet, Clément *187*
Douking, Georges *80*
Douy, Max *82, 114*
Dreyfus, Jean-Paul *29*
Dropy *95*
Dubas, Marie *182, 198*
Duc, Hélène *41, 42, 44, 65, 148, 186*
Duclos, Jacques *215*
Ducreux, Louis *164*

Dufilho, Jacques *196*
Dufresnes, François *147*
Duhamel, Georges *14*
Duhamel, Marcel *24, 34, 36, 168, 169, 210*
Dullin, Charles *2, 11, 12, 16, 23, 55, 56, 58, 60, 61, 70, 77, 81, 113, 164*
Duncan, Raymond *47*
Dunham, Katherine *166, 188*
Dunoyer de Segonzac, André *92*
Duras, Marguerite *1, 125, 217*
Dürrenmatt, Friedrich *206*

E

Einstein, Eddie *95*
Eisenstein, Sergei *20*
Ellington, Duke *154, 162, 163*
Éluard, Paul *120*
Éparvier, Jean *142*
Epstein, Jean *80*
Erdos, Diane (Miss Vice) *165, 217*
Ernst, Max *148*
Étiévant, Yvette *41*

F

Fabrègues, Jean de *37*
Fadeïev, Alexandre *120*
Fargue, Léon-Paul *4, 5, 18, 21, 22, 48*
Fath, Jacques *184, 203*
Faulkner, William *23, 170*
Faure, Renée *204*
Fautrier, Jean *41, 217*

Ferré, Léo *2, 179, 191, 201*
Fèvre, Louis-Armand *200*
Feydeau, Georges *61, 77*
Filipacchi, Henri *36*
Fitzgerald, Ella *158*
Fitzgerald, F. Scott *19*
Flon, Suzanne *41*
Fombeure, Maurice *3, 93, 148, 192*
Fourastié, Jean *216*
Fourcade, François *41*
Fourcade, Nicole.
  See Philipe, Anne
France, Anatole *9*
Fuchmann, Lazare *26*

G

Gable, Clark *163*
Galey, Matthieu *47*
Gallieni, Michel. See Ré, Michel de
Gallimard, Gaston *12, 21, 80, 168, 187*
Galster, Ingrid *176*
Gance, Abel *80*
Gantillon, Simon *17*
Garbo, Greta *129*
Gast, Michel *174*
Gaucher (bookbinder) *92*
Gaulle, Charles de *117, 118, 143*
Gauty, Lys *182*
Gélin, Daniel *84, 94, 95, 106, 166, 218*
Genet, Jean *31, 49, 50, 114, 163*
Genevoix, Maurice *207*
Gerassi, John *40*
Ghéon, Henri *9*
Gibeau, Yves *194, 197*

Gide, André *8, 9, 10, 13, 18, 21, 58, 59, 126*
Gilles. See Villard, Jean
Gillespie, Dizzy *155, 158*
Gille, Vincent *125*
Giraudoux, Jean *55, 61, 95, 109*
Goffin, Robert *155*
Goldmann, Stéphane *190*
Gougerné, Yvonne *56*
Gourmont, Remy de *8*
Gracq, Julien *207*
Grappelli, Stéphane *154*
Gréco, Juliette *xv, 42, 47, 48, 65, 66, 68, 94, 99, 128, 130, 131, 132, 134, 135, 141, 144, 151, 158, 162, 165, 179, 181, 182, 183, 184, 185, 186, 188, 194, 195, 217*
Grémillon, Jean *34*
Grenier, Jean *98, 106*
Grenier, Jean-Pierre *192*
Grimault, Paul *29*
Gris, Juan *19, 72, 73*
Groupe Octobre *25, 26, 28, 32, 34, 35, 48, 129, 180*
Grout, Marius *69*
Guérin, Roger *194*
Guilbert, Yvette *185*
Guionnet, Louis *131, 132, 135, 136, 151*
Guionnet, Marcelle *131, 135, 136, 151*
Guitry, Sacha *63, 65, 205*

H

Haedens, Kléber *x*
Haedrich, Marcel *x*

Halluin, Jean d' *167, 168, 169, 170*
Hanoteau, Guillaume *12, 14, 21, 29, 31, 36, 37, 52, 73, 81, 82, 84, 85, 184, 193, 197*
Harrison, Rex *166*
Hawkins, Coleman *153, 162*
Hébertot, Jacques *107, 108, 109, 112*
Hemingway, Ernest *19, 68*
Henriot, Émile *vi*
Hepburn, Katherine *163*
Hilling, Jacques *196*
Hill, Teddy *155*
Hitchcock, Alfred *197*
Hodges, Johnny *158*
Honegger, Arthur *56*
Hugnet, Germaine *74*
Hugo, Valentine *73*
Hussenot, Olivier *192*

I

Ionesco, Eugène *2, 203, 205, 209*
Isou, Isidore *145, 148*
Itkine, Sylvain *25, 79, 91*
Ivernel, Daniel *172*

J

Jacob, Max *2, 73, 91*
Jacques (Tabou server) *143*
Jamois, Marguerite *17*
Jarry, Alfred *7, 74, 139*
Jaspers, Karl *101*
Jdanov, Andrei *119*
Jeanson, Francis *84, 85*

Jeanson, Henri 65
Joliot-Curie, Irène 120
Jollivet, Simone 70
Jouhandeau, Élise 11
Jourdain, Francis 13
Jourdan, Louis 188
Jouvenel, Henry de 36
Jouvenel, Renaud de 36
Jouvet, Louis 14, 16, 21, 59
Joyce, James 19
Joyeux, Odette 160
Julien. See Maistre, Aman
Juquin, Pierre 121, 122

K

Kahnweiler, Daniel-Henry 72
Kanapa, Jean 124
Karl, Roger 15
Kast, Pierre 197
Kechelievich, Olga 56, 79
Kierkegaard, Sören 100
King Oliver 155
Koestler, Arthur 123
Kosakiewicz, Olga 35, 56, 59, 60, 61, 70, 77, 114
Kosakiewicz, Wanda 35, 70, 77, 79, 81
Kosma, Joseph 182, 186, 187, 194
Kravchenko, Andreïevitch 122

L

Labisse, Félix 56, 164
Lacan, Jacques 19, 73, 162
Lacombe, Georges 108
Laforgue, Jules 185, 192
Lamy, Jean-Claude 27
Larbaud, Valery 9
Larbaud, Valéry 18
Larguier, Léo 1, 8, 23
La Rochefoucauld, François de 159, 163
Latour, Geneviève 193, 207, 210
Laubreaux, Alain 61, 85
Laudenbach, Roland 49
Laurent, Jacques 2, 169, 217
Léaud, Pierre 36
Lebel, Jean-Jacques 73
Le Bon de Beauvoir, Sylvie 1
Le Chanois, Jean-Paul. See Dreyfus, Jean-Paul
Leduc, Henri 129
Lefebvre, Henri 124
Le Feuve, Joëlle 48
Léger, Fernand 120
Legris, Roger 25
Legros, Albert Jules 147
Leibowitz, René 99
Leiris, Louise 72, 73, 74, 77
Leiris, Michel 20, 61, 72, 73, 74, 75, 76, 77
Lemarchand, Jacques 139, 208, 210
Lemarque, Francis 190
Lenormand, Henri-René 17
Letraz, Jean de 61
Leuris, Pierre 206, 208
Limbour, Georges 73
Lion, Margo 108
Lollobrigida, Gina xv
Longon, Guy 137
Lopez, Arturo 184
Loris, Fabien 31

Lualdi, Antonella *174*
Lucas, Bernard *131, 132, 135, 136, 137*
Luguet, André *164*
Lukacs, Georges *126*
Lunceford, Jimmie *157*
Luter, Claude *135, 153, 155, 156, 157, 165, 166, 179, 188*

M

Maar, Dora *32, 33, 48, 74*
Mac Indoe, Sir Archibald *196*
Mac Orlan, Pierre *2, 155*
Malclès, Jean-Denis *192*
Malraux, André *36, 58*
Malraux, Claude *36, 120*
Malraux, Roland *36*
Malson, Lucien *137*
Mara, Sally.
 See Queneau, Raymond
Marceau, Marcel *179, 191*
Marcel, Gabriel *ix, 17, 71, 101, 110, 112, 124*
Marchal, Georges *108*
Marcy, Robert *41*
Marie-Oliver,
 See Kosakiewicz, Wanda
Marquand, Christian *65, 174*
Marsan, Jean *41*
Martin du Gard, Roger *9*
Martineau, Henri *37*
Mascolo, Dyonis *125*
Masson, André *72*
Matisse, Henri *19, 92*
Matricon *147*
Matta, Roberto *130, 206*

Maulnier, Thierry *37, 43, 45, 47*
Mauriac, François *18, 125, 175, 176*
Maurras, Charles *21, 22, 37*
Maxence, Jean-Pierre *37*
McCoy, Horace *168*
Merleau-Ponty, Maurice *48, 57, 77, 99, 123, 130, 164*
Metchersky, Boris *16*
Meunier, Maurice *194*
Mezz Mezrow *158*
Milhaud, Darius *18, 187*
Miller, Henry *68, 170*
Milza, Pierre *64, 75, 96, 123*
Miquel, Louis *107*
Mireille (Mireille Hartuch) *155*
Mirò, Joan *72*
Mnouchkine, Ariane *14*
Modigliani, Amedeco *3*
Mongin, Henri *124*
Monnerot, Jules *ix*
Monnier, Adrienne *17, 18, 20, 208*
Montand, Yves *163, 185*
Montassut, Guy *137*
Montero, Germaine *183*
Montfort, Eugène *9*
Montherlant, Henry de *61, 62*
Moody *162*
Moore, Tommie *188*
Morane, Jacqueline *112, 114*
Morht, Michel *59*
Morin-Pillière (Mme) *41, 42*
Mossé, Sonia *35, 36, 91, 182*
Mougin, Henri *124*
Mouloudji, Marcel *35, 43, 45, 49, 51, 52, 55, 68, 73, 75, 76, 77, 91, 179, 181, 183*
Mounin, Georges *ix*

Mourre, Michel 147
Moussinac, Léon 26
Moysès, Louis 47, 184
Munch, Charles 56

N

Nadar, Félix 200
Nadeau, Maurice 50, 102
Nat, Lucien 13
Nattier, Nathalie 65
Navy, Yvon 114
Néron 113, 114
Nery, Jean 109
Noailles, Anna de 13
Noailles, Marie-Laure de 163
Noël, Léo 201
Nohain, Jean 182
Nonosse 147
Norman, Véra 172
Noudelmann, François 59, 115

O

O'Brady, Frédéric 41
Oettly, Paul 107
O'Neill, Eugene 17
Ory, Pascal 122, 123
Oswald, Marianne 182

P

Pabst, Georg-Wilhelm 182
Pac Pacco 147
Page, Hot Lips 162
Palmer, Lilli 166
Papatakis, Nico 65, 189, 190, 191, 195, 213
Pardo, Gégé 36
Pardo, Julien 36
Parker, Charlie 153, 158, 162
Parker, Daniel 170, 172
Pasquali, Fred 172
Passeur, Renée 163
Passeur, Steve 108
Patterson, Henri 194
Paulhan, Jean 40
Paul (Tabour barman) 143
Pelletier, Henri 51
Pénet, Martin 180, 183
Pépita 217
Péret, Benjamin 210
Pérodo (Mme) 153
Perret, Édith 164
Petit, Georges 9
Phélip, Gonzague 208
Philipe, Anne 41
Philipe, Gérard 41, 87, 95, 106, 108, 109, 110, 190, 203, 204, 205, 206, 207
Philippe, Cécile 189, 197
Philippe, Pierre 199
Picabia, Francis 21
Picard, Yvonne 58
Picasso, Pablo 2, 32, 33, 34, 48, 51, 72, 73, 120, 122, 187, 192
Pichette, Henri 2, 130, 146, 190, 203, 204, 205, 206, 207
Pierauld, Guy 196
Pierreux, Jacqueline 36
Pinard, Marcel 211
Pineau, Christian 145
Pirandello, Luigi 17

Piscator, Erwin 26
Pitoëff, Sacha 81, 114
Planchenault, Bernard 194
Pomerand, Gabriel 145, 147, 148, 217
Pontabry, Germaine 36
Pontabry, Robert 36
Pouillon, Jean 57
Poulbot, Francisque 2
Pound, Ezra 19
Pré, Catherine 95
Prévert, Jacques 20, 25, 26, 27, 31, 34, 45, 46, 47, 129, 157, 168, 180, 190, 194, 197, 200
Prévert, Janine 35
Prévert, Pierre 25, 34, 157, 200
Prévost, Jean 91
Proust, Marcel 93

Q

Queneau, Raymond 74, 77, 130, 138, 144, 156, 157, 167, 168, 185, 188, 195, 198, 199, 210
Quentin, Bernard 132
Quercy, Alain 145
Queval, Jean 156
Quillet (bistro owner) 93

R

Radiguet, Raymond 145, 187
Raphaël, Maurice 168
Raya, Nita 160
Redman, Don 157
Reggiani, Serge 183
Reinhardt, Django 154, 155

Ré, Michel de xv, 66, 68, 95, 132, 134, 190
Renard, Jules 13
Renaud, Henri 137
Renaud, Madeleine 25, 32, 73
Renoir, Jean 25, 80
Reutlinger, Charles 200
Reverdy, Pierre 73
Ribemont-Dessaignes, Georges 20
Richard, Marius 18
Richard, Marthe 93
Rich, Claude 133
Riffault 93
Riopelle, Jean-Paul 217
Ripault 36
Rivière, Jacques 9, 11
Roach, Max 158, 162
Robert, Jacques 167
Robert, Marthe 48
Robert, Yves 179, 190, 193, 196, 197, 198, 199
Roche, France 94, 164
Roche, Maurice 206
Rocher, René 81
Rolland, Jacques-Francis 130
Rolland, Romain 9
Rollan, Henri 106, 108
Romains, Jules 18
Romance, Viviane 46
Romi 200
Ronet, Maurice 166, 217
Rospoli (Princess) 163
Rougé, Edmond 170, 173
Rougeul, Jean 30, 68, 190
Rouleau, Raymond 81, 112
Roussel 92
Roussin, André 78, 197
Royal, Ernie 162

Roy, Claude *18, 88, 123, 125*
Ruyters, André *9*
Ryce-Anger *149*

S

Sablon, Jean *155, 180*
Sabouraud, Brigitte *201*
Sachs, Maurice *48, 62*
Sadoul, Georges *95*
Saint-Denis, Michel *81, 181*
Saint-Georges de Bouhélier *17*
Saint-Laurent, Cécil.
   See Laurent, Jacques
Salacrou, Armand *73*
Salacrou, Lucienne *73*
Salis, Rodolphe *2*
Sapritch, Alice *41*
Sarcey, Yvonne *18*
Sarment, Jean *17*
Sartre, Jean-Paul *v, vi, vii, ix, x, xi, xiv, xv, 18, 34, 35, 39, 40, 41, 45, 47, 49, 51, 52, 53, 55, 56, 57, 58, 59, 61, 67, 68, 69, 71, 74, 75, 77, 78, 79, 80, 81, 85, 86, 88, 89, 98, 99, 102, 105, 113, 122, 123, 126, 127, 130, 131, 138, 140, 142, 157, 171, 185, 195, 199, 214, 217*
Satie, Erik *18*
Sauvage, Catherine *179, 201*
Sauvage, Léo *131, 139*
Sauvage, Pierre *140*
Schiaparelli, Elsa *162*
Schlesser, Gilles *180*
Schlumberger, Jean *8, 9, 12*
Schwob de Lur, Annabel *xv, 68, 159, 213*

Scipion, Robert *35, 41, 44, 52*
Seghers, Pierre *120*
Sentein, François *37, 40, 43, 44, 45, 49, 52, 61, 88*
Serge, Jean *112*
Serreau, Jean-Marie *210*
Shakespeare and Company *19, 20*
Sicard, Solange *45, 65, 93, 190*
Signoret, Simone *46, 94, 95, 162, 163, 164, 190, 191*
Sigurd, Jacques *108*
Simone *13*
Singer, Winaretta *20*
Sirinelli, Jean-François *121, 122*
Sismondi, Jean-Charles de *110*
Sorokine, Nathalie *67, 68, 70*
Soupault, Philippe *18*
Spinelly *164*
Stein, Gertrude *19, 33*
Stéphane, Roger *87*
Strindberg, Johan August *85*
Suarès, André *9*
Sullivan, Vernon. See Vian, Boris
Suzanne (Tabou dancer) *144*
Sylvia, Gaby *81, 83, 94*

T

Tamiz, Edmond *196*
Tanous, Jean *156*
Tarn, Pauline. See Vivien, Renée
Tatum, Art *158*
Taylor, Freddy *155*
Tchimoukow, Lou (known as Lou Bonin) *24*
Tedesco, Jean *80*
Tessier, Valentine *13, 21, 80*

Théâtre de la Cité 60
Théâtre de la Madeleine 63
Théâtre de Paris 60
Thimoukow, Lou 28
Timsy Pimsy 137
Toklas, Alice B. 19
Touchard, Pierre-Aimé 31
Toulet, Paul-Jean 37
Toulouse-Lautrec, Henri de 2
Toulouse-Lautrec, Marie-Pierre de 163
Tourenne, Patrice 197
Tourenne, Paul 191
Tournier, Michel 102
Tours, Grégoire de 5
Toursky, Alexandre 132, 135
Toutoute. See Gréco, Juliette
Tranchant, Jean 182
Trenet, Charles 155, 182
Trépel, Mireille 190
Triolet, Elsa 190
Turlais, Jean 85

V

Vadim, Roger 130
Vailland, Roger 41, 130, 136, 163
Vaillant-Couturier, Paul 26
Valéry, Paul 18
Vallès, Jules 139
Vallon, Louis 143
Van Dongen, Kees 3
van Rysselberghe, Maria 13
Varte, Rosy 196
Vaucaire, Cora 179, 183, 201, 217
Vaudoyer, Jean-Louis 64
Védrès, Nicole 36, 130, 163

Vercors (Jean Bruller) 120, 122
Verne, Jules 198, 209
Vian, Alain 137
Vian, Boris x, xiii, 21, 46, 47, 51, 94, 99, 128, 130, 131, 134, 137, 138, 144, 145, 147, 150, 151, 153, 156, 157, 158, 159, 160, 162, 164, 166, 167, 168, 169, 171, 172, 173, 179, 197, 203, 205, 217
Vian, Lélio 137
Vian, Michelle 169
Vidal, Henri 65, 107, 108
Vidalie, Albert 48, 197
Vienot, Christian 137
Vilar, Jean 10, 139, 146, 203
Villard, Jean 181
Vitaly, Georges 108, 190, 203, 205, 211
Vitold, Michel 81, 112
Viton, Marie 107, 109
Vitrac, Roger 20, 28, 132, 133
Vivien, Renée 19

W

Wahl, Jean 101
Waldteufel, Émile 185
Warnod, André 2
Wiener, Jean 187
Wilde, Oscar 7
Wilder, Thornton 19
Willy, Colette. See Colette, Sidonie-Gabrielle
Witold, Jean 134
Wols 68, 131
Wright, Richard 163

Y

Yvain, Maurice *163*

Z

Zacharias, Bernard *165, 188*
Zegel, Sylvain *164*
Zette. See Leiris, Louise

www.ingramcontent.com/pod-product-compliance
Lightning Source LLC
Chambersburg PA
CBHW031614210526
45464CB00004B/1569